D1460228

Watercolour Landscapes

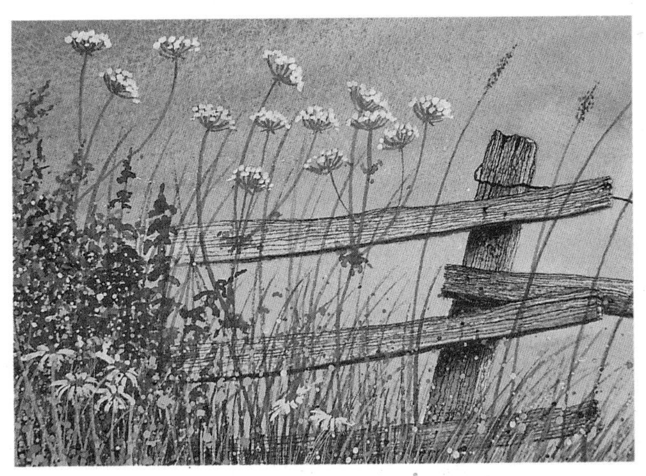

IN DETAIL

✦✦✦✦✦✦✦✦✦✦✦✦

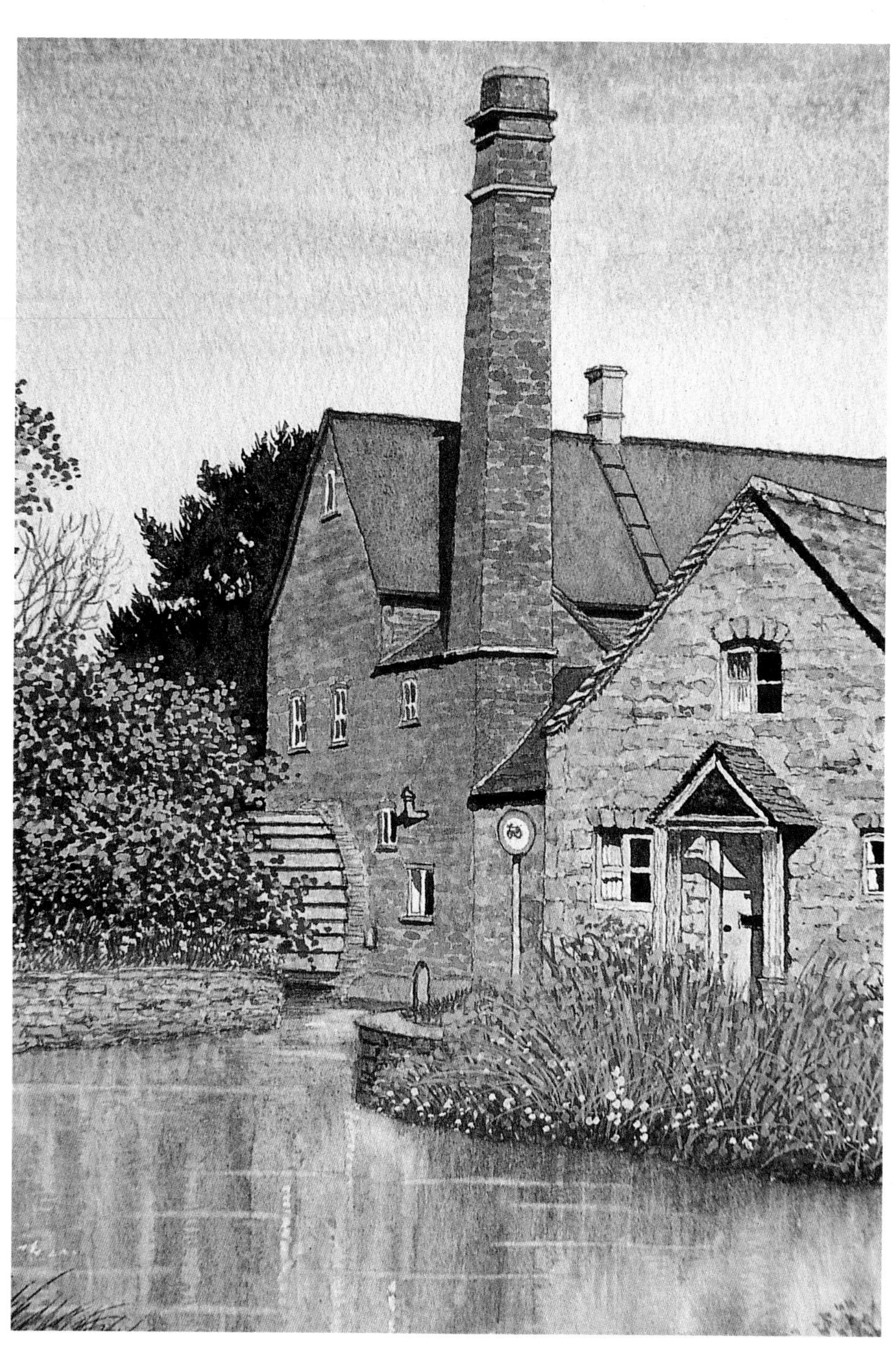

Watercolour Landscapes
IN DETAIL

✦✦✦✦✦✦✦✦✦✦✦✦

MICHAEL WARR

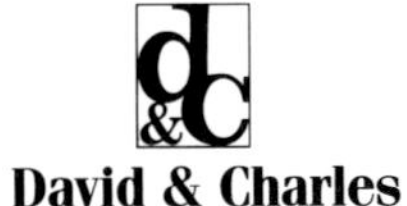

David & Charles

For Muriel

Acknowledgements

I would like to thank the following for help in the production of this book: Geoff Holmes (photography); Colab, Coventry (photographic processing); Jakar International (main UK importers of Caran d'Ache); Daler-Rowney (art materials); John Hall, Yorkshire Bank plc; Alison Elks at David & Charles; Cooper Wilson Design; and Muriel Smith for assistance and encouragement.

A DAVID & CHARLES BOOK

First published 1993

A catalogue record for this book is available from the British Library.

ISBN 0 7153 0051 2

Designed by COOPER WILSON DESIGN
Typeset by ABM Typographics Ltd, Hull
and printed in Hong Kong by
Wing King Tong Co., Ltd
for David & Charles
Brunel House Newton Abbot Devon

Contents

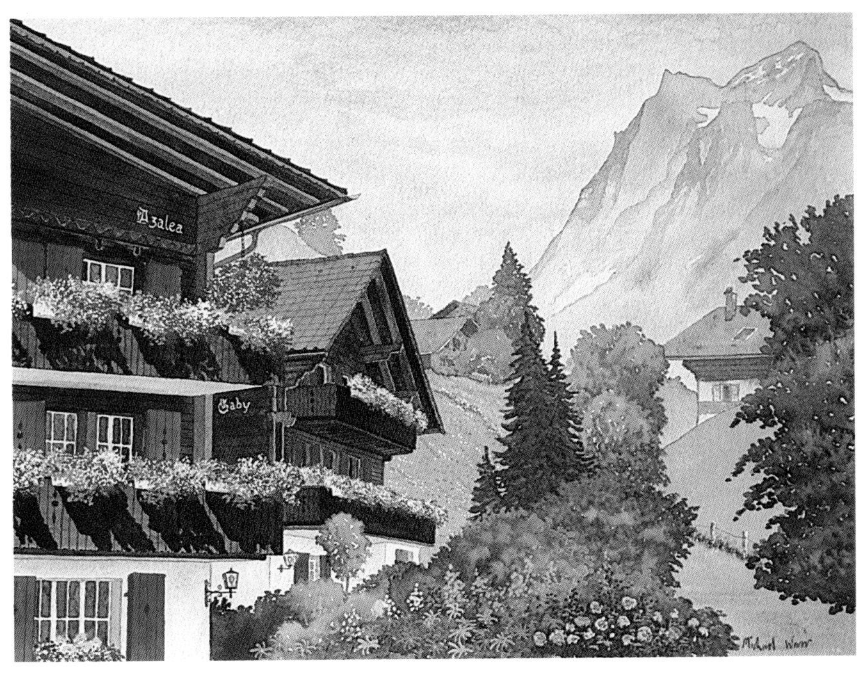

Introduction

When my publisher asked me to produce a book about painting watercolour landscapes in detail, I responded with delight and enthusiasm because landscape is a wonderful subject to be involved with, especially when watercolour is being used; it is a beautiful medium for depicting the everchanging moods of nature experienced in the great outdoors.

The first watercolour landscapes to be produced in their own right were painted at the beginning of the sixteenth century by a German artist, Albrecht Dürer. Up until this time landscape had simply featured as an accompaniment to figures in classical compositions.

Outdoor painting was completely unknown until about 1830 when a group of French artists took their equipment into the countryside at Barbizon, a village just south of Paris. The then art 'experts' considered these landscape artists to be completely mad, but they felt that it was an excellent way to study nature and the landscape, which indeed it was. There is no finer activity than to sketch and paint outdoors.

All this activity by artists, as well as by writers and poets, led people to appreciate the beauty of landscape. Mountains, for instance, were considered by the local inhabitants to be an ugly nuisance; to reach a destination they either had to be climbed over or walked around. Gradually, as artists and writers began to travel and record their findings, so interest in the landscape began to develop. In the middle of the nineteenth century, English and German artists painted the American West. They exhibited their paintings in London and Paris, which enabled the peoples of Europe to see the grandeur of the New World. By this time landscape painters had established themselves in importance and their services were used extensively to record scenes in many parts of the world.

Many styles and 'isms' have come and gone since the mid-nineteenth century, but I agree with William Coldstream of the Euston Road Group when he declared: 'The only thing to do with landscape is to sit down in front of it and paint it'. This does not necessarily mean that we should reproduce everything that we see, but painting a landscape in a representational way becomes an engaging challenge, and with only watercolour paints at our disposal the game of creating a picture is a very interesting one.

My own roots lie in the tradition of landscape painting. Having been born and raised in the countryside, trees and fields were the subjects that surrounded me as a child. Many years later, when a converted barn became my studio, recollections of landscape came flooding back. The views from the studio windows looked out on three centuries of transport system – canal, railway and roads. Many possibilities for landscape painting began to unfold. It was then that the idea of combining detailed farming subjects with landscape developed – I was surrounded by it. Detail in the nearby rustic objects led me to paint the surrounding landscape; the combination of worn and weathered wood, plus rolling landscape, became exciting and irresistible. Because there were so many subjects to be tackled, the use of watercolour as a medium seemed to be a natural choice. Its speed of execution and drying is a distinct advantage when many sketches and studies are being produced quickly.

Total involvement with the landscape became necessary: I walked on it, and sat and laid on it during all types of weather in order to experience and soak up the atmosphere. One morning, while I was observing a sunrise from the studio window, twin lambs were born right outside; it was a marvellous feeling – the real countryside was there just below me. Gradually, I drew or painted all of the nearby subjects from many viewpoints. An interesting exercise was to sit directly on the ground among a clump of ox-eye daisies and to draw them. Being completely surrounded by subject matter – the flowers were actually above me – produced a wonderful feeling of harmony with nature.

Response to landscape should be personal. After all, through our paintings we ought to express a true inner feeling and not simply record a 'mere scene'. Although we may wish to paint a landscape with detail, it is important to retain creativity in our minds and to be ready to respond to any idea which may help the painting. At the end of the day, we are judged by what we produce with paint on paper, not by what is out there in reality. I believe that painting should be a fusing together of technique – which is a knowledge of one's materials gained by use and experiment – plus ideas, imagination and emotion which comes from within the artist. Too much emphasis on technique can produce work which is too clinical, but if technique is ignored completely, expression of an idea is not possible. In other words, a balance should be sought. Any good landscape painting ought to take on a style or identity of its own rather than being merely a record of a certain locality.

With this in mind, it is important to train the eye to see potential pictures within the landscape. Try to see things from an unusual viewpoint or look at subjects which have never received consideration in your landscape paintings before. Keep a fresh eye.

Sometimes having a knowledge of the activities of the people in certain areas can be helpful. Remember that people as well as nature form the landscape of a region. Buildings in particular can help to identify an area; styles of architecture are often easier to recognise than a range of mountains, but however much knowledge is gained, a quote from the English painter J. M. W. Turner is worth remembering: 'Paint what you see, not what you know to be there.'

Watercolour as a medium is used in many ways – no two watercolour artists will agree on a given formula. There appear to be two schools of thought: the so-called 'purists' who claim that it is sacrilege to use watercolour in any form other than the completely translucent – that is, the use of white paint or 'body' colour is absolutely taboo – and a school which says 'anything goes'. I am pleased to belong to the latter school of thought. The purists spend a lot of time telling artists not to do one thing or another. Discussing what can be done by exploiting the medium to the full is a much more positive attitude. All sorts of interesting visual effects can be obtained by adding gouache and inks to watercolour, as well as using masking fluid and wax resists. These and other techniques will be described later on. This approach does not indicate a lack of respect for the beauty of a luxurious, translucent watercolour wash; after all, this method is the backbone of good watercolour painting in any form, but it is important to keep an open mind on the creative possibilities by experimenting a little. In order to produce detailed watercolour paintings, the use of body colour is often necessary; do not feel guilty about this. If the end result justifies the means, then that is fine. Very often a painting is successful by the inclusion of an extra ingredient. So many watercolours I have seen in exhibitions are dull; they require sparkle, which can be achieved by taking the above advice.

Travel is an extremely good stimulus for a landscape painter; the excitement of pastures new, reaction to a fresh environment and the discovery of differing colour harmonies in a landscape lead the artist to see with new eyes. Unfamiliar people and their customs add an extra dimension to your work, and provide plenty of ideas for when you return home.

Drawing for Landscape

Painting landscape with detail requires careful observation of the selected scene. An excellent way in which to do this is through drawing. Drawing is the foundation stone of painting; it provides much of the information required to begin a painting. If the visual problems are solved at an early stage by making a drawing, total involvement can be enjoyed when painting. There is nothing worse than being dogged by problems of a basic nature when the paint should be flowing.

Visual information in the form of sketches together with written notes are useful for recording a scene quickly. This information can be used later when you are painting indoors. It is not always possible to produce finished paintings on location for reasons of time, weather, etc, and sketches act as excellent reminders of initial reactions and ideas.

The drawing materials I use encompass the whole range, but it is all down to personal choice. When you are on location, you might think that a couple of pencils will do, but as you will see, it is important to have a reasonable range available.

My equipment is carried in a travel bag which has a divided inner section and zip pockets. This provides some sense of order, preventing everything being jumbled together in one area. A small lightweight folding stool is useful for painting outdoors. It is important to be comfortable when drawing or painting, as your concentration should be directed at your work and not at feeling sorry for yourself. A real luxury is a small light drawing-board.

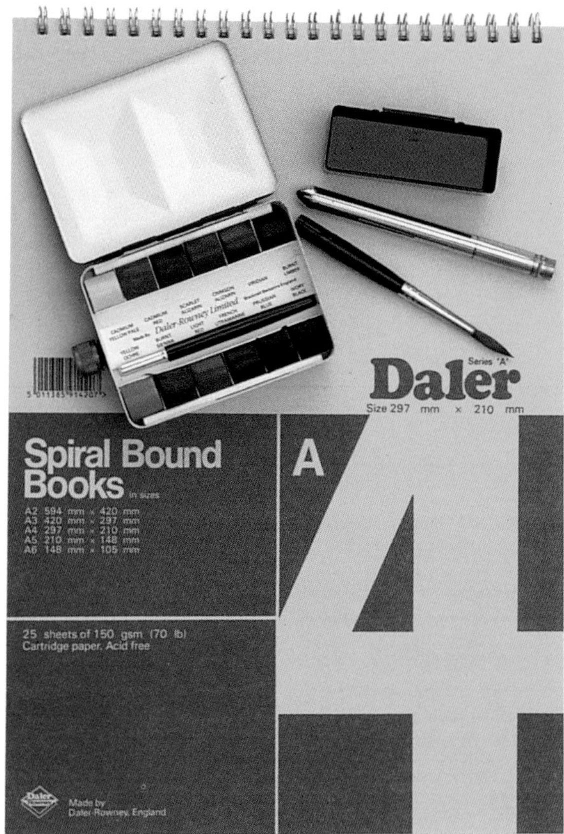

Portable watercolour equipment, which includes a Rowney pocket-size box of pan colours complete with lid palette and water container. Two telescopic round pointed sable brushes and an A4 sketch-pad

GRAPHITE PENCIL

The graphite pencil is the most basic of all drawing instruments and is probably the most misused. A wide range of differing grades is available, making it very confusing for the beginner. By using a soft pencil, you will be able to obtain all of the luscious dark tones which a hard one will not achieve. To simplify matters, I have devised a table of 'hard' and 'soft' pencils (see opposite).

Differing grades of graphite pencils in sets, including water solubles, extender for short pencils, plastic eraser, fine-grade file and craft knife

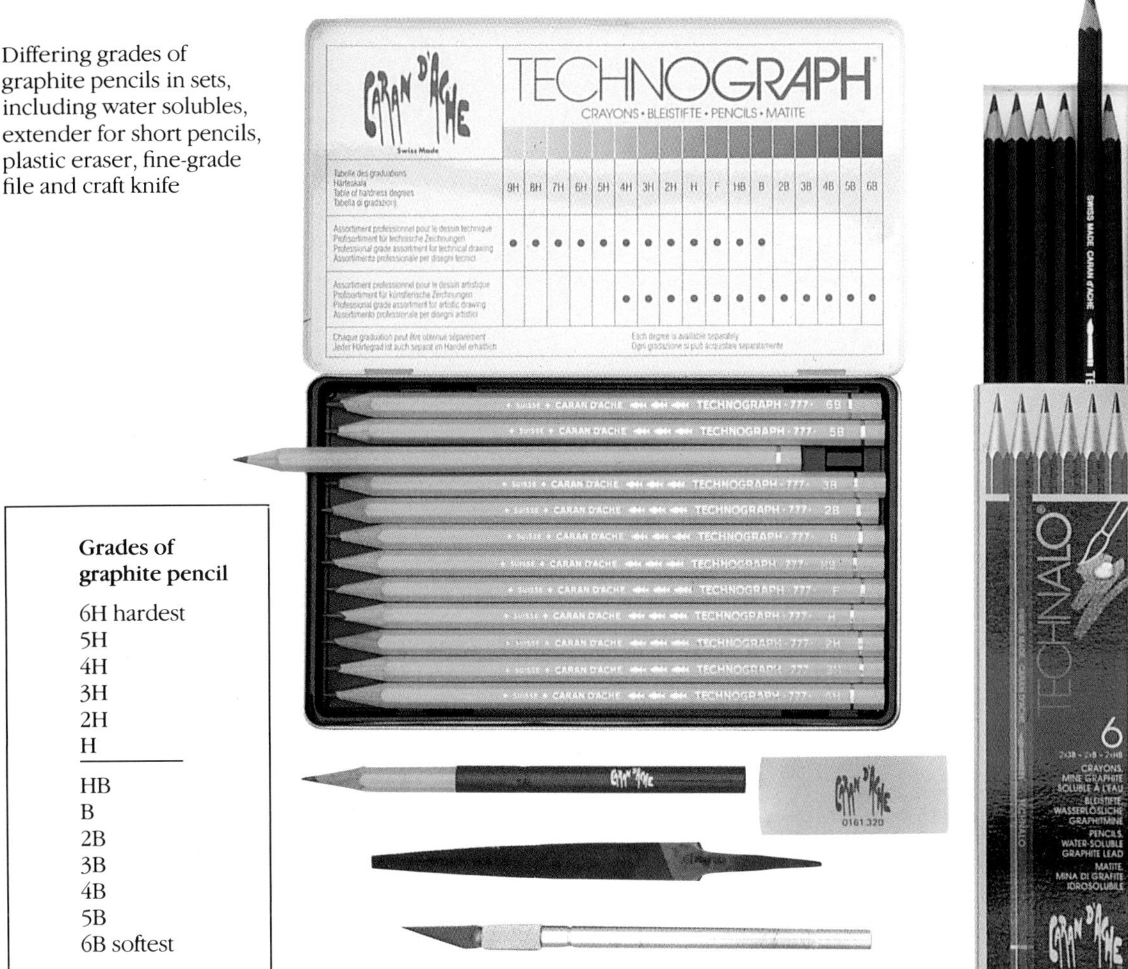

Grades of graphite pencil

6H hardest
5H
4H
3H
2H
H

HB
B
2B
3B
4B
5B
6B softest

The H pencils above the line are hard and normally used by designers in industry or architecture, while the B pencils below the line are soft, making them flow easily and as a result suitable for the free-hand sketching artist. The higher numbers in the H range are the hardest pencils, whereas the higher numbers in the B range are the softer ones. It is possible to obtain a wide variety of tones or shades with the softer grades. A good drawing needs all the tones from white, light grey, mid-grey and dark grey through to almost black.

Many students complain that their drawings are grey. Normally, it has nothing to do with their inability to draw, but is the result of the wrong choice of materials – for example, a 6H pencil will not produce the very dark tones.

It is important to keep pencils sharp; blunt leads hinder the attempt to make good drawings. Pencil sharpeners are useful, but they have an irritating habit of breaking the lead just as a suitable point is obtained; a craft knife is far more efficient and easier to control. A small file is an excellent aid in maintaining a point while you are working (in between the times when the pencil needs sharpening). It is not a good idea to sharpen a pencil down to a stub so that you cannot see the point as you draw, but if you do so, the life of the pencil can be extended by using a metal holder, thus enabling it to be used almost down to the end.

It is not cheating to use an eraser – it is the simplest way to eliminate unwanted lines. Plastic erasers are very easy and clean to use. They do not seem to damage the surface of the paper if they are used carefully.

Surfaces on which graphite pencil may be used vary enormously. Cartridge paper or illustration board provide the most suitable backgrounds, but interesting effects can be obtained by drawing on to textured surfaces such as watercolour paper, rough cartridge paper and pastel papers.

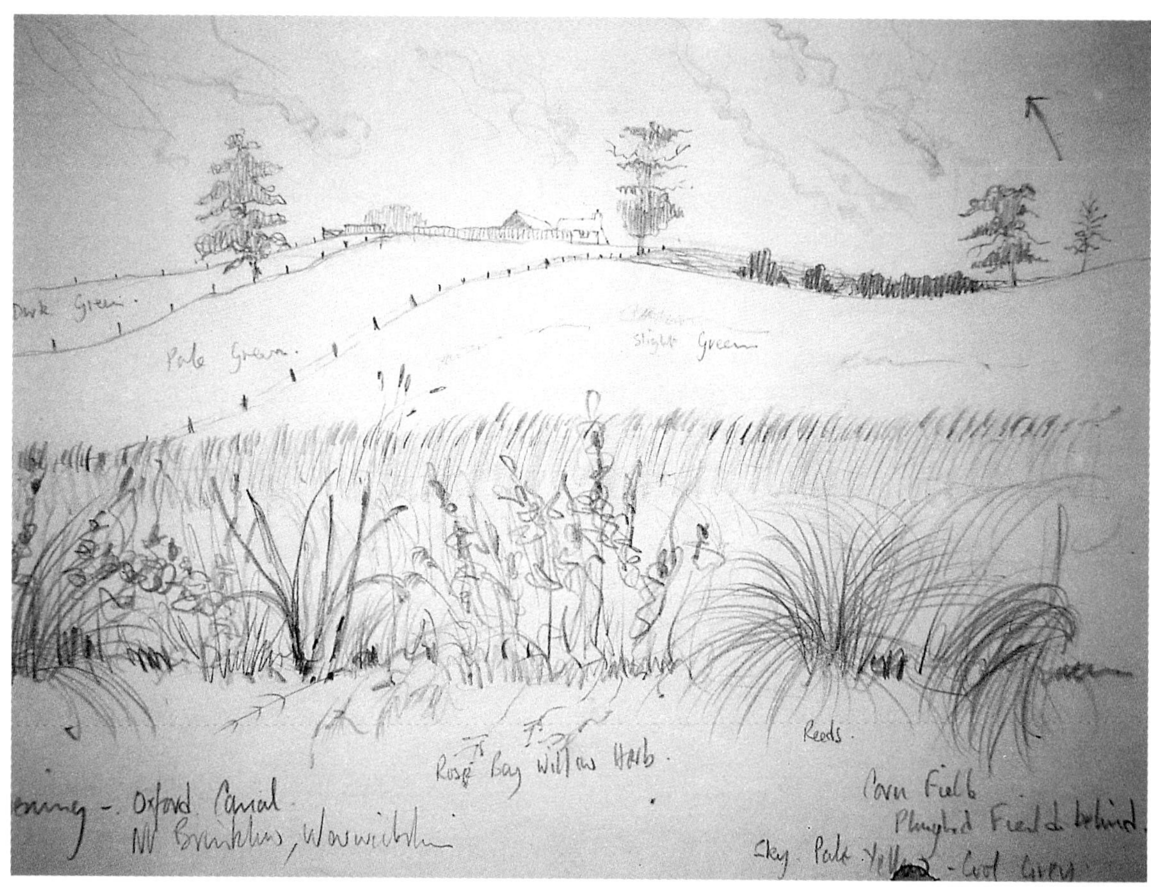

A graphite pencil-drawing made in the early evening, while I was sitting on the deck of a moored boat on the Oxford Canal. Many written notes accompany the drawing, including information about the species of canalside plants and wild flowers. The arrow (right) denotes the cloud direction

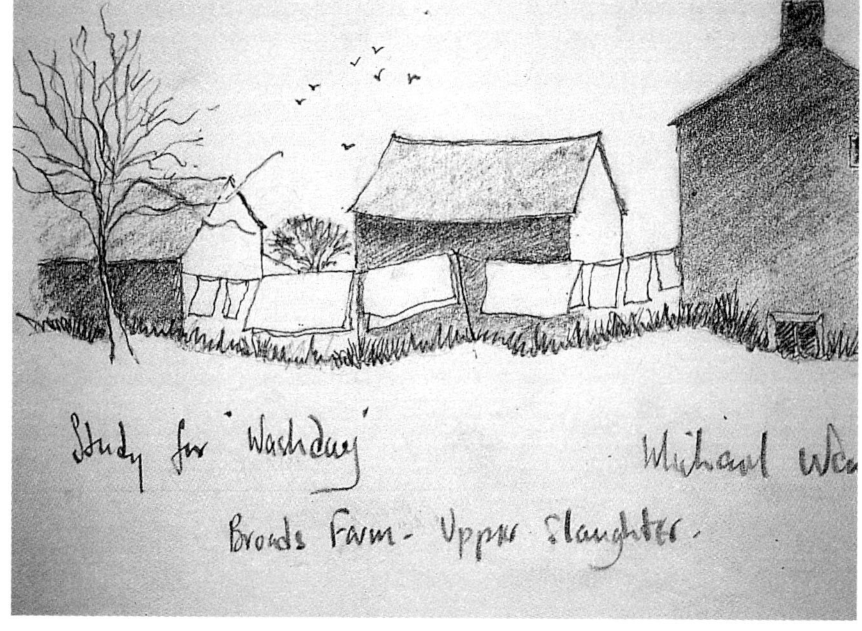

The use of a soft 4B graphite pencil enables us to see the 'white' washing in this drawing of a farm in the Cotswolds

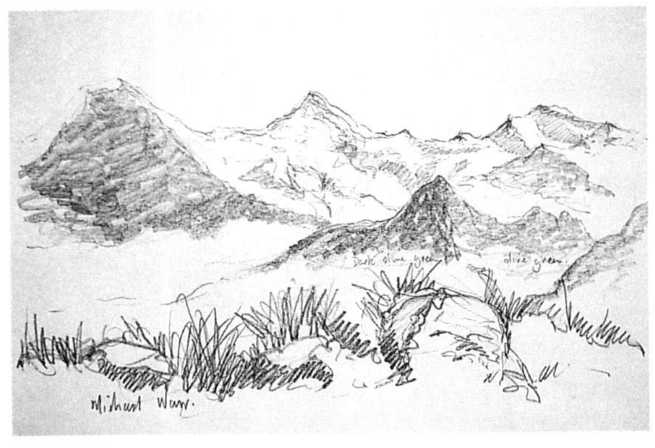

HB, 2B and 4B graphite pencils are used to produce a sketch of mountains in Switzerland

COLOURED PENCILS

Caran d'Ache produce a comprehensive range of coloured pencils in a quality suitable for artists. The permanence of a coloured pencil is important as no one likes to see a piece of work disappear after a matter of weeks. Coloured pencils offer the precision of a graphite pencil combined with colour. The leads are not too hard and not so soft that they crumble the first time they are used. Coloured pencils are useful when making studies of detailed subjects; the colours can be overlaid to produce colour mixing effects.

Sometimes, when working in the studio, it is difficult to remember a certain colour which could be the key to a whole composition. Being able to record colours and subjects quickly on location is a distinct benefit. There is a tremendous advantage in being able to work without the fuss and paraphernalia of painting equipment, particularly if you are on the move. In studio conditions it is possible to produce highly finished drawings with a good range of coloured pencils.

Again, as with graphite pencils, it is essential to keep a sharp point, and a craft knife rather than a pencil sharpener is far more suitable.

The surfaces on which coloured pencils work best are exactly the same as those for graphite. It is worth remembering, though, that unlike graphite pencils, coloured ones cannot be erased easily. Careful scraping with a sharp blade is the best method.

WATER-SOLUBLE GRAPHITE PENCILS

These are excellent if you wish to add a slight watercolour effect to a drawing. A full range of tonal values can be exploited if water is added with a round pointed brush; the result is a monochrome wash drawing. Caran d'Ache produce these in grades HB, B and 3B which are adequate for satisfactory results.

If a lot of water is to be used, heavier weight watercolour paper is recommended as a surface.

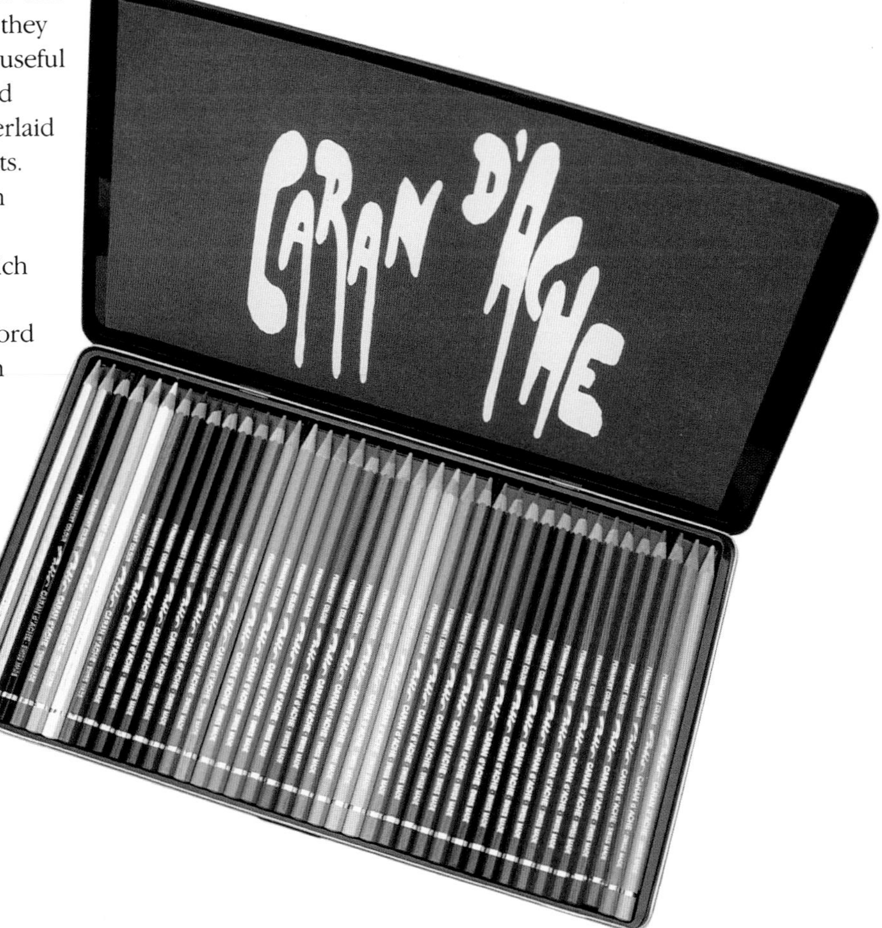

Caran d'Ache Pablo range of artist's-quality coloured pencils

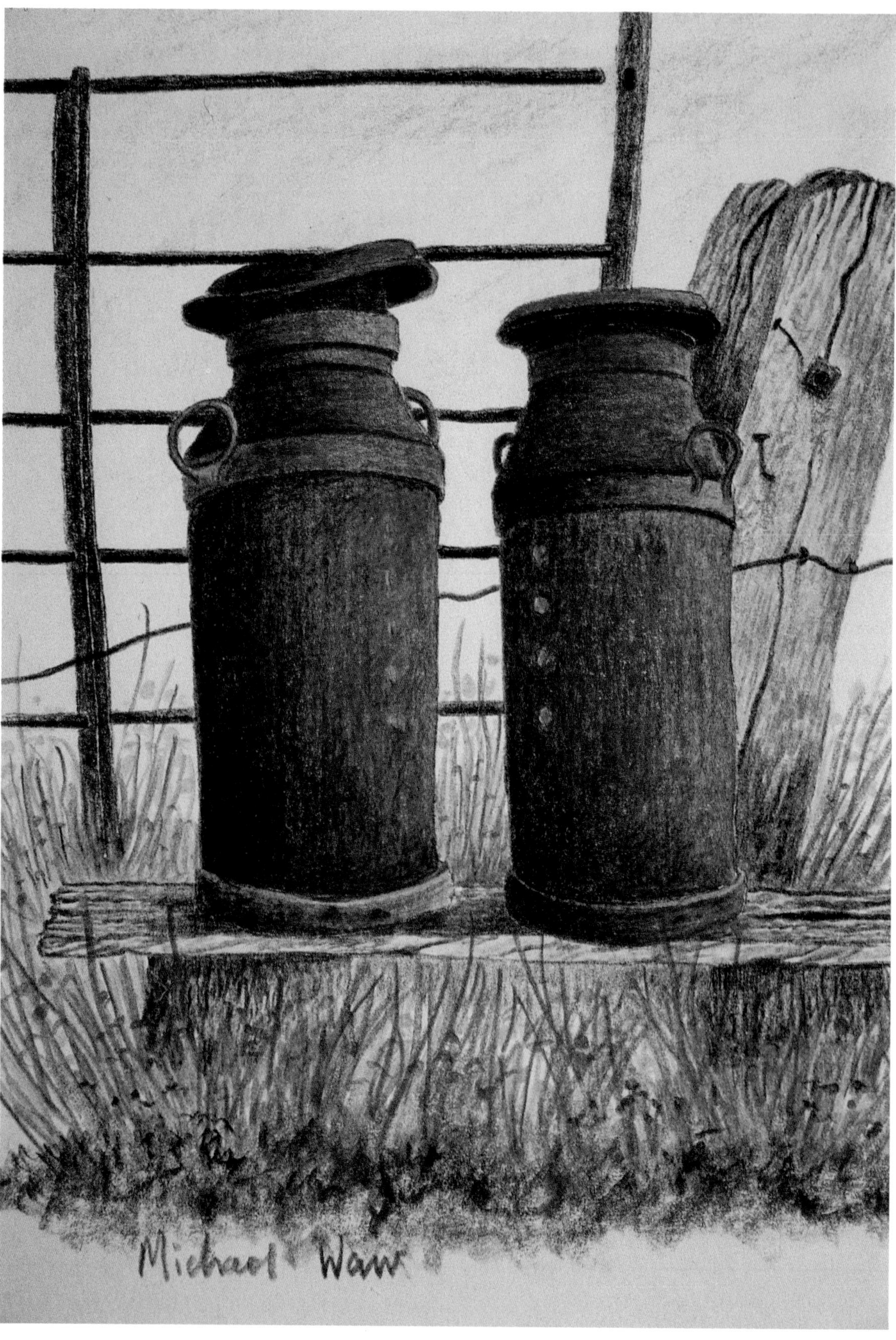

Left: This detailed drawing is produced with Caran d'Ache coloured pencils. The milk-churns, discovered in the corner of a landscape, provide excellent source material for possible inclusion in a large landscape painting at a later date. They may well serve as foreground subjects and the detailed information will be invaluable

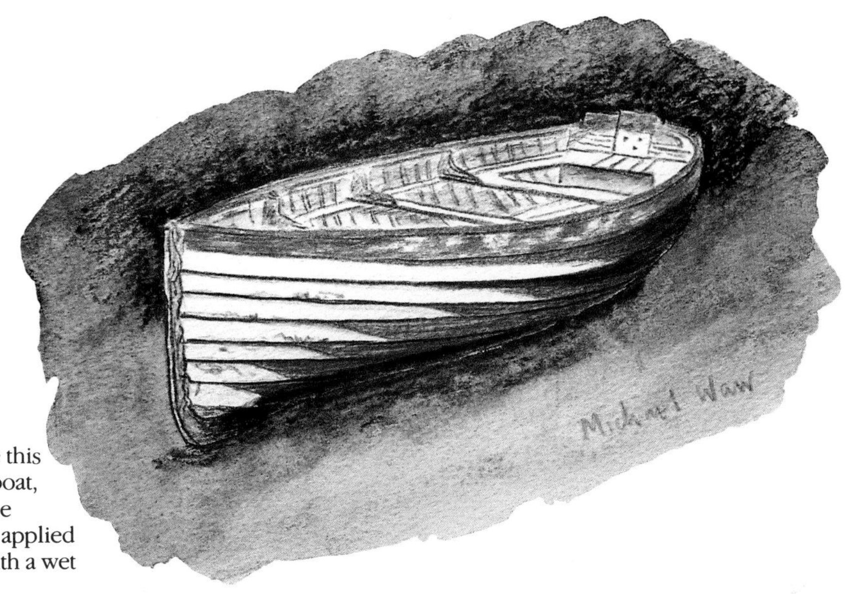

Right: Two coloured pencil techniques are used to produce this subject. Dry pencils create the boat, while water solubles provide the background colours, which are applied to a dry surface and softened with a wet round pointed sable brush

WATER-SOLUBLE COLOURED PENCILS

Caran d'Ache produce coloured pencils which are water soluble. If a colour drawing is required quickly, but there is time to use a brush and water, these are ideal. It is a great joy to apply water-soluble colour to dry watercolour paper and then to wash on water with a large round pointed brush – the results are astonishing. The drawn image softens immediately, colours merge and a whole new feeling about the work transpires. Equally, if the paper is dampened first and then lines are drawn with pencil, the effect produced is soft lines and some colour wash. When the paper dries it is possible to rework the study by adding lines and accenting certain areas as desired.

A fairly heavy watercolour paper such as Bockingford or Waterford 140lb or 200lb is the best surface for these techniques.

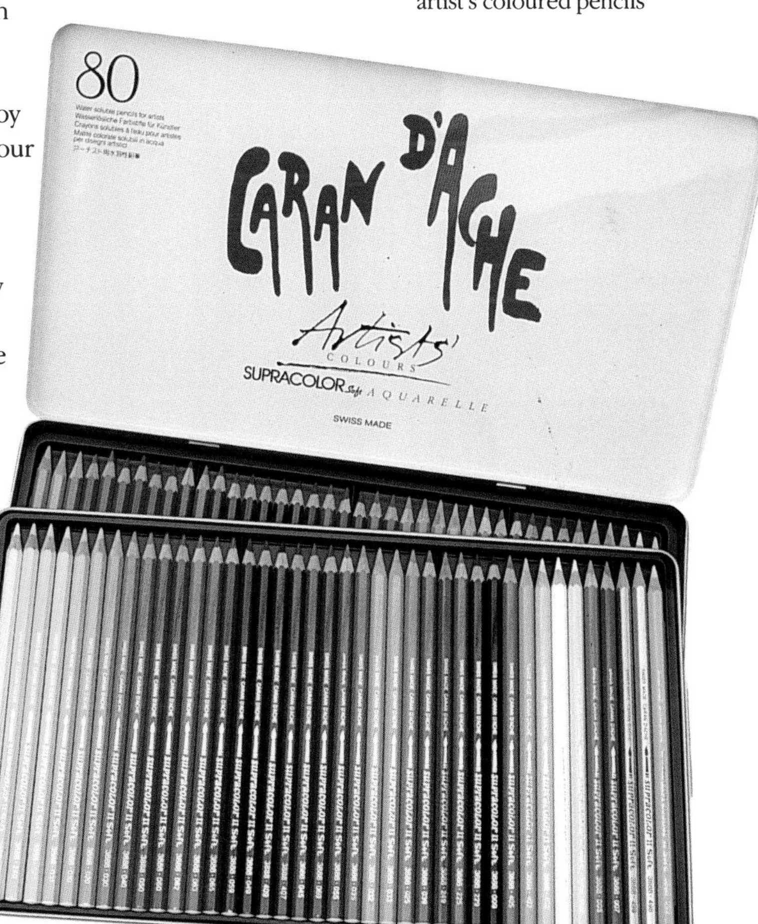

Water-soluble Caran d'Ache artist's coloured pencils

Right: Water-soluble coloured pencils worked on to damp paper created this study of a lake and mountains in the Alps. Blocks of colour shown on the left are in their dry form. The boats were added when the paper was almost dry, making them appear a little sharper

Caran d'Ache water-soluble artist's crayons

WATER-SOLUBLE ARTIST'S CRAYONS

Produced by Caran d'Ache, these work in a similar way to water-soluble pencils, but because they are much larger, their use for the first broad impressions of landscape is excellent. They can be broken into short lengths and used on the side; this way large areas of paper are covered quickly. There is no need to sharpen water-soluble crayons and ideal surfaces to work on are heavier weight watercolour papers, both white and tinted.

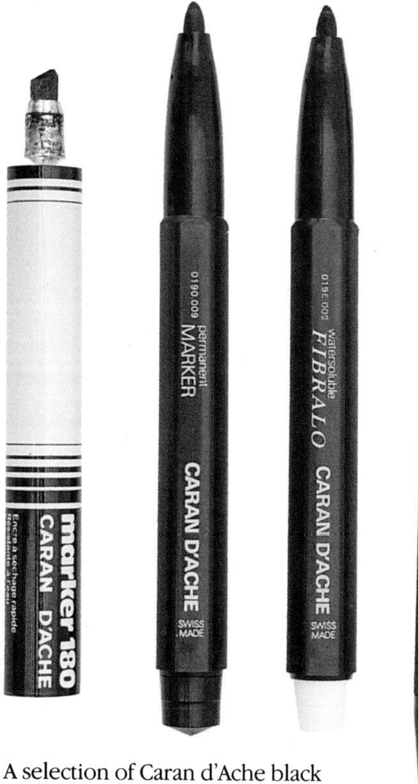

A selection of Caran d'Ache black water-soluble fibre-tip pens

FIBRE-TIP PENS

Fibre-tip pens are available in many sizes and colours; the choice is enormous, but I use a small range of black ones produced by Caran d'Ache. They offer a three-year storage guarantee which is a real advantage. The fibre-tip's instant use is very appealing; it does not need to be sharpened and it moves over a paper surface easily, whether it is smooth cartridge or rough-textured watercolour paper. Because of their flowing quality, fibre-tip pens are able to record initial reactions with an almost unrivalled immediacy. Caran d'Ache produce fibre-tips and markers with both water-resistant and water-soluble inks; the latter is the most useful for artwork.

The best method of application is to draw first and then to add water with a round pointed brush. Interesting results gradually transpire as the black lines change to subtle greys with a hint of pink and green. This effect introduces mood and atmosphere into the drawing, triggering off ideas which may be included in a painting later on.

White and tinted watercolour papers of a reasonable weight make good surfaces for this method of working.

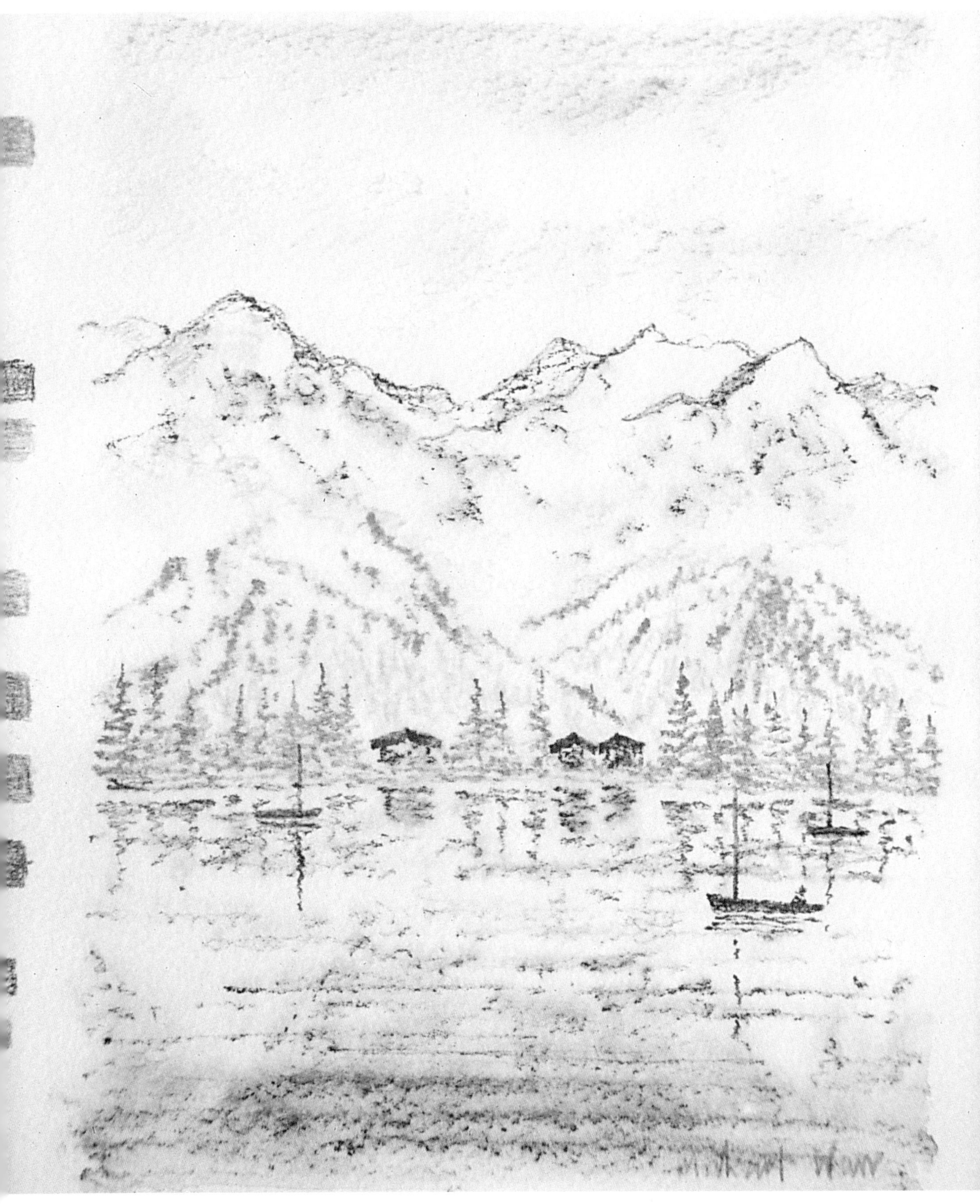

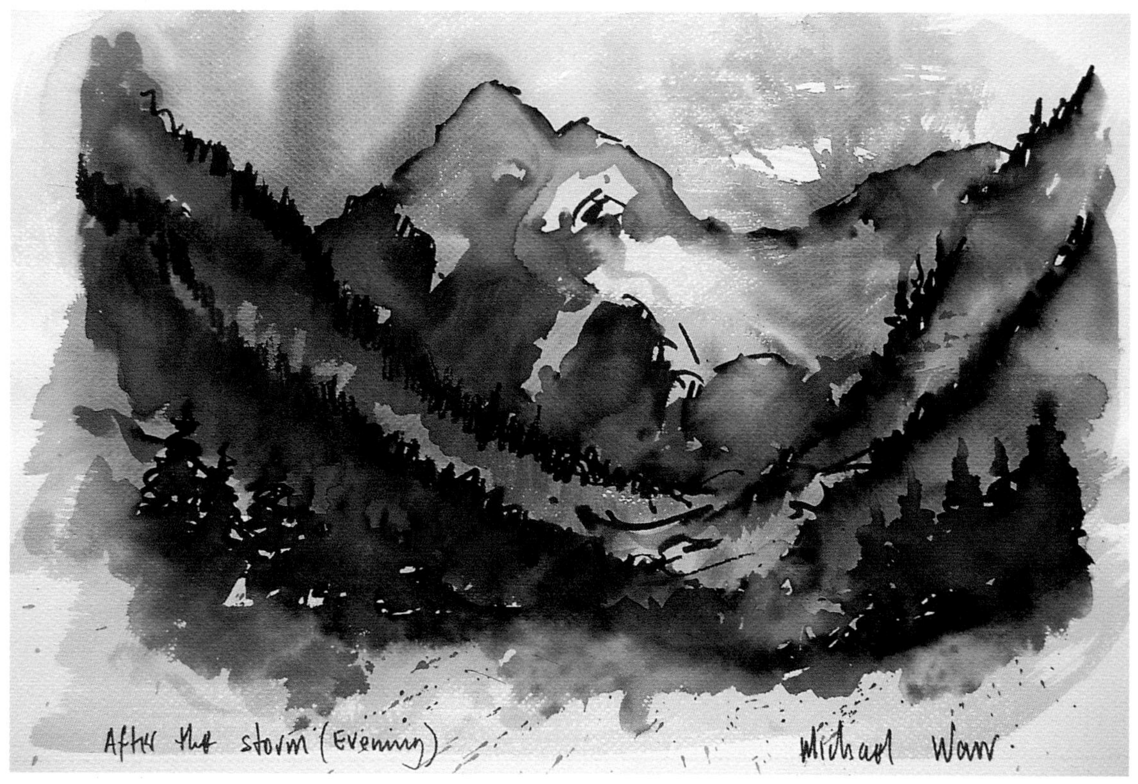

A quick sketch made with a Caran d'Ache black water-soluble fibre-tip pen and gouache. As wet colour is added to the sketch, so the hard lines diffuse, creating a pleasing atmospheric effect

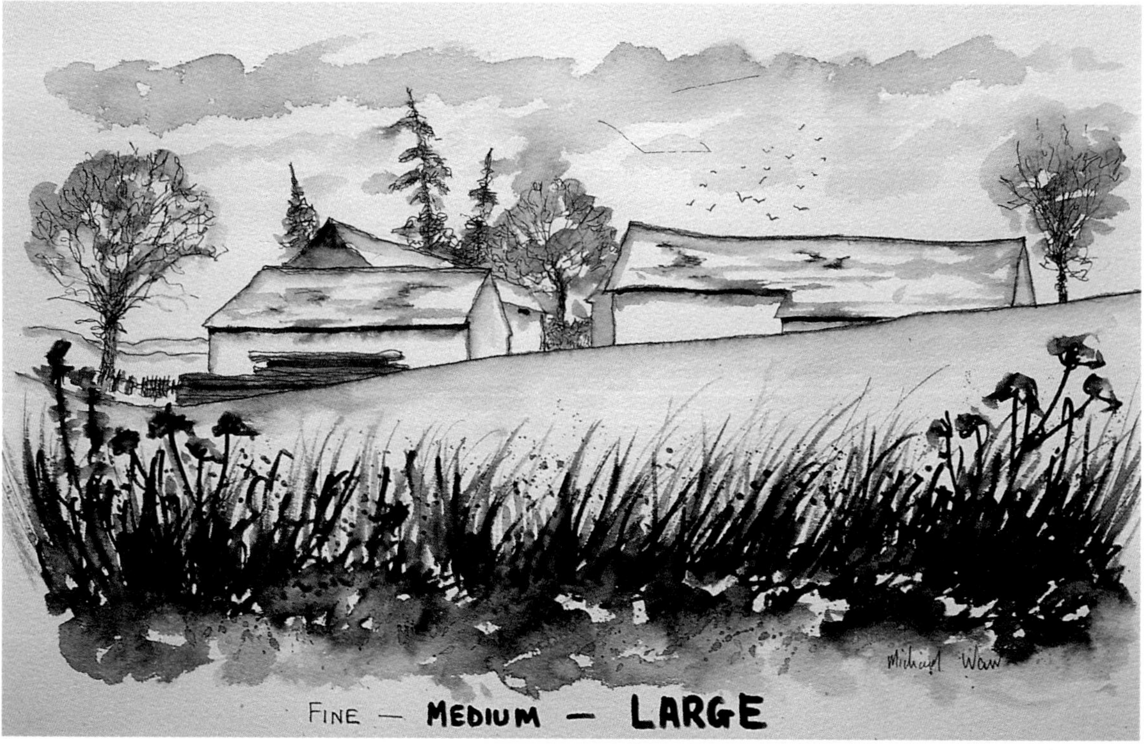

A landscape drawing which features buildings, illustrating the use of a range of black Caran d'Ache fibre-tip pens. The lettering underneath shows the thicknesses of the three pens used – fine, medium and large. Slightly differing colours emerge as water is added with a large round pointed Dalon brush

PEN AND INK

One of the simplest ways to draw with ink is to use a mapping pen. This is a cheap dip-pen and is useful when the beginner is introduced to ink. The nib of a mapping pen fits into the holder when it is not in use, providing protection against damage. A rather sophisticated way of applying ink is to use a Rotring reservoir pen. The ink is discharged through an orifice via a small tube. There is a considerable size of line range available, but the 0.35mm line thickness is suitable for the free-hand artist. Rotring also supply a full range of inks for their pens; as it is necessary to keep the pen extremely clean, they also produce a complete cleaning kit. The ink used with these pens is permanent and is not water-soluble, so it is difficult to erase. Light scratching is the best method to erase unwanted lines.

When working with ink, good results are best obtained by drawing on to cartridge paper or illustration board. Softer watercolour papers are not very suitable as the surface tears very easily and the fluff produced will clog the nib.

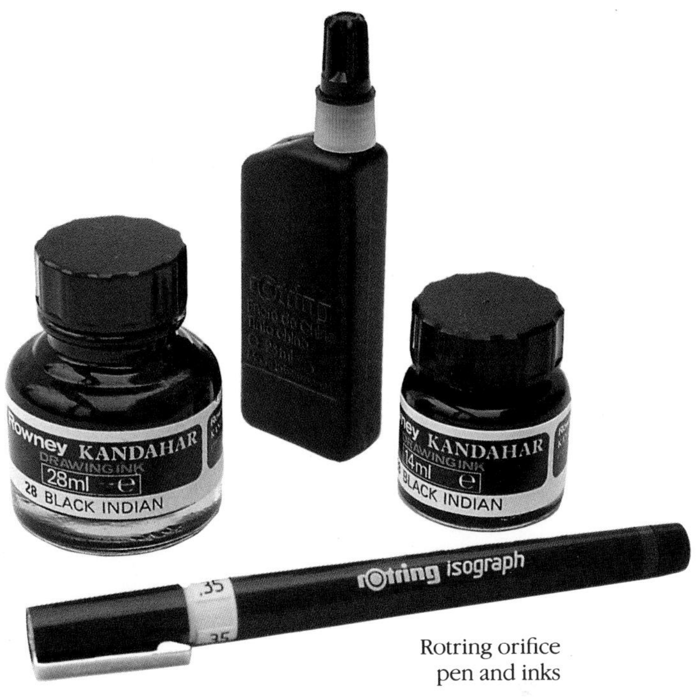

Rotring orifice pen and inks

LINE AND WASH

Line and wash is a method of combining ink or pencil lines with colour. The lines can be produced either before or after applying watercolour washes – it is a matter of personal choice. In both cases it is preferable to use waterproof inks if ink lines are being employed, unless special effects are required (see water-soluble fibre-tip pens, p14). Watercolour paper, illustration board or good quality cartridge paper make suitable surfaces for the pencil line and wash technique, but watercolour paper is not recommended for ink line work. Illustration board or good quality cartridge papers are far more suitable.

It is possible to use combinations of the aforementioned media in one piece of work with great effect. Apart from capturing the detail required, combined techniques and media can produce interesting results in their own right. It is worth experimenting with mixtures of graphite and water-soluble pencils, fibre-tip pens and water-soluble crayons – in fact, the whole works. Presentable and finished pieces of work can be achieved quickly, providing excellent information for more detailed and complex paintings which may be produced later on.

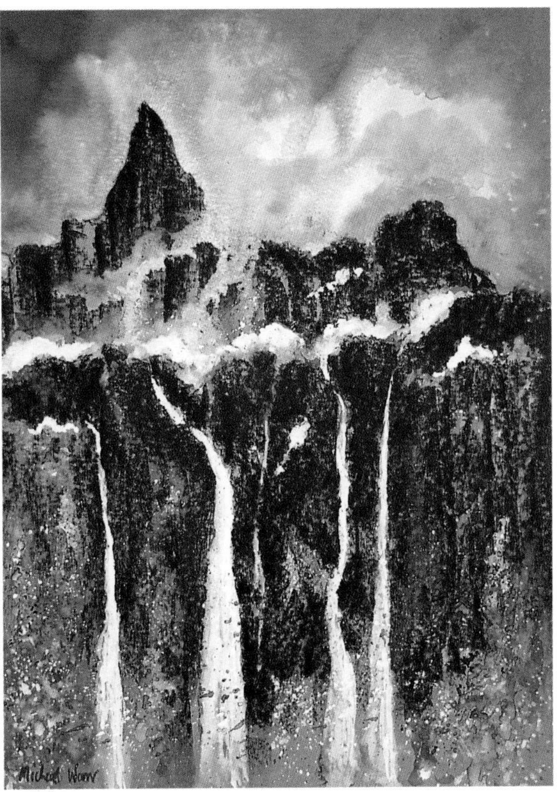
Here is an example of mixed media being employed to depict clouds clinging to a mountain in the French Alps. A storm has recently passed, leaving behind interesting atmospheric conditions and an abundance of flowing water. The picture includes Caran d'Ache graphite and water-soluble pencil, together with watercolour and gouache on grey tinted board

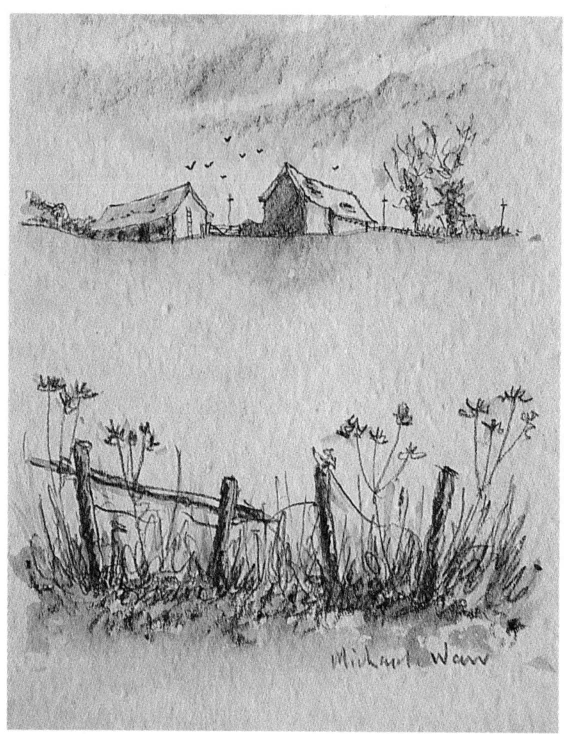

Water-soluble graphite pencil on dry watercolour paper over which clear water is washed with a round pointed Dalon brush.

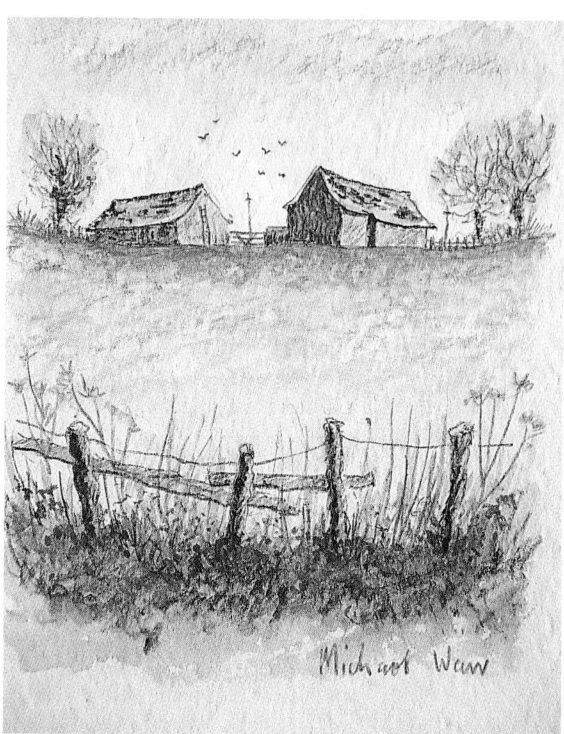

Water-soluble coloured pencil applied to already damp watercolour paper; the technique produced a 'soft' colour sketch.

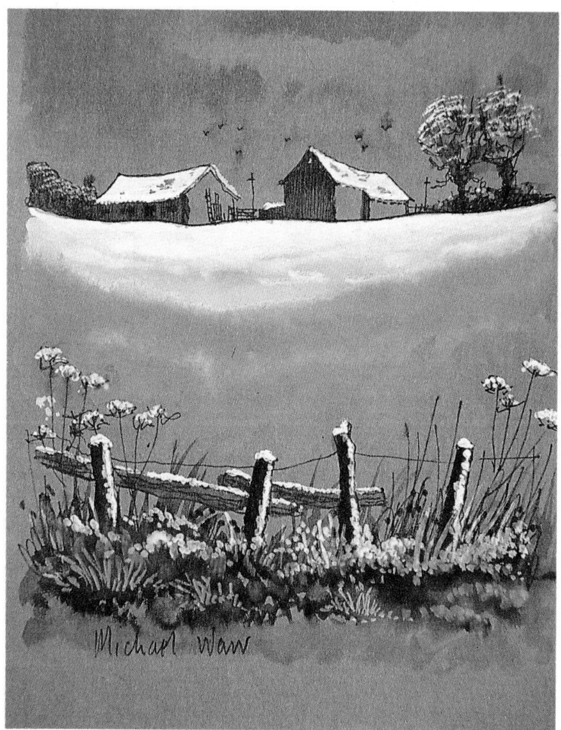

Winter's icy mantle is portrayed here by combining water-soluble fibre-tip pen and white gouache. Coloured card provided the surface, creating a feeling of warmth to balance the cold colours.

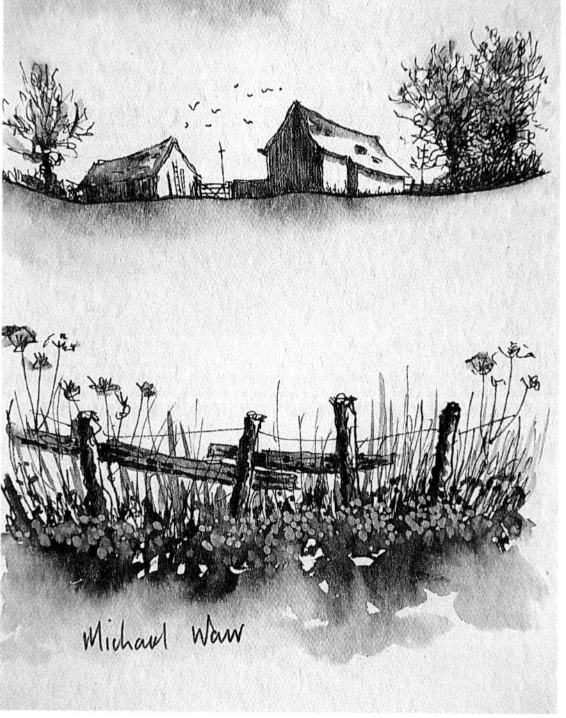

Starting with dry paper and then using a water-soluble fibre-tip pen washed over with clear water created this effect. When the sketch was dry, a little gouache added extra interest in the foreground.

Simple Perspective

Perspective is always a difficult subject for art teachers as there are so many aspects that can be covered. It is possible to enter the realms of architectural perspective with its complicated methods of working out not only the perspective of an irregular-shaped building, but its shadows as well! However, before you are discouraged from looking at the subject of perspective, I will discuss it in simple terms. Nobody could be more untechnical than myself so it was necessary for me to develop an easy method of coping with perspective.

The first rule to remember is that any line we see at eye level will be completely horizontal. Angles seen above eye level will appear to go down and away from us, while angles seen below eye level will appear to go up and away from us (see diagram). Try to keep this in mind when you are drawing and painting; it will act as an excellent guide.

The method of dealing with perspective on page 20 is the only other thing that you need to worry about. Over the years I have found it to be completely foolproof.

This house in Stuttgart, Germany, offers very interesting perspective. Protruding balconies always present a tricky challenge to the painter. The initial drawing was produced by using my 'simple' method of checking angles. There is plenty of 'going back and forth' here. Although the building lines are severe, trees on either side help to soften these and to place the house in its garden setting

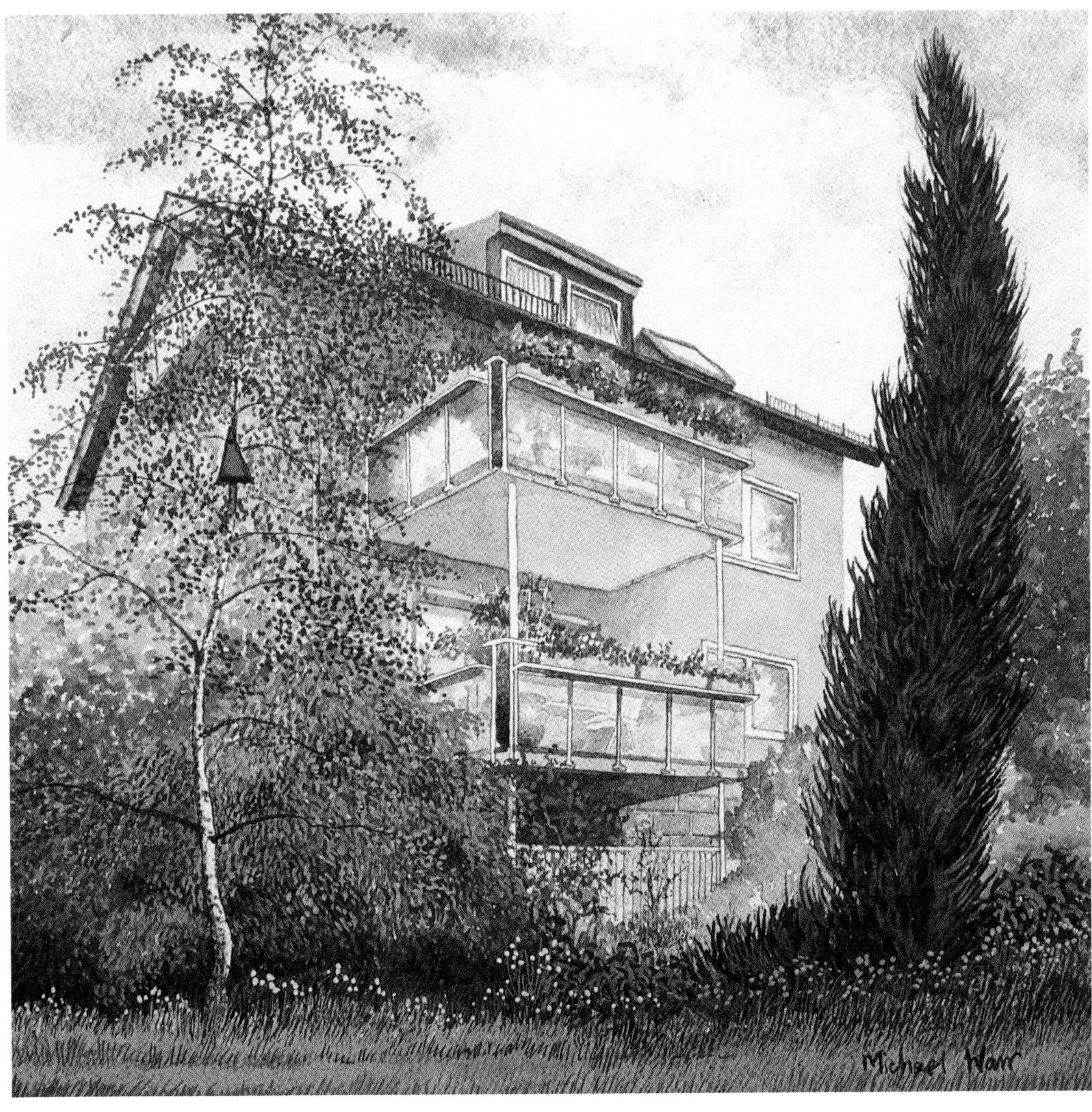

The following illustrations explain my simple method of checking angles. The method is equally suitable for buildings, interiors and objects

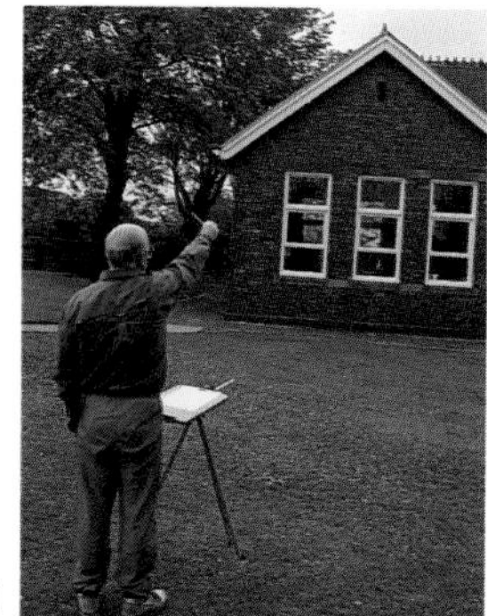

1

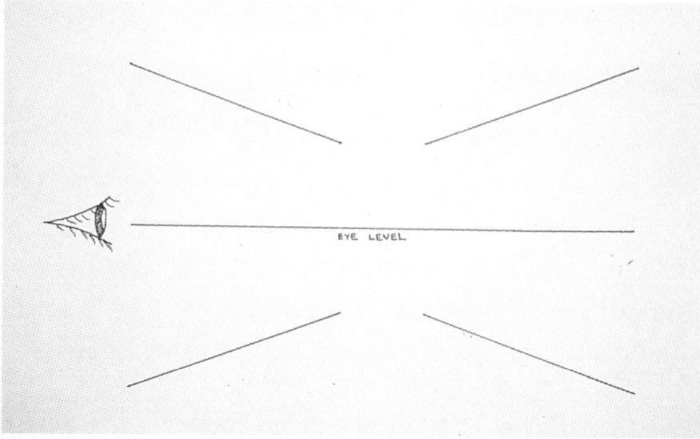

Diagram showing lines above and below eye-level

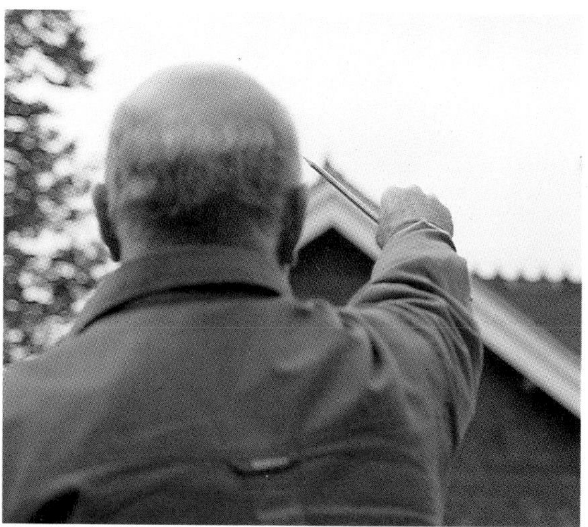

2

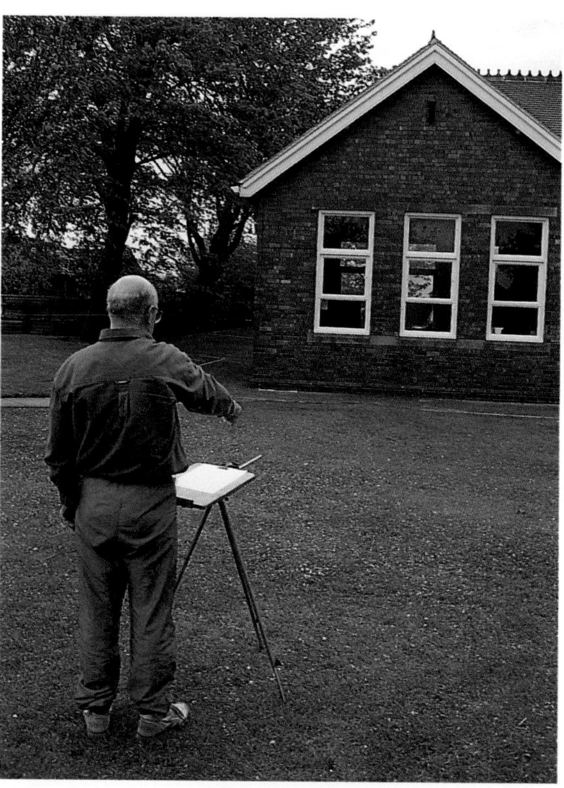

3

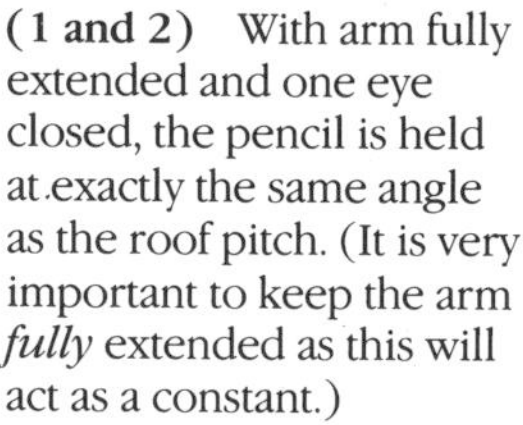

(1 and 2) With arm fully extended and one eye closed, the pencil is held at exactly the same angle as the roof pitch. (It is very important to keep the arm *fully* extended as this will act as a constant.)

(3) Keeping a *stiff* wrist, the pencil is gradually moved down towards the paper. (It is important to allow the wrist to remain stiff, which ensures that the pencil is still at the same angle.)

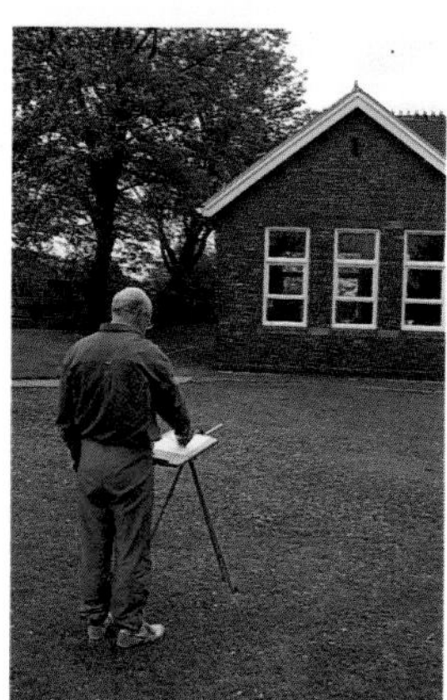

4

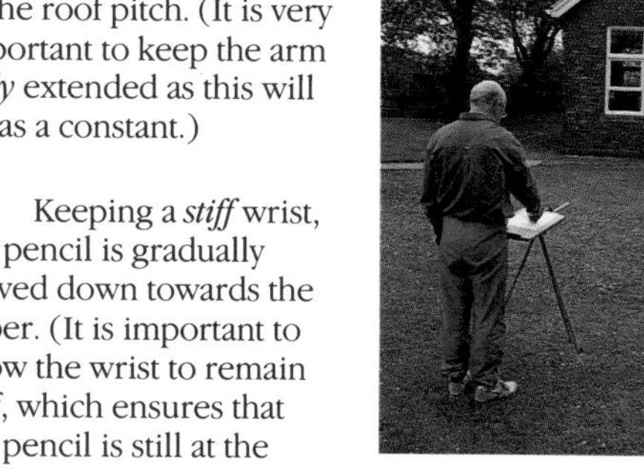

(4 and 5) The pencil arrives at the paper surface, enabling an already drawn angle to be checked. (If a line is not already drawn, it is possible simply to mark the two points with another pencil, or, with practice, to dip the point of the used pencil which makes a mark, and a faint mark can be made with the other end; the two points are then joined with a line.)

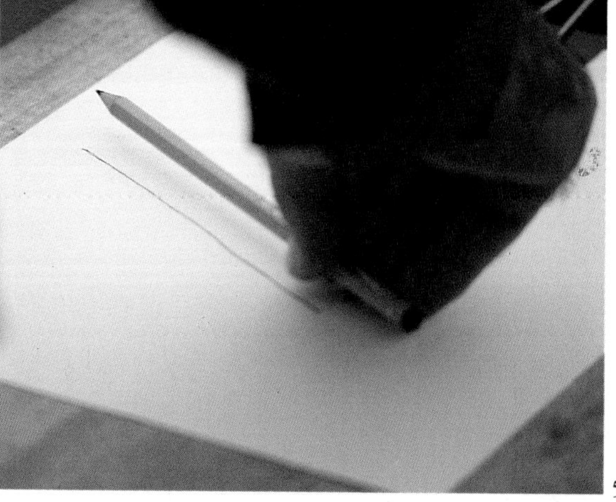

5

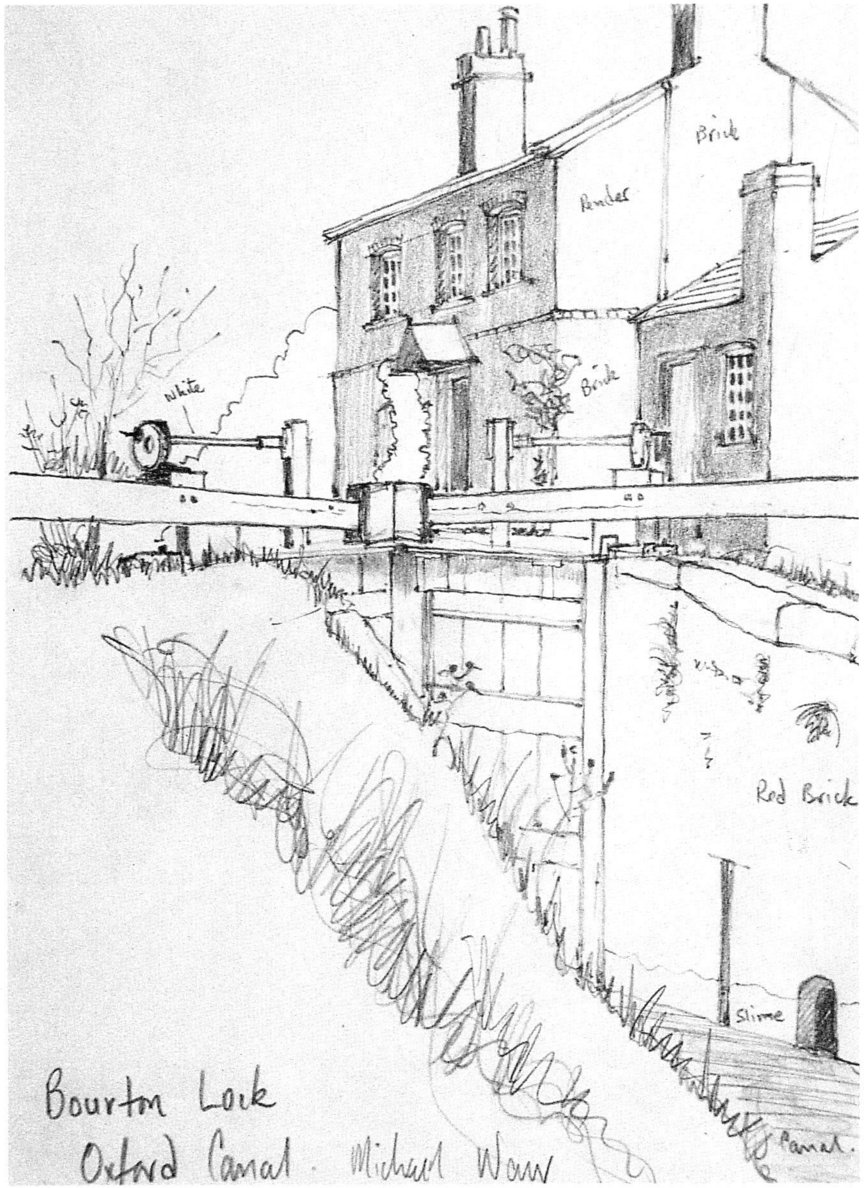

Lock gates and an old lock-keeper's cottage provide interesting perspective in this graphite pencil-drawing. Studies of this type are a useful exercise in observation; practice is essential for maintaining accuracy in paintings

Composition

For many amateur artists composition is an overrated part of painting, but it is one of the most important factors in picture making. For some artists the word 'composition' is yet another part of the jargon connected with drawing and painting. Nothing could be further from the truth – a successful painting depends so much on good composition. It is something we have control over – an area in landscape where we can reorganise nature to suit ourselves, enabling us to express inner feelings and ideas about the landscape which we see in front of us. Finding a suitable viewpoint for a landscape painting is of vital importance. It is generally the first step we take.

The next consideration is to create a focal point. The focal point of a picture is the subject that draws our attention – it gives the painting a point. Where this point is placed is important for good composition. It should not be in the middle of the picture, or near to the side or to the bottom of the painting. There is nothing worse than seeing a tree standing on the base of a picture.

Deciding how to compose paintings comes with practice, of course, but developing sensitivity towards the rectangle in which we work helps enormously;

in other words, try to see landscape shapes with rhythm and harmony. To do this, it is necessary to use artistic licence, because rarely do we find everything in nature placed exactly where we would like it to be. This is where the artist has an advantage over the photographer, because the photographer is normally limited to portraying what lies in front of the camera. With painting, however, selection enters very much into the composition; we have to decide what we include or leave out. Decision-making is one more facet of composing a painting.

Foregrounds are difficult to execute – ask any professional painter, they can be the very devil. Texture in the immediate foreground can be useful; it enables the eye to stumble over the base and into the rest of the picture without too much distraction.

We could discuss many mathematical theories about composition, such as the Golden Section developed by the Greeks, but the aim here is to keep things as simple as possible. Developing an intuitive approach to composition is the best idea, allowing a natural response to the organisation of space. Eventually, composing a picture should become second nature.

Unusual Viewpoints

Sometimes it is worth looking at a subject from an unusual angle or viewpoint. This is not suggested in order to be gimmicky, but as an exercise to stimulate ideas and creativity in the approach to landscape. By changing the way we see and by producing a different angle on a scene in a drawing or painting, we are able to introduce drama into what otherwise might be very ordinary. If by doing this we are able to stimulate someone else into sharing the same viewpoint and pleasure, we have achieved something very worthwhile.

One of my favourite ideas is to look through a fence or gap at the scene beyond. The item through which the scene is surveyed can create a natural frame for the subject or produce a picture within a picture. These elements are all part of picture making and are useful as compositional aids (which are illustrated more fully on pp 22–25). The texture of the close-up subject can be exploited to the full, whether it is brick, stone or wood; it is great fun to depict these with paint as well as the landscape beyond.

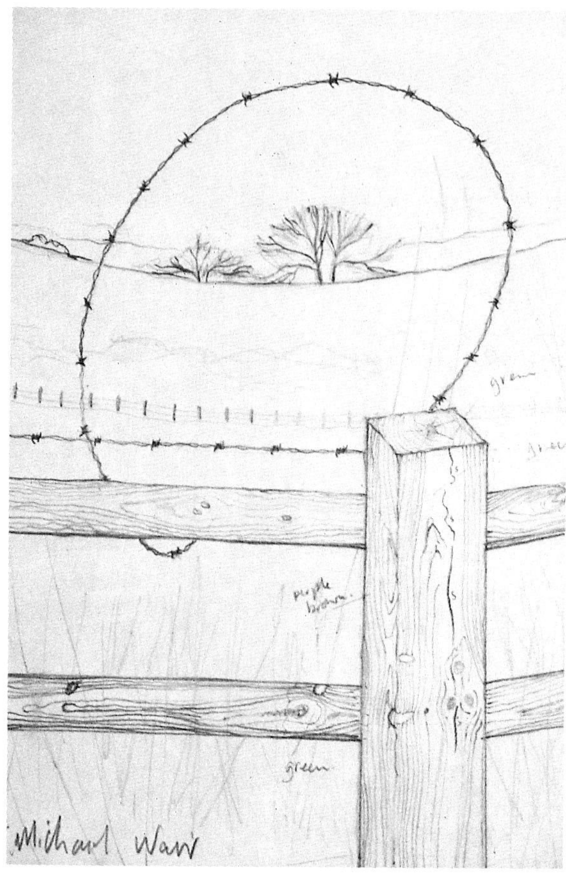

Above: Barbed wire which has snapped under tension and formed a coil provides a frame for distant trees. This idea, recorded with graphite pencil, later became a finished watercolour painting

Opposite above: A view of a distant village in the Cotswolds. Some close-up details are indicated on the left and attention is paid to the shapes of the local stone in the foreground

Opposite below: Distant farm buildings are seen through this fence in Lincolnshire. Large lumps of ploughed soil form the foreground. The whole idea creates an interesting composition

Looking through a window can provoke many interesting thoughts; on the other side there may be a garden, the sea or even a desert. Combining the window-frame and sill with whatever is outside instantly provides an interesting picture. Items on the window-sill may be included, providing yet another dimension to the composition. Jugs, for instance, will contrast with the landscape, while plants will harmonise with it. Another way of using this idea is to paint the warmth of a room inside contrasted with a wintery view outside.

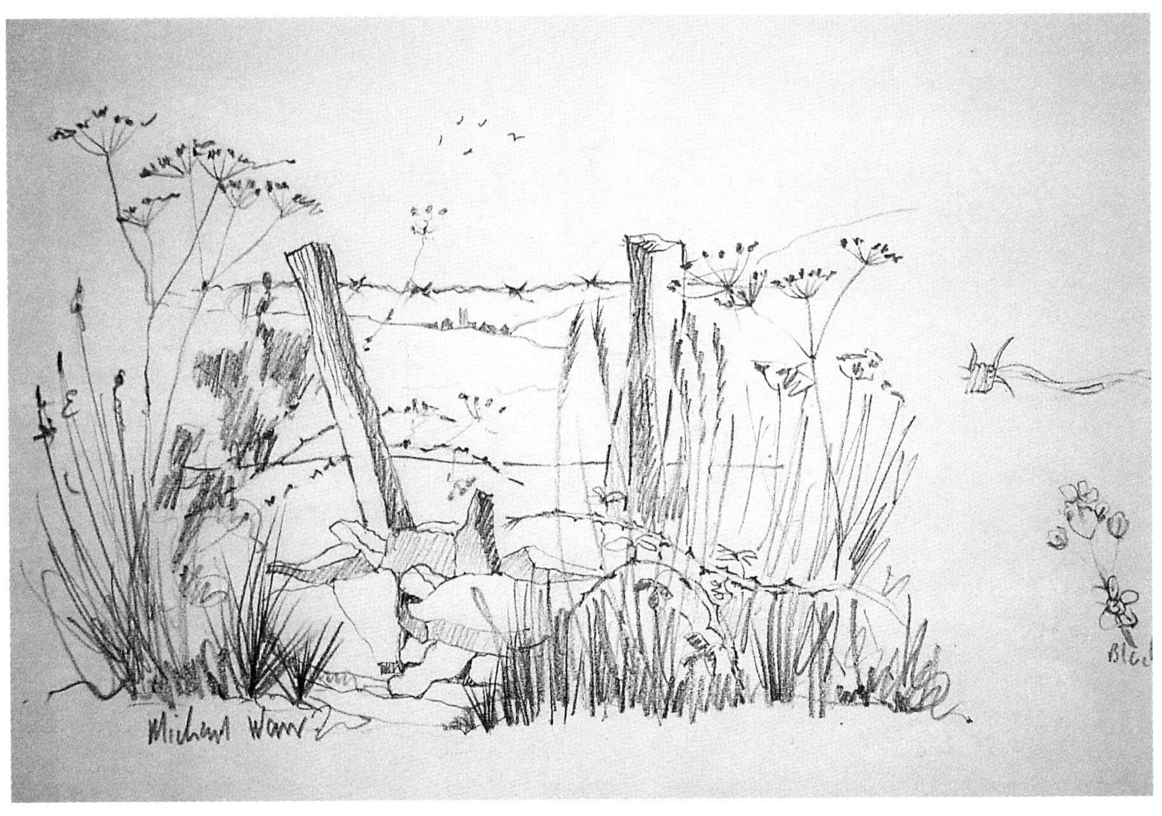

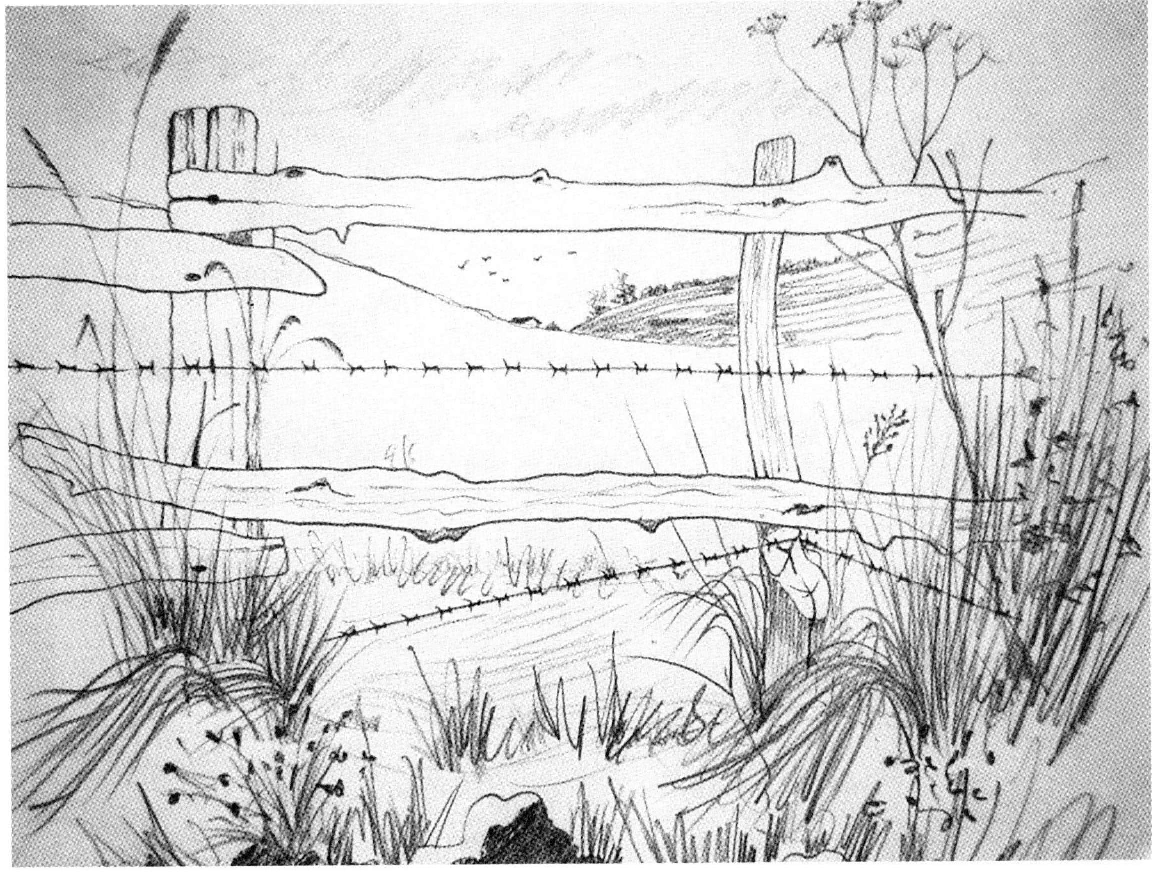

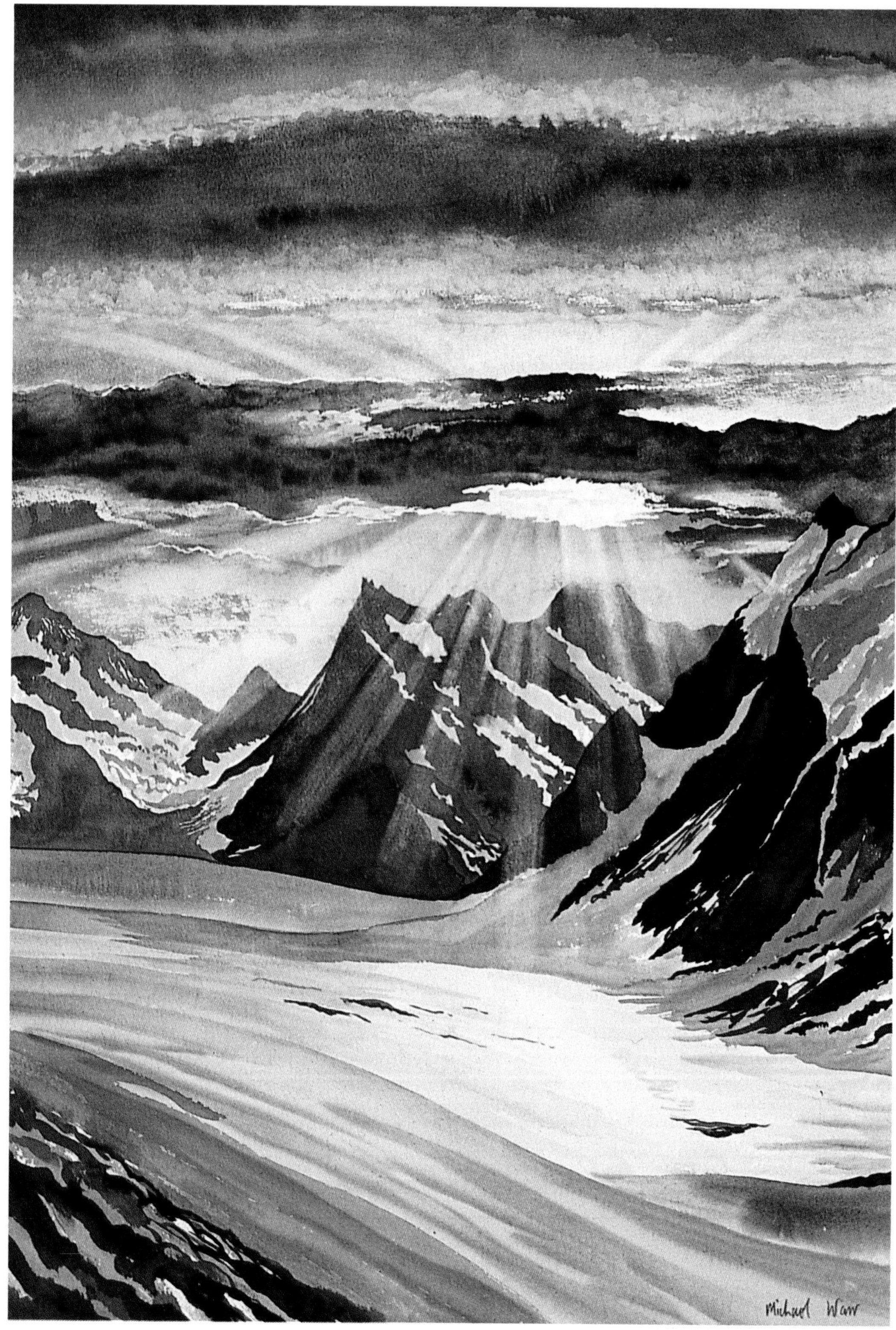

On the Glacier
This unusual view of the Aletsch Glacier was produced as a result of a helicopter trip over the Swiss Alps. The painting was made in the studio from some very shaky drawings and photographs

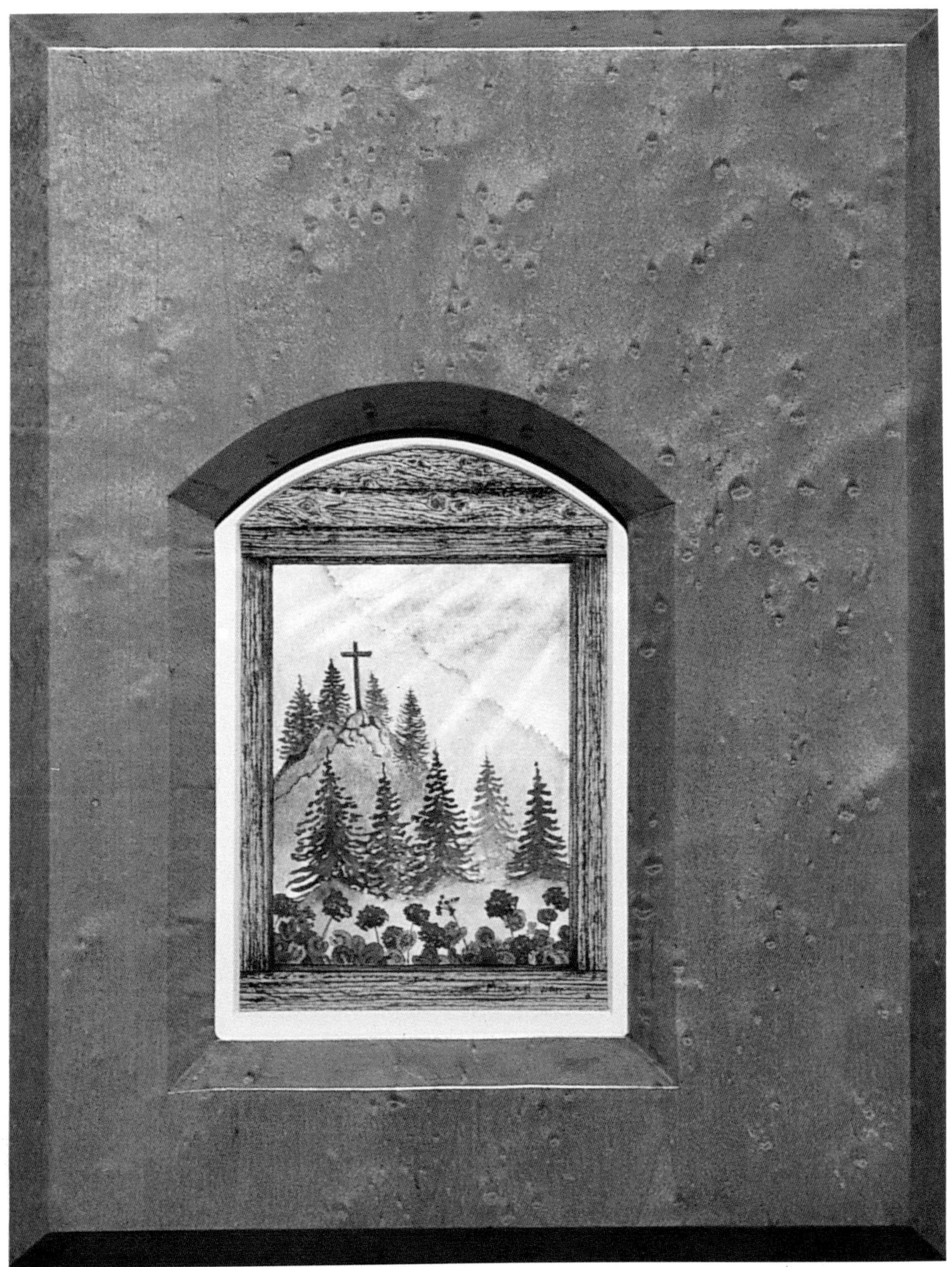

Through a Window
The drawing for this small painting was made during a meal in a restaurant on the menu, which was the only surface available. The view, containing a wooden cross and nearby geraniums, is in Ticino, the Italian-speaking part of Switzerland. Later the bird's-eye maple frame was purchased at an antiques fair and the finished painting was produced to suit

Animals, Buildings and People

When you are looking for suitable landscape subjects, it is not long before animals, buildings or people are encountered. Many students have said to me that they do not include animals, buildings or people in their paintings because they cannot draw them. Avoiding these subjects is very sad as they form an integral part of landscape painting, particularly if detail is required. Amateur artists seem to think that they will suddenly acquire the ability to draw these subjects like an expert. It simply will not happen; constant practice is necessary. The longer that these subjects are avoided, the longer it will be before they can be included in your paintings.

Buildings are perhaps the first to be attempted. Remember the advice on perspective (see p19), which is the main problem when drawing architectural subjects, and try to keep those few basic rules in mind.

While buildings stand still, animals and people do not, so they tend to be more difficult to draw. In short, more practice is needed in this area. It is very beneficial to carry a sketchbook always and to use it for reference material; quick drawings can be produced in restaurants, visits to farms and on vacation, etc. It is possible to build up a wealth of information in this way, which will be useful for inclusion in paintings at a later date.

Right: Precarious pantiles on the outbuilding of a Lincolnshire farm are drawn with a range of graphite pencils. Careful drawing of the buildings is required to capture their fragility

Below: These two hillwalkers make excellent subjects for a combined figure and landscape painting. A wet day produces an atmospheric effect, enabling some of the subjects to merge, as there is mist in the background. The foreground remains reasonably sharp, creating contrast. This type of painting can be produced by referring to stored drawings and placing them together in one composition

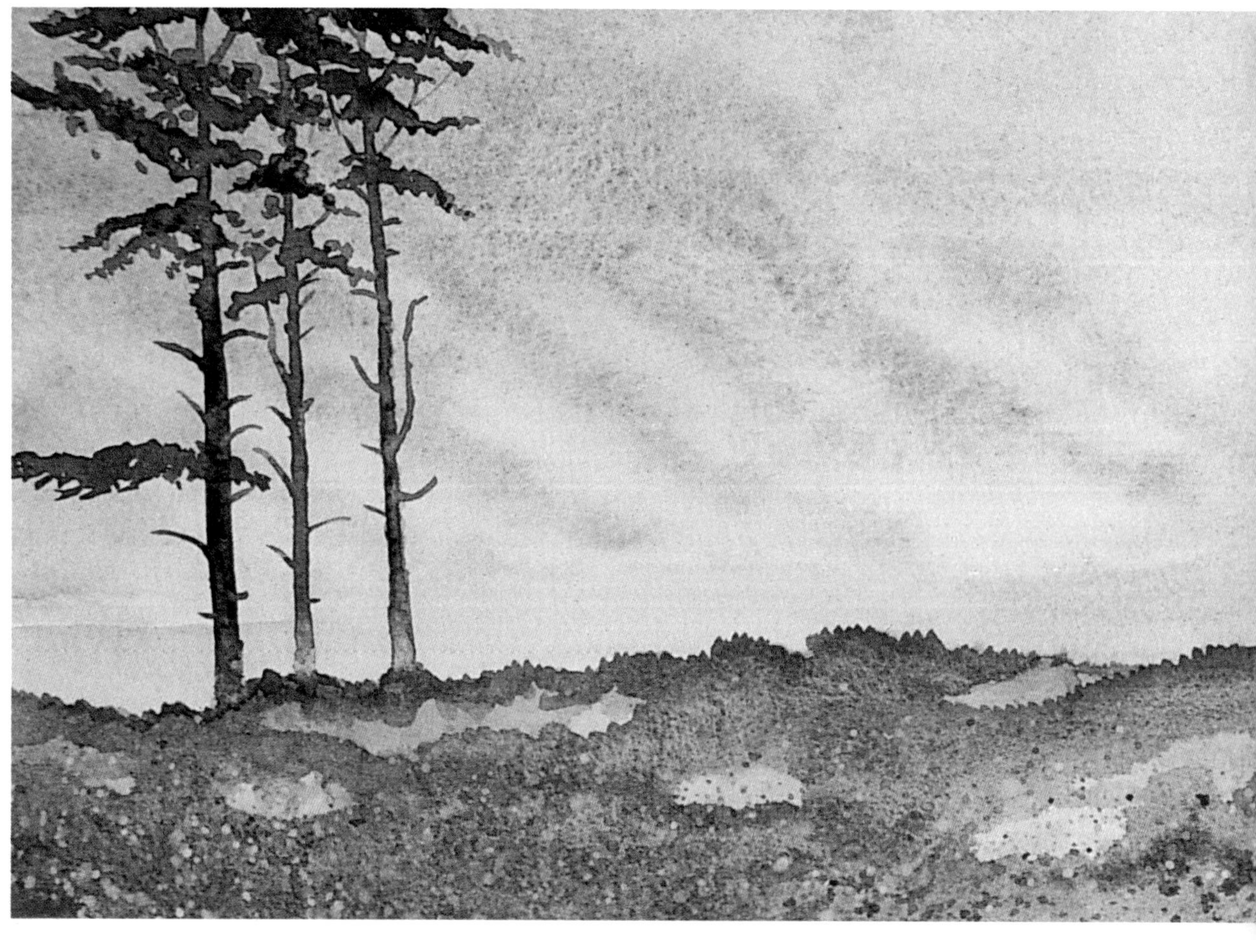

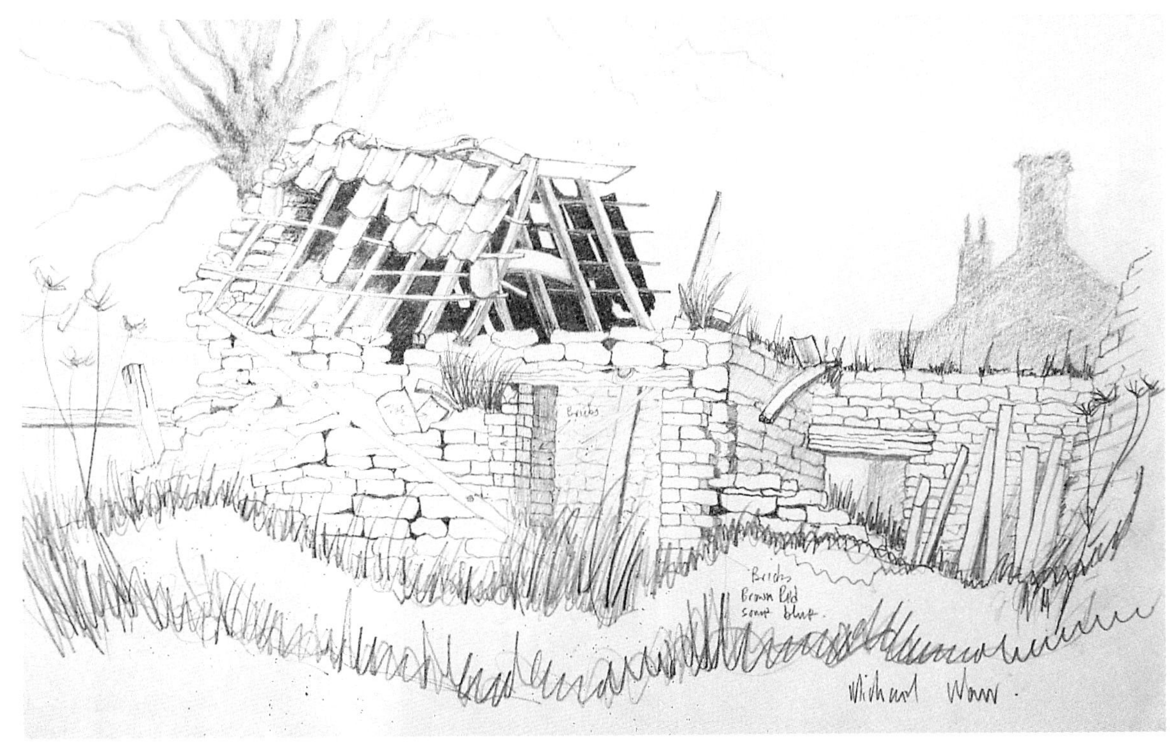

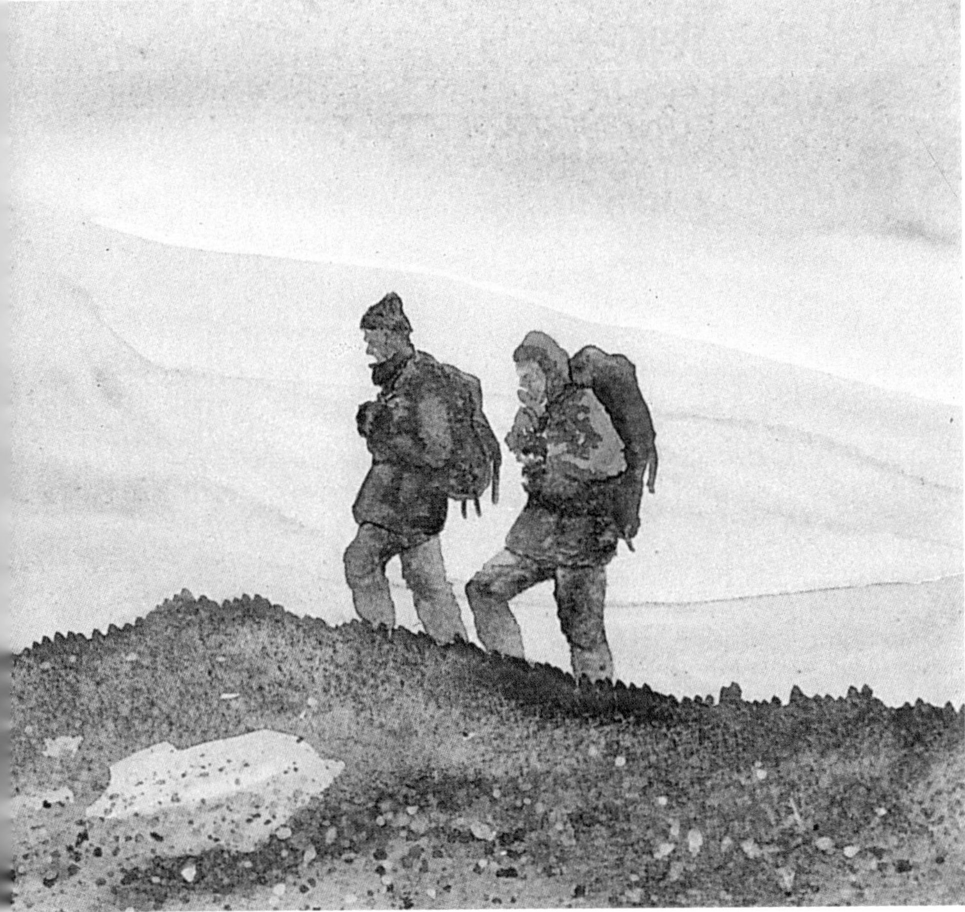

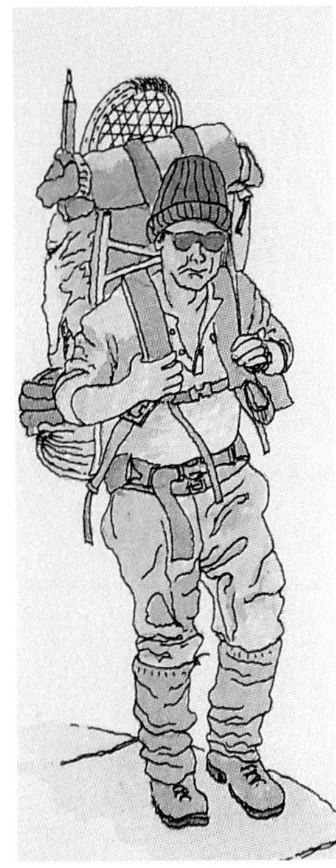

Ink line and wash study of a Californian back-packer. The colour is applied to a light pencil-drawing and, when it is completely dry, the 'lines' are strengthened with a Rotring pen and waterproof ink

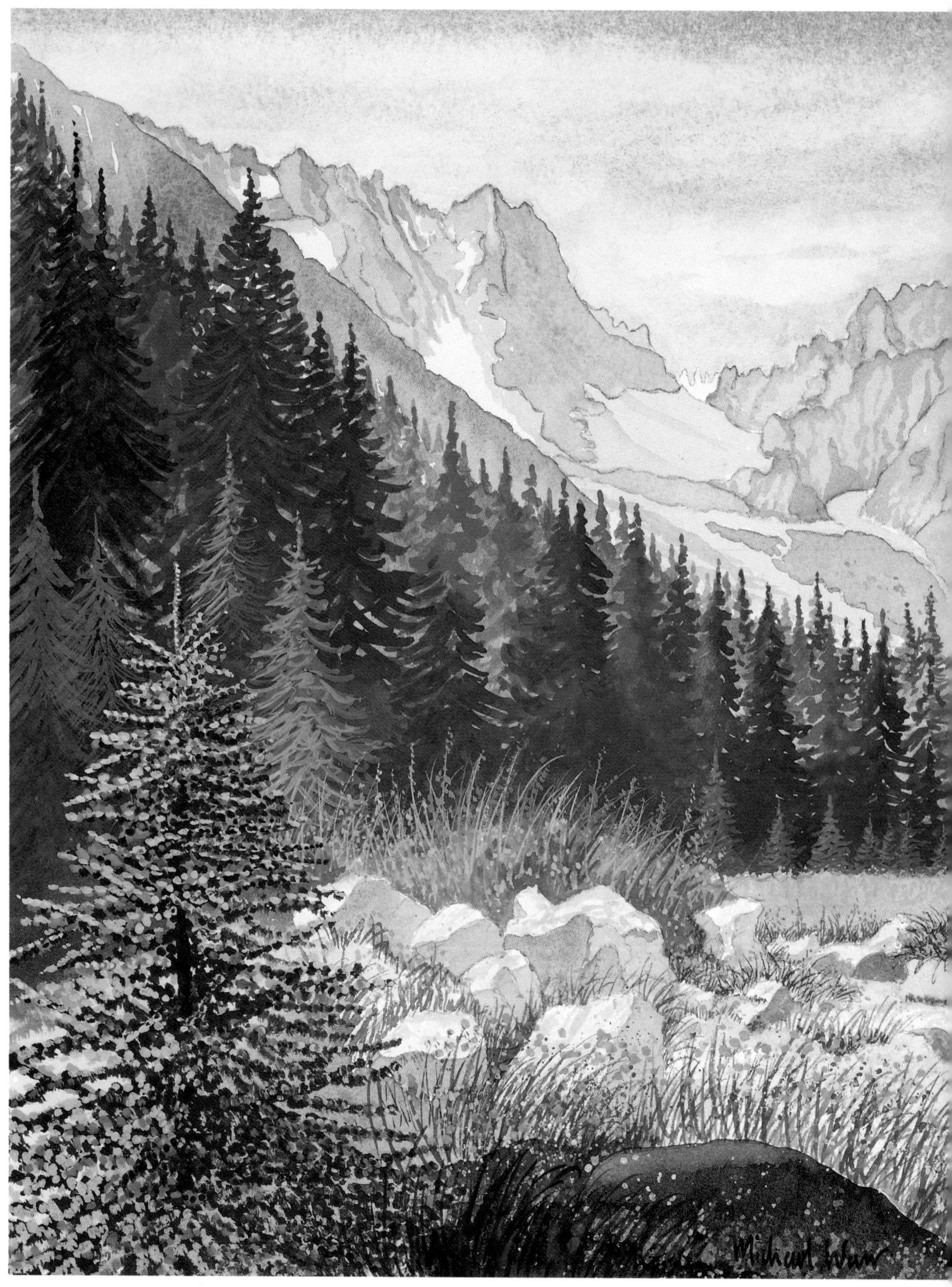

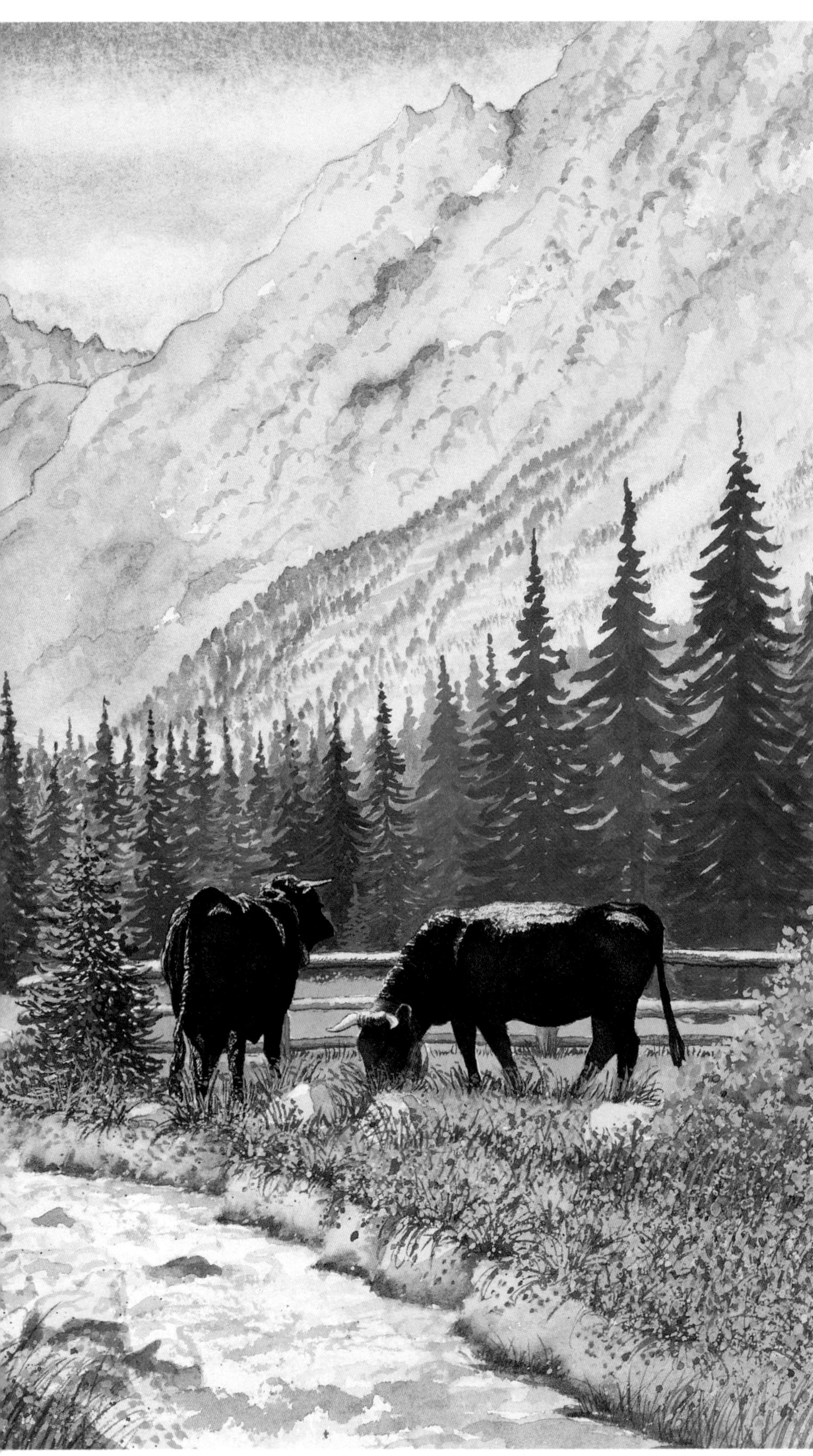

Entry into the Woods, Val d'Arpette
The sturdy alpine cattle feature as the main subjects in this painting. Their strong black forms contrast with the lighter greens in the background. Drawings of the cows were made on location, high in the Alps on the Swiss–French border. At the same time a watercolour study was produced to record the scene – the woods, mountains and stream, etc. Later, these elements were combined in this painting, which is a combination of watercolour and gouache

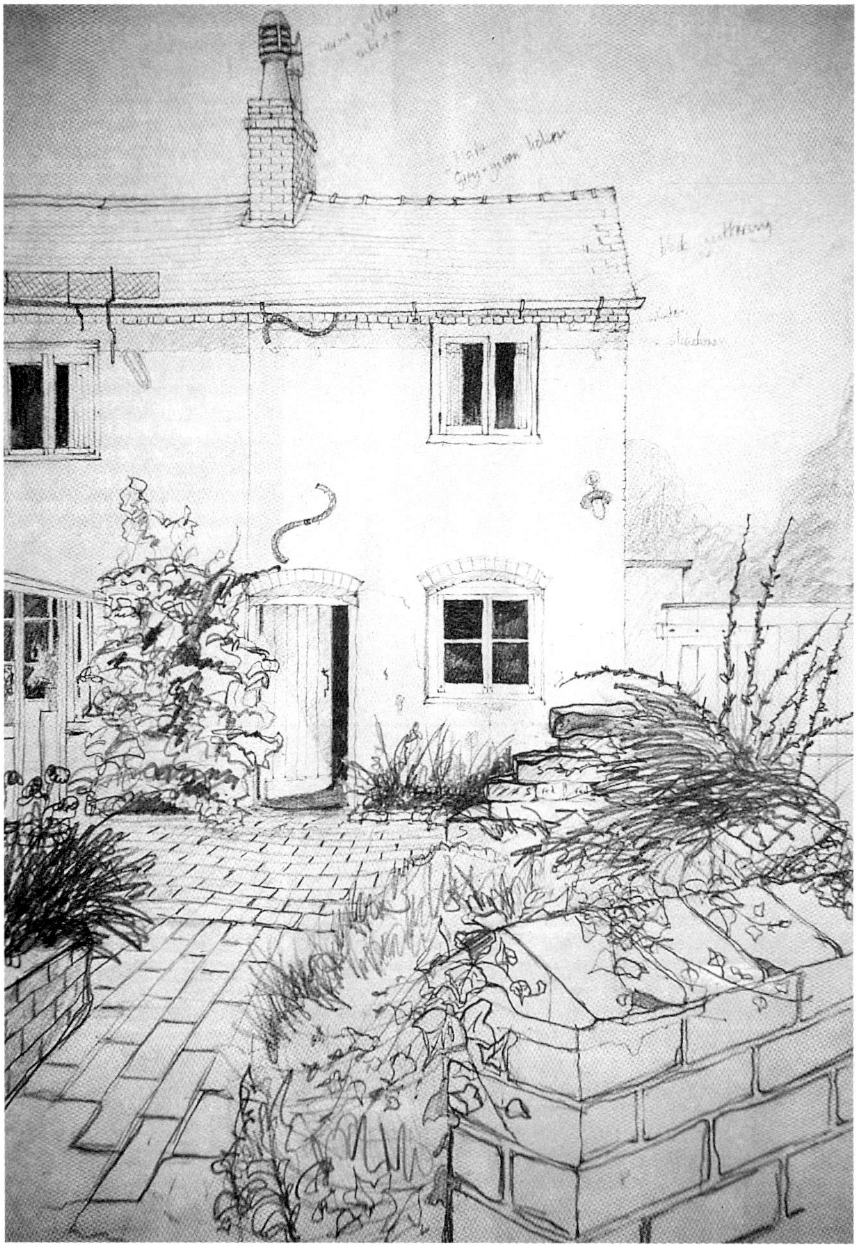

Dark tones in the windows of this old farmhouse are produced with a soft 6B graphite pencil

Below: A monochrome wash drawing produced with Caran d'Ache water-soluble crayon. The crayon was scribbled on to the paper (right), and water was added and transferred with a no 1 round pointed sable. This is a very simple way of creating a wash drawing. The only requirements are one crayon, a drop of water and a round pointed brush

Graphite pencil-drawing of a grazing sheep

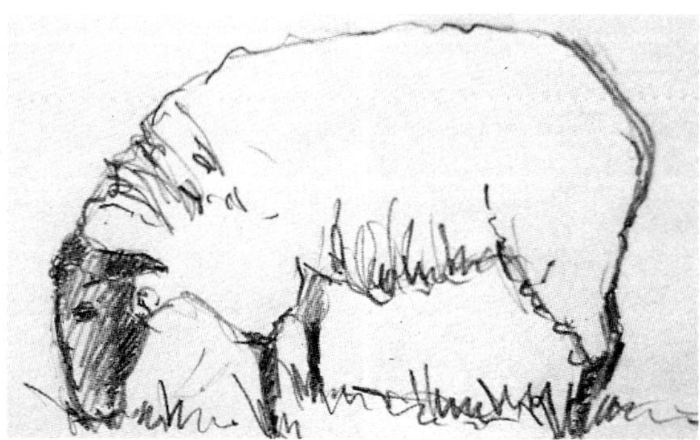

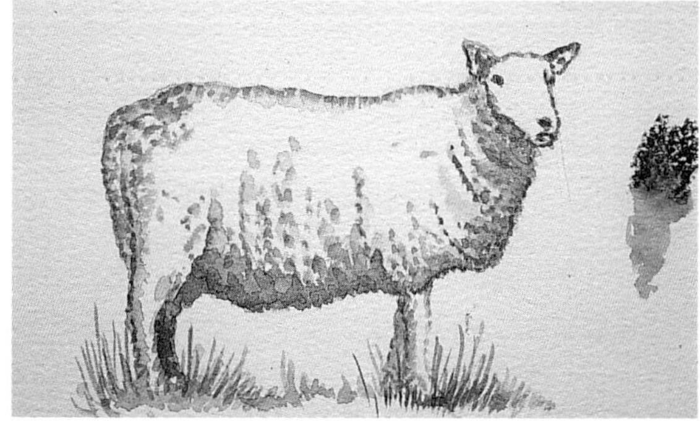

Materials and Equipment

The materials and equipment required for painting detail in watercolour vary little from those used for loose wet-into-wet styles. It is the range of brushes that tends to be more extensive. Besides having large round pointed wash brushes, a selection of small sizes is also necessary. A few extra colours can help in detailed work and these are listed on p32.

The suggested materials are kept to a minimum, but are adequate for producing detailed work. Having too much choice can be as bad as not having enough.

Watercolour

PAINT

Watercolour is a beautiful translucent medium, but because of this quality there is not the same scope for error as there is with an opaque medium. This does not mean that minor mistakes cannot be corrected, but it is not possible to put light colour over dark. Normally, light washes are applied first, with a gradual movement to the dark tones. If watercolour is applied to white paper, it retains translucency, giving it a special quality which no other medium has. However, if white pigment is added to the pure colour, it becomes gouache, a medium which will be discussed separately.

Artists constantly discuss the quality of the watercolour paint which they use. I prefer Rowney Artists' quality; the pigments are finely ground, making the colours more intense and easier to mix. Good watercolour paints consist of finely ground pigment with gum arabic as a binder; the water-soluble gum acts as a light varnish, giving the colours extra brightness and sheen.

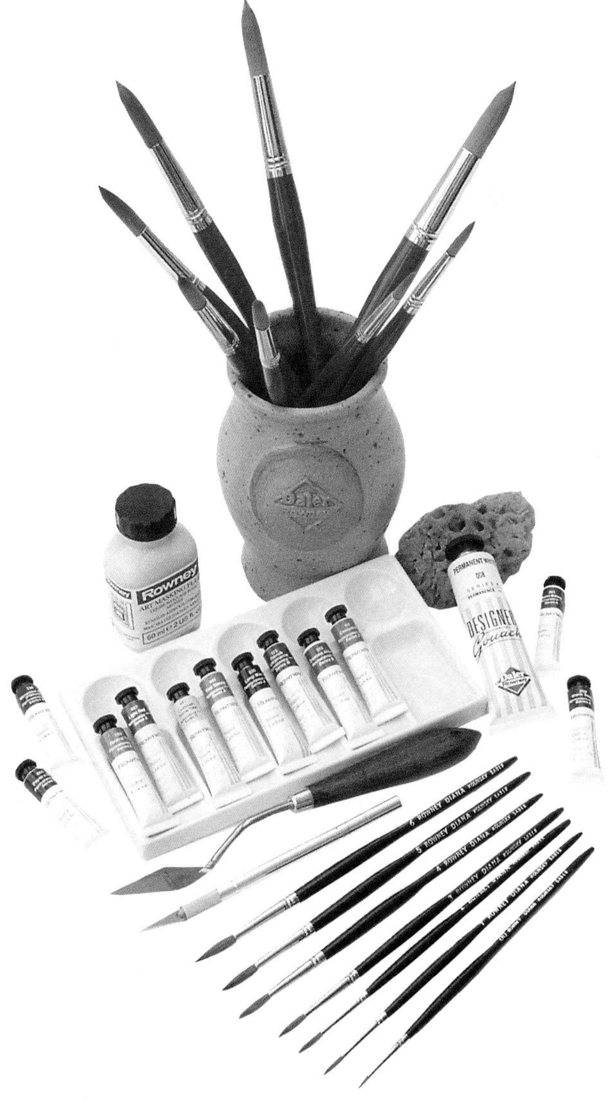

Watercolour equipment comprising round pointed brushes, nos 00 – 20. A selection of Rowney artist's tube colours, ceramic well palette, white gouache, masking fluid, sponges, painting knife and craft knife

Watercolour can be applied to a surface in many different ways. I sometimes use the paint in a free-flowing manner, creating large washes, and at other times I employ the dry-brush technique, which is very useful for conveying detail.

There are differences between what artists regard as their palette or colour range. The paintings in this book contain the following colours:

french ultramarine	light red
coeruleum	raw sienna
monestial blue (phthaloxcyanine)	cadmium yellow pale
Payne's grey	crimson alizarin
lamp black	warm sepia
neutral tint	titanium white gouache

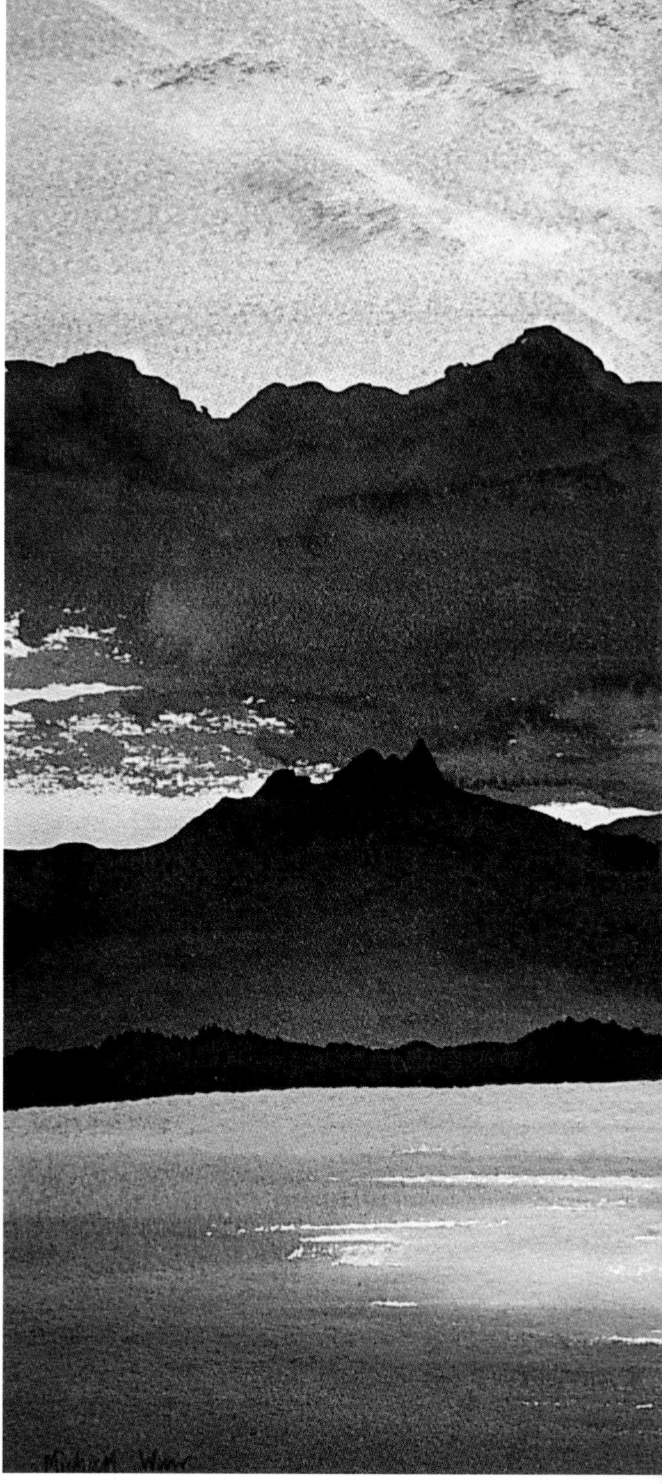

PAPER

Watercolour papers are many and varied – there is an astonishing choice. Because the range is so great, experience of using differing weights and textures of paper is the best way of discovering the most suitable ones for individual use. Basically, there are three types of real watercolour paper: hot pressed or HP, 'not' (not hot pressed), and rough. Hot-pressed paper is very smooth; 'not' is popular because its semi-smooth surface will take large even washes, but a dry brush dragged across it will produce a texture; rough paper has a 'tooth' to it and is useful for conveying texture of all kinds. It is important not to be intimidated by textured papers, but to attack them with gusto.

The weight or thickness of paper is easily explained. It is measured by size and ream. For instance, one ream of imperial size 250lb Bockingford paper weighs 250lb. Incidentally, 250lb Bockingford was used for the paintings illustrated throughout this book.

BRUSHES

Kolinsky sables are the best watercolour brushes, but these tend to be expensive. Fortunately, these days it is possible to obtain good alternatives in the form of synthetic fibres; they make an acceptable substitute for sable. The paintings in this book have been produced by using a selection of both sable and synthetic brushes. The smaller sizes (nos 000-6) are Rowney Kolinsky sables, while the larger ones (nos 7-20) are Rowney Dalon synthetics. There is not a great deal of difference in price between the

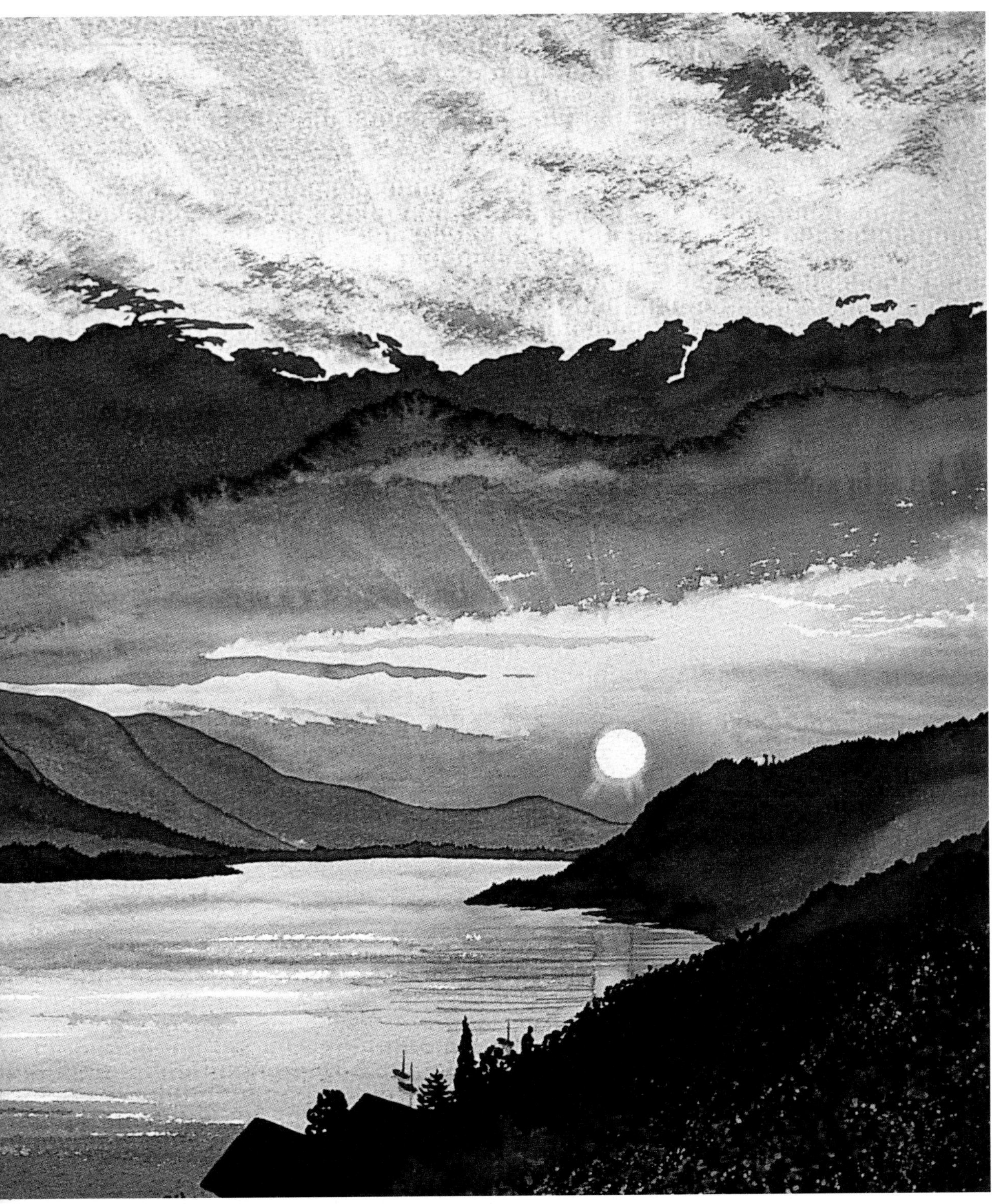

smaller sizes of sables and synthetics, but there is a huge difference between the larger ones. Smaller brushes are used for detail and it is desirable that the point is retained. I have found sables to be better in this respect; the synthetics wear quickly when they are used on roughly textured paper.

Mountains in the Sky
A glowing watercolour painting produced with the colours and brushes discussed in this section. The title is derived from an idea that the shapes of the mountains echo those of the clouds

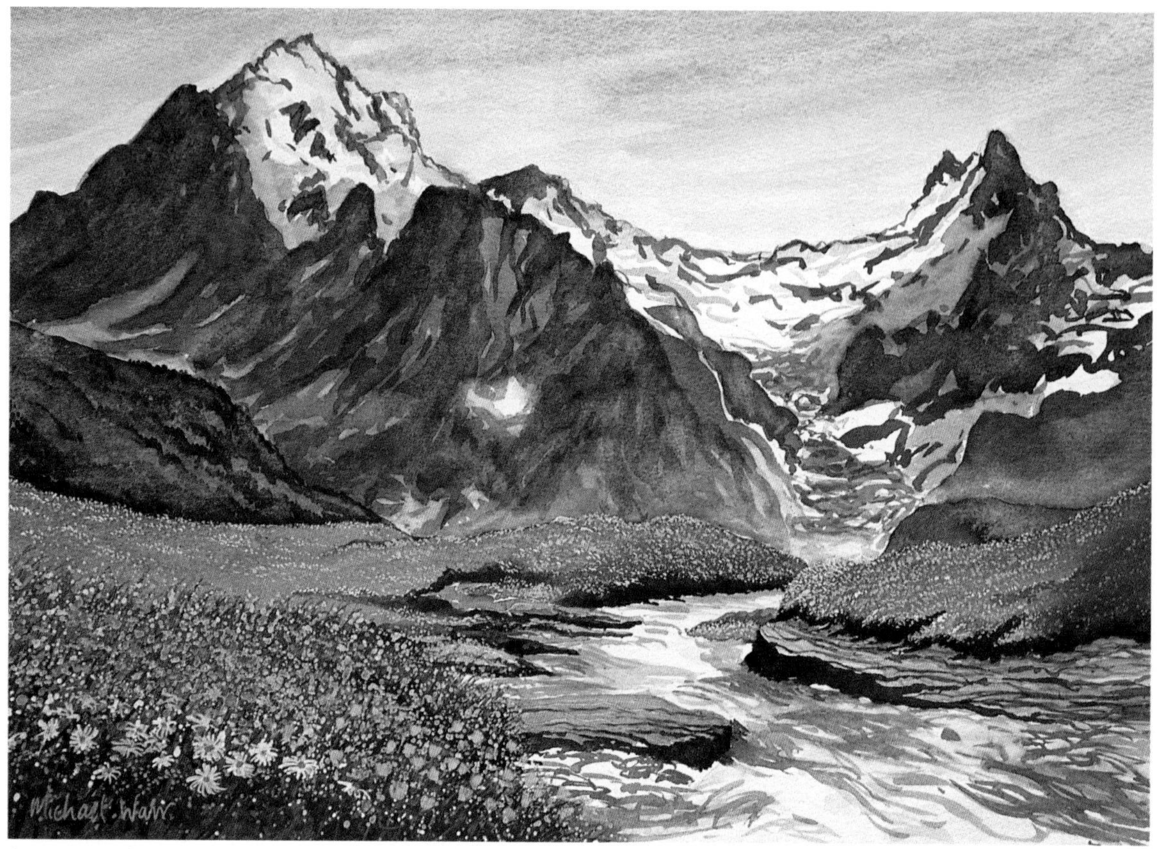

A watercolour study, this painting was done on location. The foreground was strengthened by the use of gouache

PALETTES

Watercolour palettes come in many shapes and sizes. The recessed or well types are the most suitable and are made from plastic or ceramic material. I prefer the ceramic ones as the paint does not 'skid' about on them. When large amounts of colour are required, coffee-jar lids or saucers make good palettes.

EASELS

A stable easel or surface is essential for producing good detailed watercolours. In the studio, a drawing-board placed at an angle on a table-top is suitable, and for outdoor use I recommend an aluminium sketching easel. These are easier to erect than the wooden ones, and being lighter in weight, they are easier to carry.

OTHER EQUIPMENT

Pieces of natural sponge are useful for applying colour or removing it, as are tissues or kitchen towelling. Rowney art masking fluid, a water-resistant liquid, is a useful aid to the detailed watercolourist, especially when the white of the paper is to be retained. Painting knives, usually associated with oil or acrylic painting, are useful for certain techniques.

Gouache

PAINTS

Gouache is opaque watercolour and, as a medium, was discovered by a European monk in the fourteenth century. He realised that by adding Chinese white to his transparent watercolours they became opaque. White gouache added to watercolours renders them very opaque, a technique I like to use in the foreground of a painting.

It is possible to work from dark to light with gouache, adding white to lighten the colours, rather than diluting them with more water. The addition of black darkens the colours and produces interesting results when mixed with red or yellow. Black, a colour considered taboo by many artists, is well worth experimenting with.

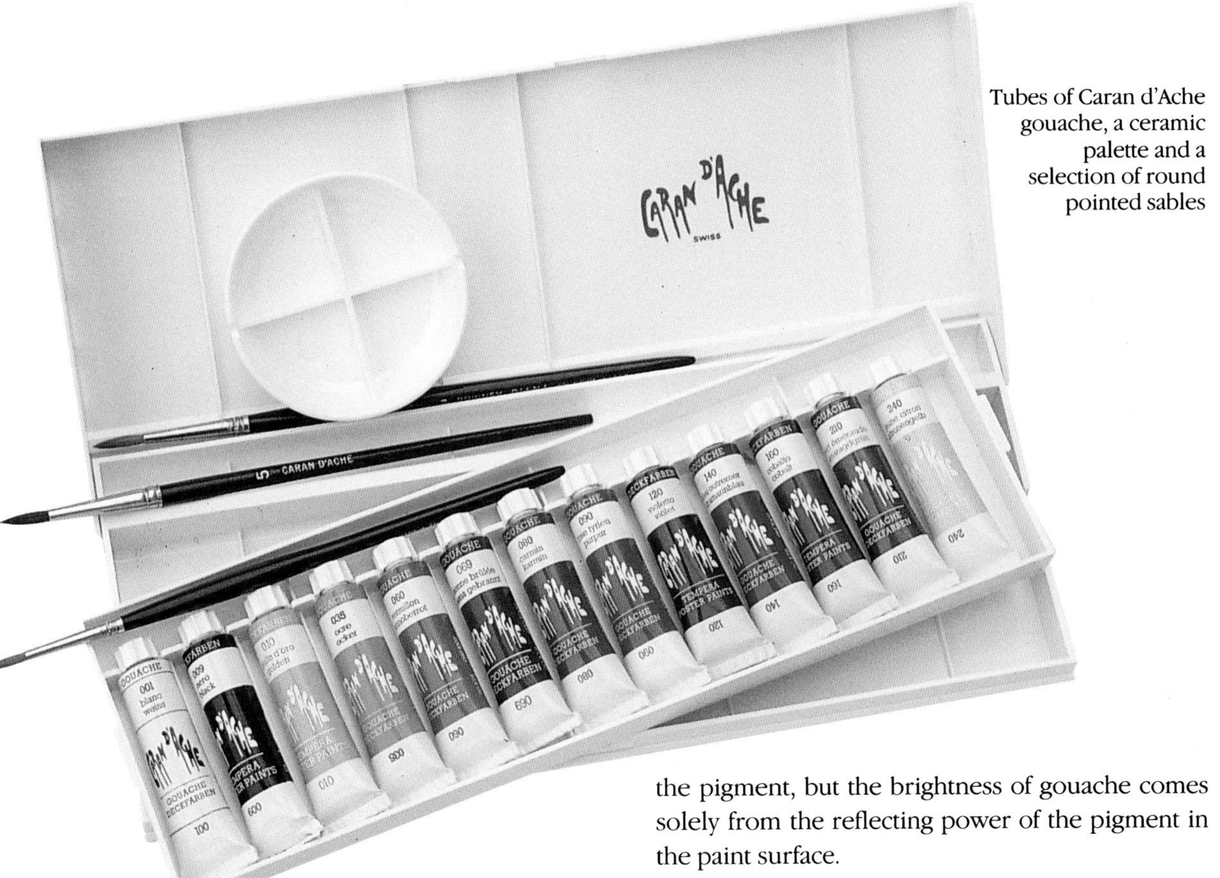

Tubes of Caran d'Ache gouache, a ceramic palette and a selection of round pointed sables

the pigment, but the brightness of gouache comes solely from the reflecting power of the pigment in the paint surface.

When using gouache as a medium in its own right, I prefer Caran d'Ache paint in tubes. Their range of twelve permanent non-fading colours is more than adequate; they comprise:

white	purple
black	violet
golden yellow	ultramarine
vermilion	cobalt
burnt sienna	lemon yellow
carmine	yellow ochre

PAPER

The same papers can be used for gouache as for watercolours, but with the addition of tinted ones, because the medium is opaque. Watercolour glows, the white of the paper underneath shining through

BRUSHES

Watercolour brushes are suitable for gouache, especially when detail is being depicted, but hog-hair oil-painting brushes can be used to apply the paint thickly.

PALETTES

These are the same as for watercolour painting, but because dilution is not so necessary with every painting, a large plate can be useful.

EASELS

Watercolour easels and surfaces are suitable for gouache.

OTHER EQUIPMENT

Because gouache is prone to lifting when washes are applied one on top of the other, the use of an acrylising medium is an advantage. This is mixed with the paint on a palette and fixes the underlying wash if desired. Sometimes the lifting effect is required. The mix of colour is very interesting, but if the end result is to be a clean one, the addition of the acrylising medium is necessary.

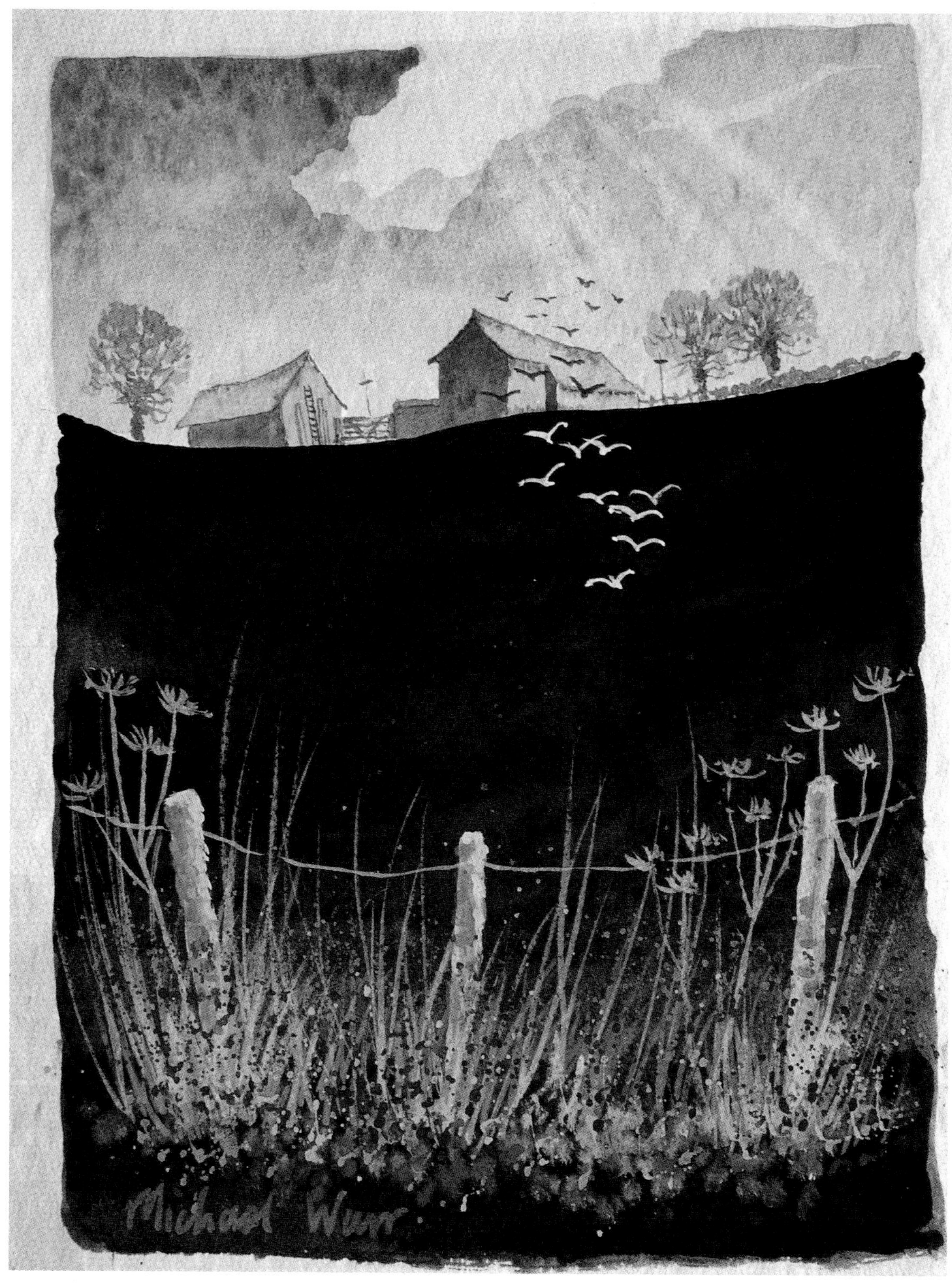

A study produced entirely with Caran d'Ache gouache. Note how the light against dark technique is used with the foreground posts and vegetation. These are painted on top of the dark brown ploughed field, as are the white gulls.

Techniques

Before introducing the step-by-step guides, I feel that it is important to discuss the techniques of detailed watercolour painting. The examples illustrated will hopefully lead to a greater understanding of the various stages in the paintings, eliminating the need to interrupt the flow of thought when describing a certain stage during a demonstration painting. Practising these techniques provides invaluable experience, which is extremely helpful when working on a finished detailed watercolour painting. Remember, by experimenting with techniques it is possible to discover ways of depicting certain features of a subject. Textures, for example, can be produced with many items other than brushes. Gimmicks are not encouraged, but creativity and discovery of the possibilities in the use of watercolour and gouache should be developed.

It is not necessary to fill every part of a painting with detail, which can result in a picture losing its impact. If detailed subjects are allowed to breathe by being surrounded with flowing washes, the poignancy they exude can have a powerful effect. Therefore, the following techniques contain a combination of detailed and free-flowing ideas. These provide the anatomy of detailed landscape watercolour painting.

Tricks of the Trade

Many times I hear the retort from students, 'So that's how it's done'. They are normally referring to a technique they have seen someone else perform or have just discovered for themselves, and nine times out of ten it is a trick of the trade. This is the use of one of the many aids which are available to watercolour painters. A number of techniques have been discovered and developed over the years to assist in the production of watercolour paintings. Some of these can be extremely helpful in the depiction of detail or textures. It is important not to let them dominate the work, but allowing them to become an integral part of a painting can certainly help to make it successful. If the tricks take over, the resulting paintings are simply a series of gimmicks. Like any aid, if it is used with taste and discretion, a trick of the trade can help in the creative process to great effect.

MASKING FLUID

Of all the resists devised for watercolour painting over the years, Rowney art masking fluid is the most effective for retaining the 'white' of the paper. Sometimes it is desirable to retain light intricate shapes and painting around them is impossible. This is where masking fluid comes into its own; being a rubber-based solution, it is impervious to water. It can be applied to the paper with many tools, including cocktail-sticks, brushes and pens. The fluid is applied and allowed to dry, then watercolour is painted over it. When this is completely dry, the masking fluid can be removed with an eraser or finger. If the paint is still wet, the colour will smudge. Applying the fluid too thickly is not recommended; a thin covering is just as effective and it should not be left on the paper for weeks – a few days is the maximum. One other word of warning: if a brush is used to apply the fluid, wash it immediately after use in warm soapy water, otherwise the brush will be useless.

CANDLE WAX

Candle wax used as a resist is extremely effective; its waxy nature enables hit-and-miss effects to be achieved. To produce an interesting texture, simply break off a piece of colourless candle and rub it on to some watercolour paper. Apply watercolour paint

Shapes created with masking fluid

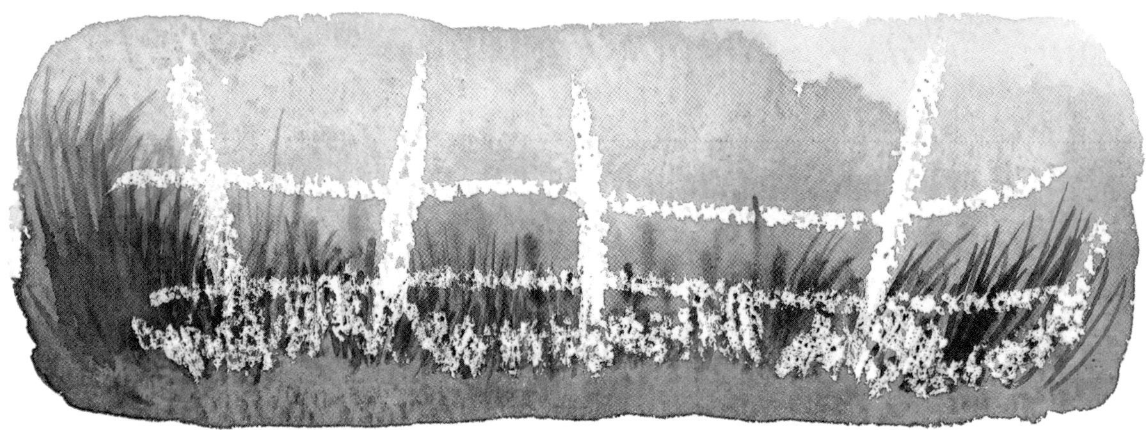

Candle wax used as an effective resist

Wintry textures produced by adding salt to a damp wash

Cloud shapes formed by blotting the damp wash with a tissue

Colour lifted with a thirsty sponge

Colour applied with a sponge

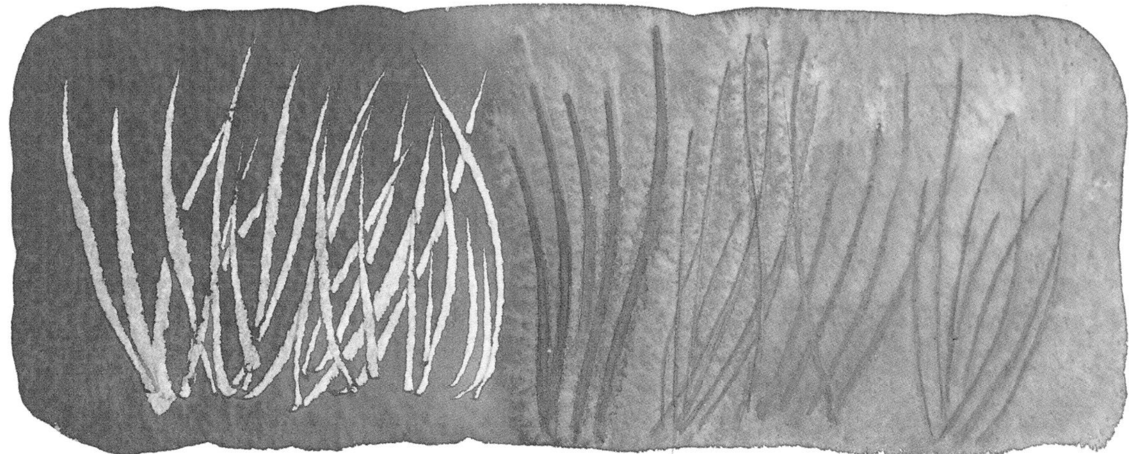

Left: Colour removed with a painting knife *Right:* Shapes created by scoring the paper prior to applying paint

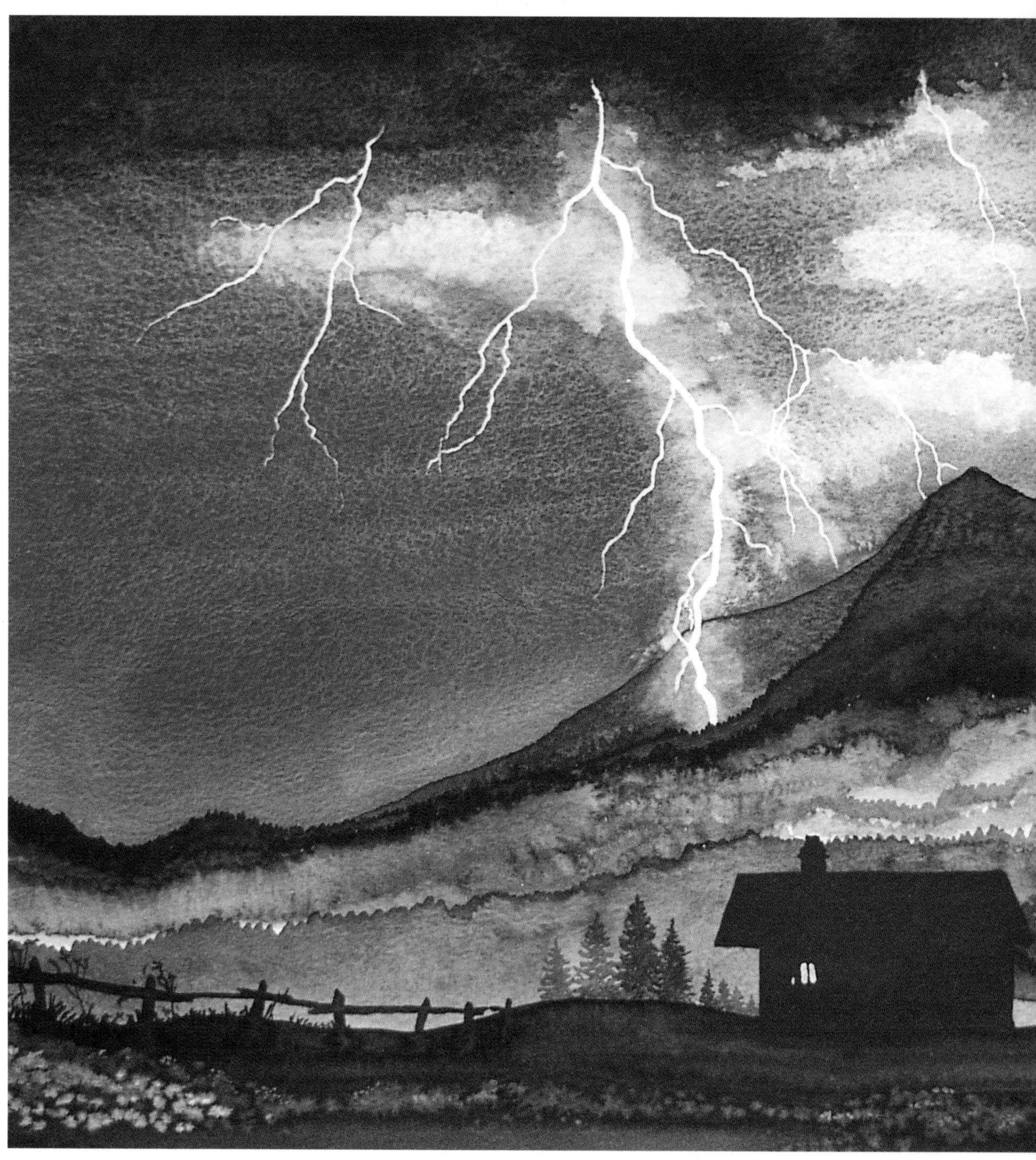

and allow this to dry. Remove the wax by placing blotting-paper or tissue on top and pressing with a hot iron.

SPONGES

A selection of natural sponges is useful for both applying paint and removing it. I say 'natural' as opposed to synthetic, because the shapes of natural sponges are far more random. When you are trying to create a natural texture, synthetic sponges, which are machine made, tend to produce results that are too even; natural sponges, on the other hand, will produce a more random, and therefore more natural result. Usually, we are trying to convey natural textures in a landscape.

Sponges may also be used to lift off or remove paint which is either wet or dry; if the paint has dried, dampen the sponge slightly in order to lift the paint.

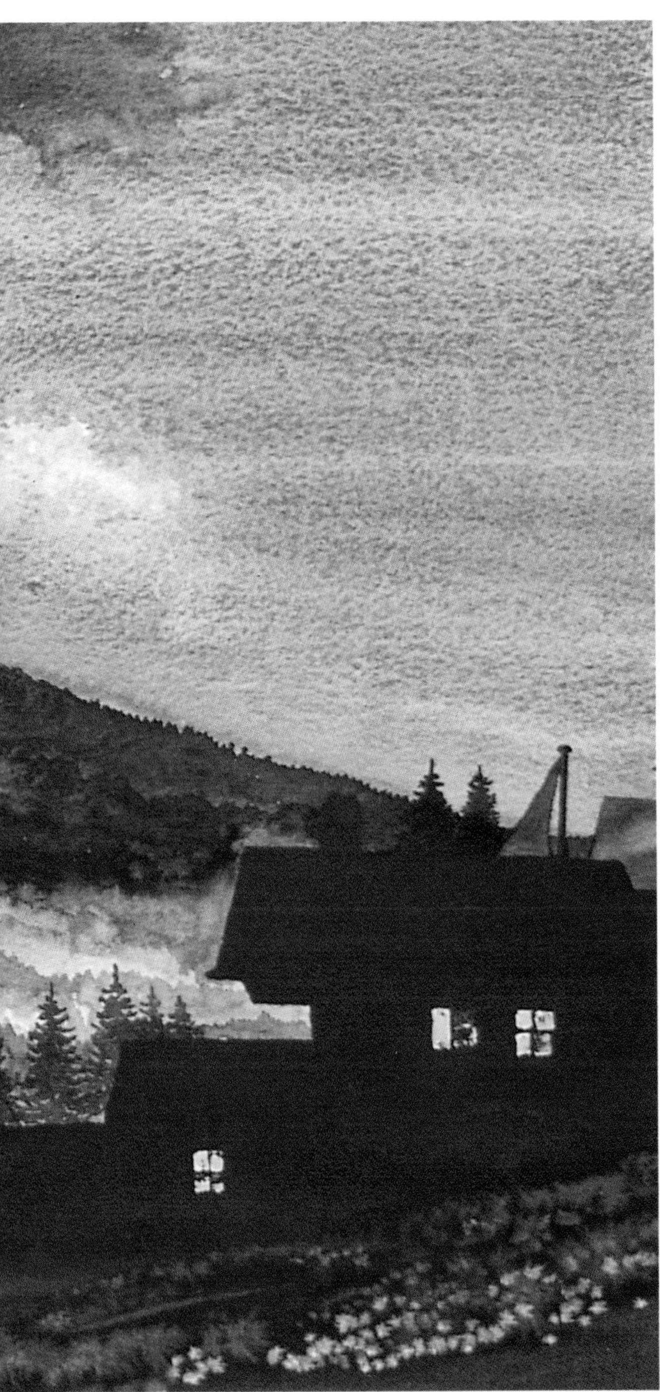

Evening Lightning
Masking fluid is a real aid in portraying the flash of lightning in this dramatic, darkly lit painting. The forks of lightning are initially masked off before any colour is applied. When it is dry, a very dark wash is brushed over the entire sky area. The landscape, which consists mainly of mountains and buildings, is painted after the sky is completely dry. When all of the contents are complete, the masking fluid is removed and the lightning forks are tinted with weak colour

MARKS WITH TOOLS

Many implements other than brushes can be used to make marks with paint. A painting or palette knife normally associated with oil and acrylic painting is useful for lifting off watercolour. It must be used while the paint is wet to create the best effects. The technique is known as 'knifing out'; it can be employed in many situations from forming shapes to suggesting textures of a wide range of subject matter.

Matchsticks and cocktail-sticks may also be used for removing wet or damp watercolour, creating similar yet different marks and shapes.

Scoring the paper before watercolour is applied can be effective. Lines and shapes scored into the surface with such items as the handle of a paintbrush, scissors, a very hard pencil or palette knife produce interesting results when overpainted with dilute paint.

Dry watercolour can be removed by scratching out with a razor blade or scalpel. The contents of a painting from cobwebs to highlights on water can be depicted in this way.

HOG-HAIR BRUSHES

These brushes are normally used for oil or acrylic painting. Some artists use them for watercolours or gouache, but I like to use them for removing watercolour rather than for applying it. The method is simple: when the watercolour paint is completely dry, wet the hog-hair bristles and rub the brush over the dry paint. It will reactivate immediately (rather like the dry paint on a palette), and the damp paint can be blotted away with a tissue or piece of kitchen towelling. Sun-rays, seen against a dark sky, may be created in this way. The technique can also be used for correcting errors by washing out an unwanted shape or area. The paper will only stand a certain amount of 'scrubbing' – do not over-rely on this method.

THIRSTY BRUSH

Round pointed sable or Dalon brushes can also be used as blotters. If excess moisture is squeezed from

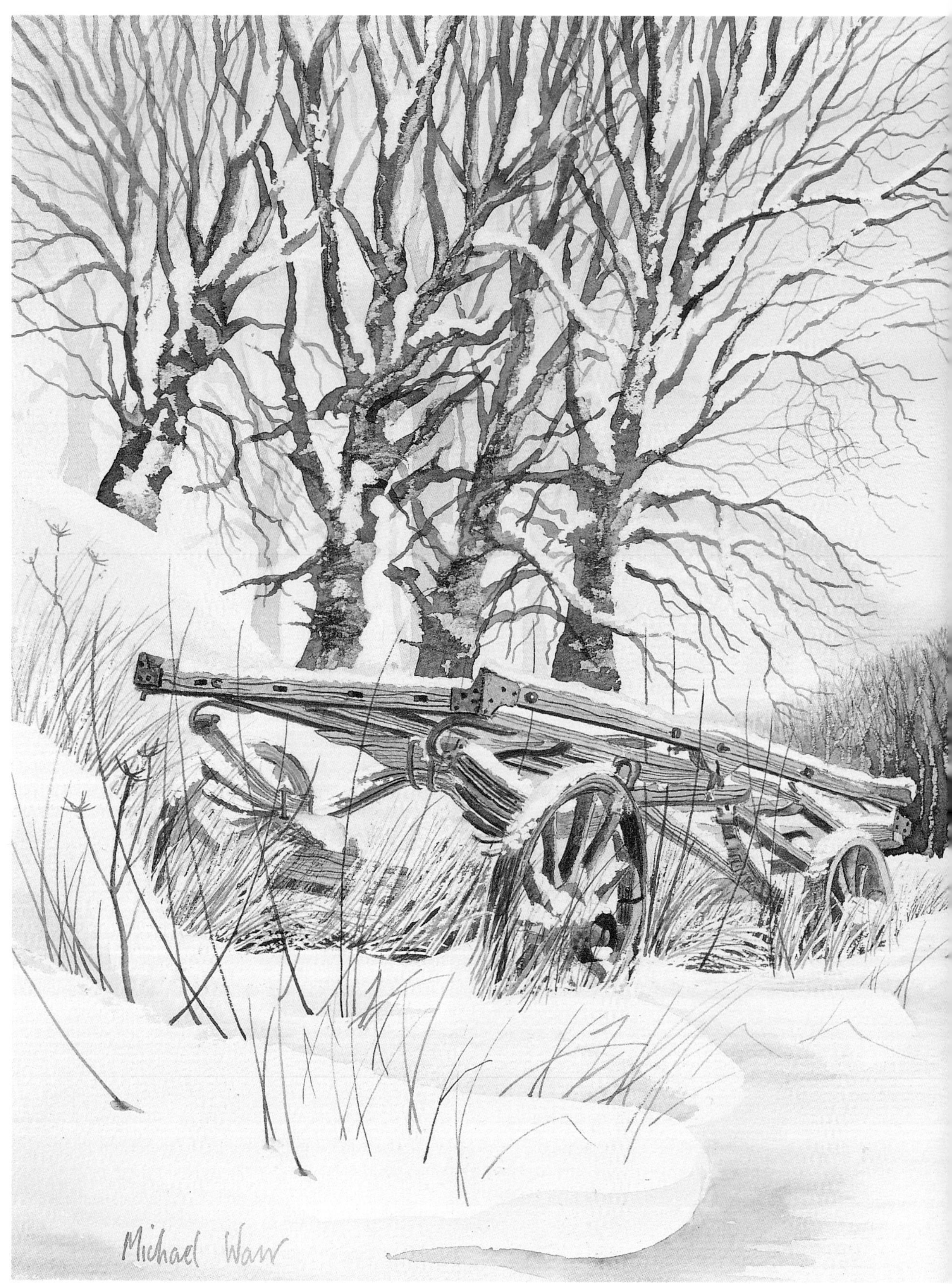
Michael Warr

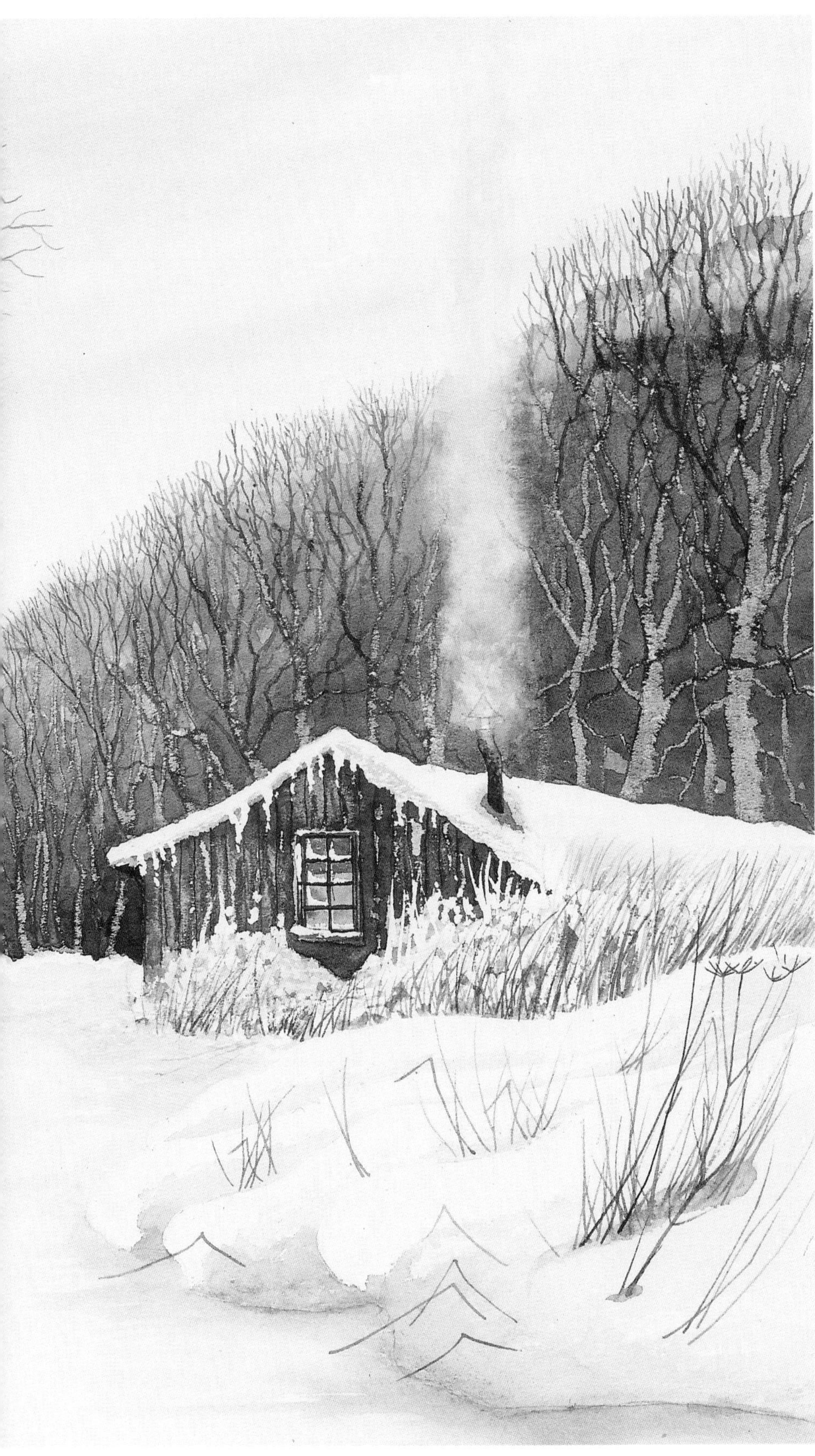

Evening Glow
A number of techniques combine to produce a wintry effect. The distant trees are created by lifting off with a painting knife, while a hog-hair brush removes colour in order to convey smoke rising from the chimney. Masking fluid retains the white of the paper, suggesting snow on nearer trees and on some parts of the old waggon

the bristles with two fingers, it leaves a brush which is almost dry. This may then be used for soaking up surplus water from a wet wash. Lines or shapes can be created in this way – for example, wire on a fence or light wisps of cloud in a darker sky. If the brush is used more than once, make sure that excess colour is removed each time and that the brush remains almost dry.

GRANULATION

Interesting effects are produced by using colours which granulate. Granulation occurs when certain colours with differing pigment weights are mixed together – for example, french ultramarine and crimson alizarin. French ultramarine is a heavier pigment colour than crimson alizarin, so when the resulting mixed colours are applied to the paper, the pigments separate: the heavier one sinks into the dents of the textured surface, while the lighter one sits on the bumps.

FLICKING AND SPATTERING

When watercolour is flicked and spattered on to a surface, the results are astonishing. The technique can be used to create textures and is especially useful for landscape foregrounds – for example, the 'out of focus' area in our immediate vision which enables the eye to stumble over and into the picture proper. This textural effect is produced by holding a brush as normal and using your index finger to tap the top of the brush handle. Watercolour leaves the bristles, hitting the paper in random form, helping to depict natural features. Running the finger along a toothbrush loaded with watercolour can produce a similar effect.

DRY BRUSH

Dry brush is a method of painting which is good for depicting detail, but it is also useful in landscape work. Excess paint is squeezed out of the brush with the thumb and forefinger and then the bristles are splayed. This allows just enough colour to pick up on the texture of the paper without flooding it. Another method is to remove excess moisture from a large round pointed brush and drag it across the paper on the side of its bristles. The process needs practice – too much moisture ruins the effect. It is important to lay down a luxurious wash before dry brushing. Used directly on to white paper, the technique is not very effective as there is no depth and the painting does not come to life underneath.

SALT

Salt sprinkled into a wet watercolour wash can produce amazing results. For example, star-like shapes that imitate falling snow can be obtained; also, water splashes and flower shapes appear as if by magic. Textures of fading colour and crumbling walls can be achieved to great effect by the sprinkling of salt into a damp wash.

The timing of salt application is critical. If the wash is too wet, sprinkled salt will soak up more moisture, producing fewer, larger shapes; it is better to wait until the wash is less wet and then to sprinkle it; the resulting texture will be a little more controlled. If the wash is too dry, the salt will not be able to soak up any moisture, and therefore a texture will not be obtained.

Salt will not react on paint which has dried and then been rewetted; the best results are obtained by sprinkling into a freshly applied wash. Do not apply too much salt in one go as it takes a little time to work. Be patient and try not to disturb the surface while you are waiting. It is worth experimenting with amounts and timing on small pieces of scrap watercolour paper.

BLOTTERS

Paper kitchen towelling, tissues, cotton wool and any type of absorbent cloth are useful for creating effects in watercolour painting. They are particularly good for producing textures when they are used for blotting or lifting off wet and/or damp paint. The marks or shapes they leave behind will vary with the choice of blotter. Any absorbent material is useful for removing excess moisture from a watercolour brush while you are working on a painting.

MIXED MEDIA

Watercolour and gouache will mix quite happily, producing many interesting effects. It is a good idea to experiment by adding black Indian ink – the textural qualities produced are astounding. Allowing watercolour, gouache and Indian ink to dry and then washing them under a tap can produce an interesting result. Line and wash is another area to be explored. This technique starts with a pen or pencil drawing to which watercolour or gouache, or both, is added. The sky is the limit with mixed media.

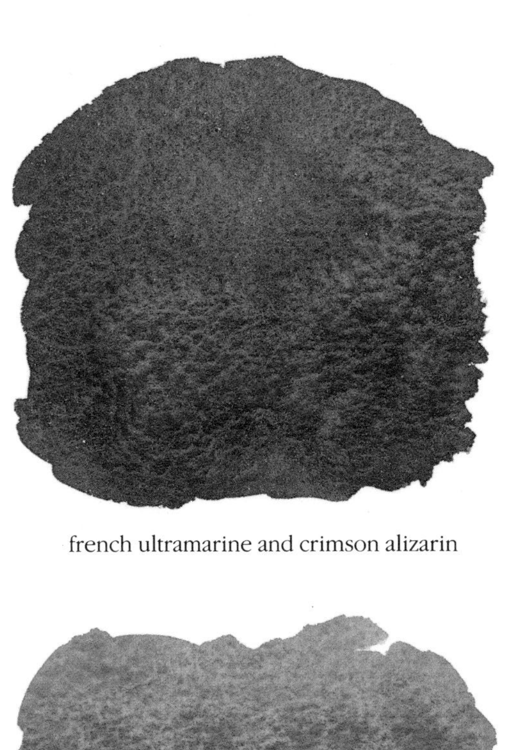

french ultramarine and crimson alizarin

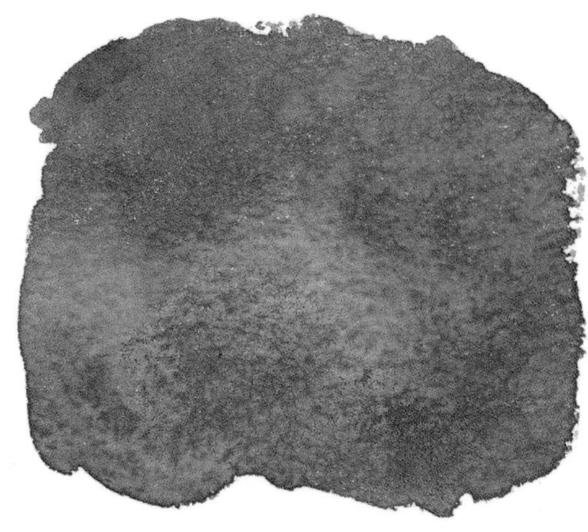

cadmium yellow pale and lamp black

french ultramarine and coeruleum

raw sienna and Payne's grey

french ultramarine and light red

french ultramarine and burnt sienna

Six examples of colours mixed together which encourage granulation. The overall colour will change if the pigment content is varied – that is, if there is more crimson alizarin and less french ultramarine, or more french ultramarine and less light red

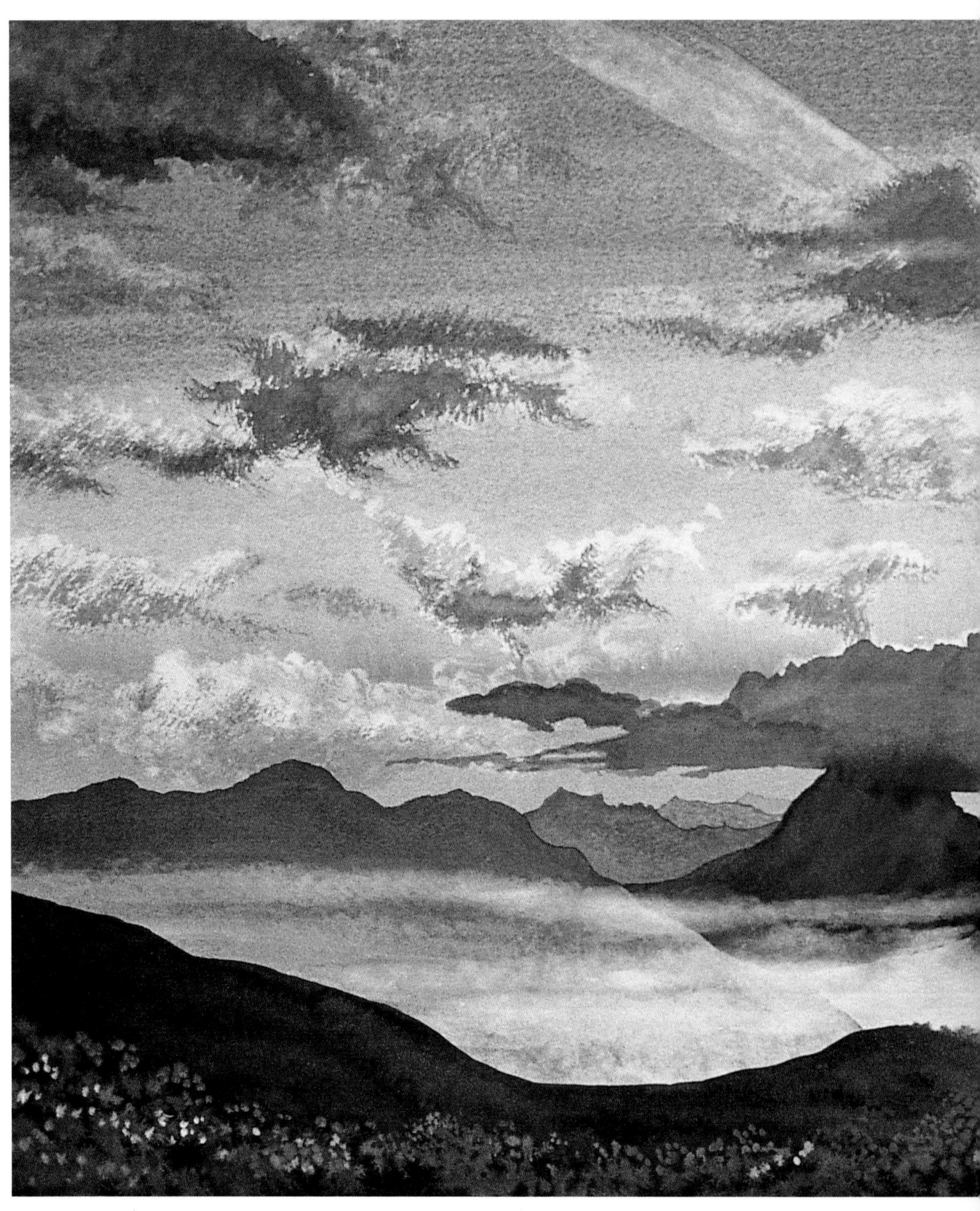

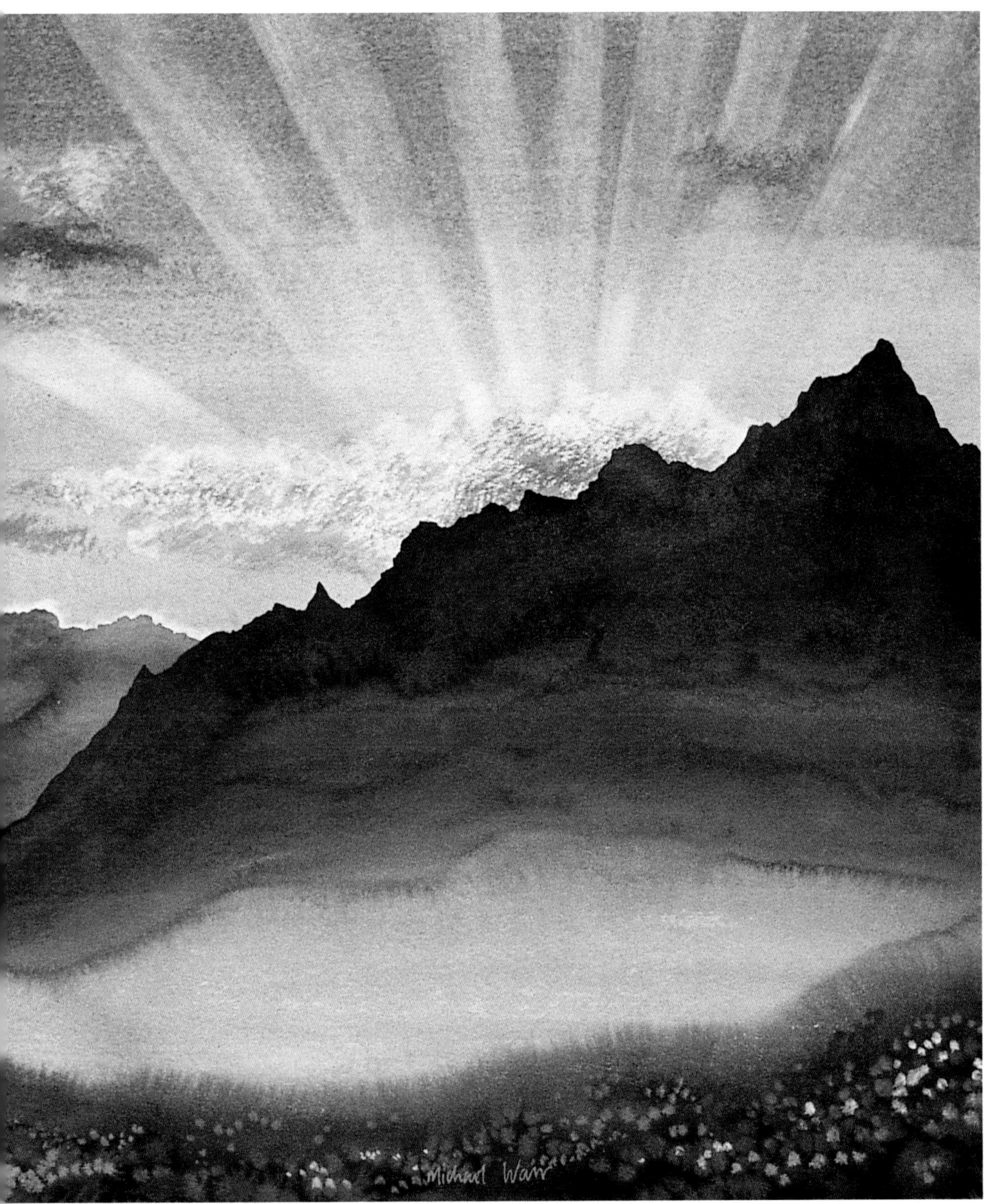

Heralding the Day (Grosse Scheidegg)
The rays of the rising sun in this painting are produced by lifting off dry paint with a wet hog-hair brush. Some of the morning mist is also created using the same method

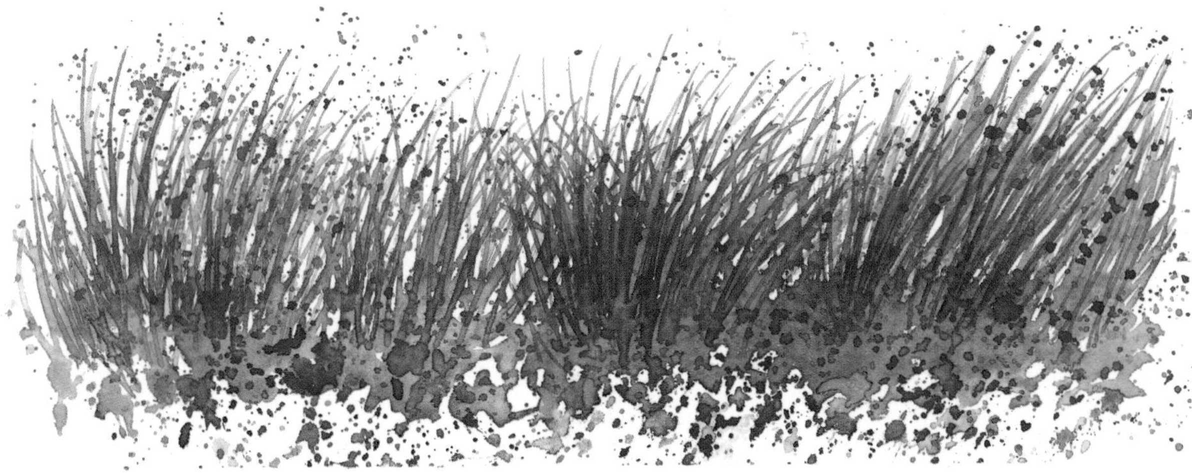

Textures created by flicking and spattering with a no 6 round pointed sable. Grasses are indicated with a no 1 round pointed sable

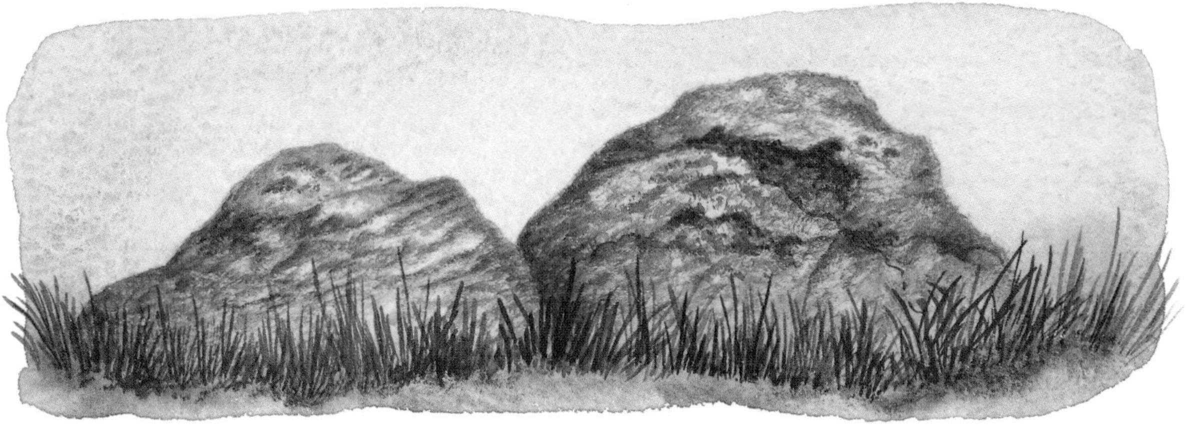

Two small rock formations painted with a dry brush. A light wash, which is allowed to dry thoroughly, provides good underpainting

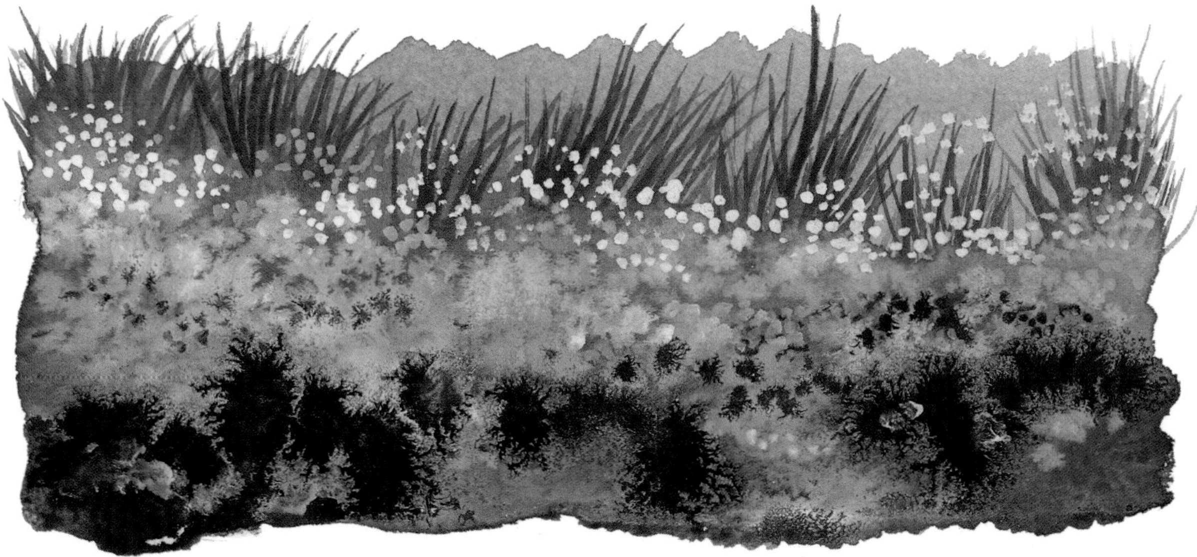

Interesting landscape foreground textures created with the use of watercolour, white gouache and black Indian ink

Sky Blues

Selecting suitable blues for skies is another problem for landscape students. This is understandable as there are so many to choose from. You must decide whether you want to include all of them in your range or whether you are going to select two or three and learn about their properties by mixing and experimenting. I prefer the latter choice, but that does not mean that the rest of the range should be ignored. It is a good idea to work through the range, discovering which ones seem most suited to individual needs. Normally, by a process of elimination, two or three blues will be found that are adequate for most of your requirements.

Some artists will argue that one blue is sufficient, but I have found from experience, especially when painting at different times of the year, that this is simply not enough.

The blues that are included in my range and which are suitable for general landscape needs are: french ultramarine, coeruleum and monestial blue.

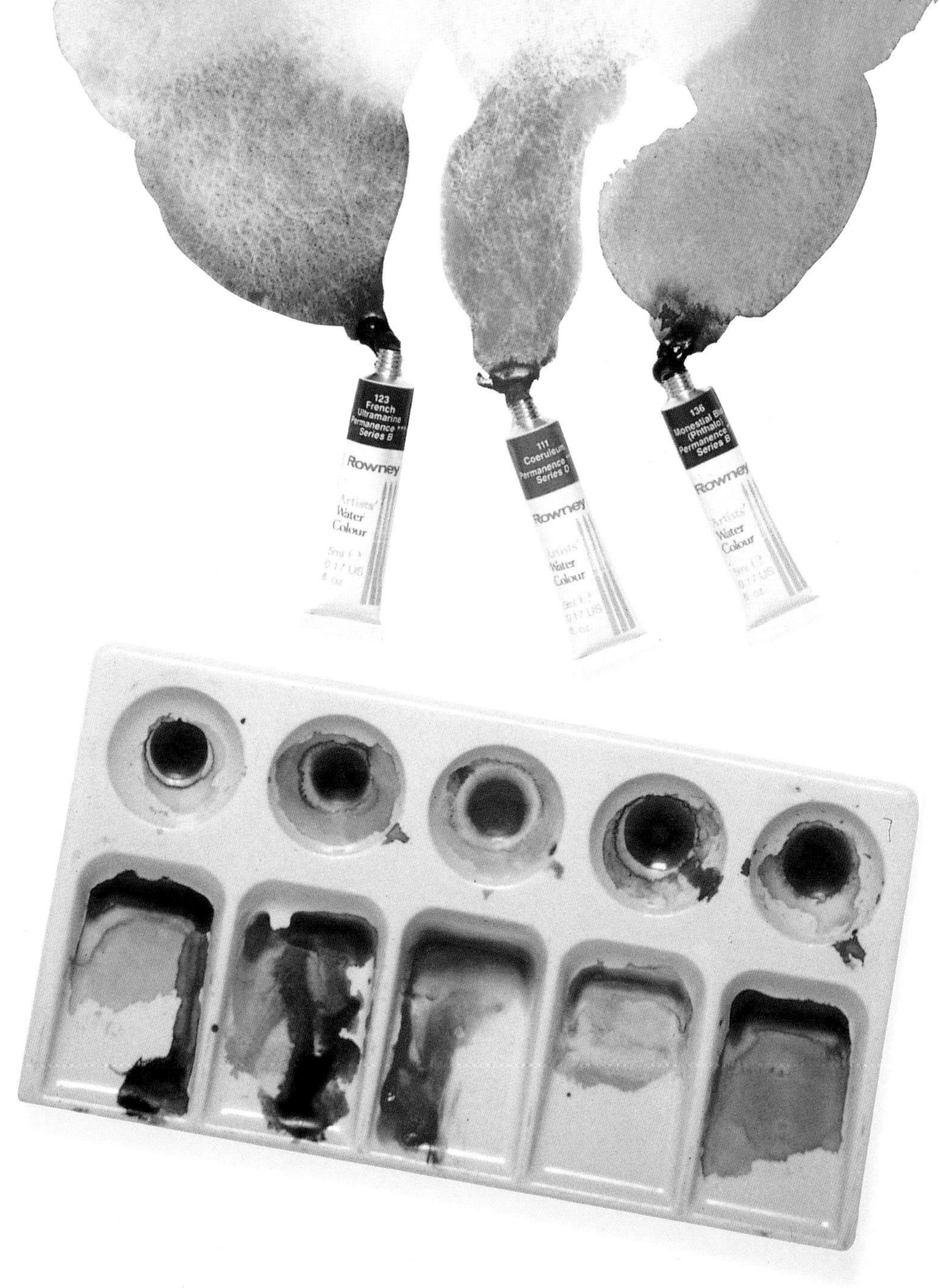

Coeruleum and monestial (phthalocyanine)

Coeruleum and french ultramarine

Monestial (phthalocyanine) and french ultramarine

Here are three examples of blues mixed together which are suitable for skies. You will find that french ultramarine is 'cool', while coeruleum and monestial (phthalocyanine) are 'warm'.

There are many variations on these recipes and experimentation with mixing is strongly recommended. More water, a little less colour pigment – keep trying until the desired results are obtained

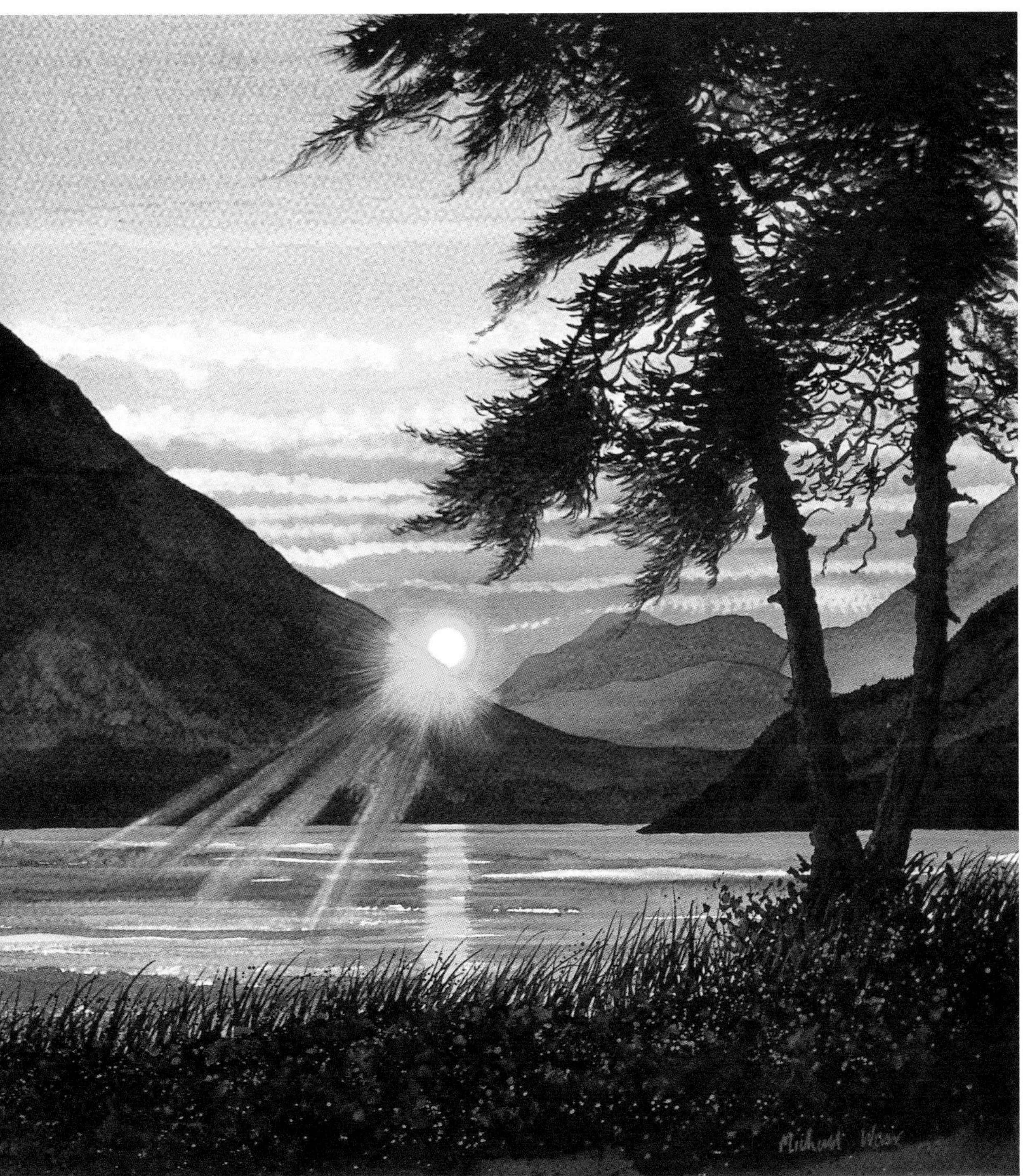

Where Dreams Come True
Many of the techniques discussed are combined in this painting of a sunset. Kitchen towelling has lifted off cloud shapes, while a hog-hair oil-painting brush, loaded with water, has lifted rays of the sun and lighter areas on the lake. There is granulation in the sky caused by mixing french ultramarine, coeruleum and crimson alizarin. Spattering and flicking occurs in the foreground and the technique of feeding gouache into a damp watercolour wash is also employed. Yellow gouache is used to strengthen colour around the sun. Back-lit subjects offer a great deal of scope for using unusual techniques

Getting to Grips with Greens

Dealing with greens is one of the major problems for students of landscape painting; they either make them too brash or too dull. More thought and careful colour mixing is often required – the use of green direct from a tube will not do. Students frequently ask for guidance on selecting and mixing greens. Mixing is important because that is where the key to producing successful greens lies. In Chapter 2, in discussing paints, I have not mentioned green as a colour because I do not carry a 'manufactured' green in my range. I prefer to make a selection of greens by mixing colours within the suggested list. An exciting and interesting range of greens can be produced by mixing unlikely colours together, as you will see. We cannot hope to emulate all of the greens that we see in nature, so it is important to interpret what is seen within the confines of the paintbox. We may have to be content with twenty shades instead of forty. In other words, the greens that we are able to produce with a small selection of colours will normally be adequate enough to make our paintings appear convincing.

The mixed greens produced here are only a few of the possibilities in a permutation which could go on indefinitely. Experimenting with mixtures is a very interesting process, leading to exciting discoveries, although too many colours mixed together will result in a muddy effect. Be selective and never mix more than three colours together.

The colours used, which are part of the suggested range for use in this book, are as follows:

cadmium yellow pale	french ultramarine
Payne's grey	lamp black
burnt sienna	raw sienna
monestial (phthalocyanine)	coeruleum

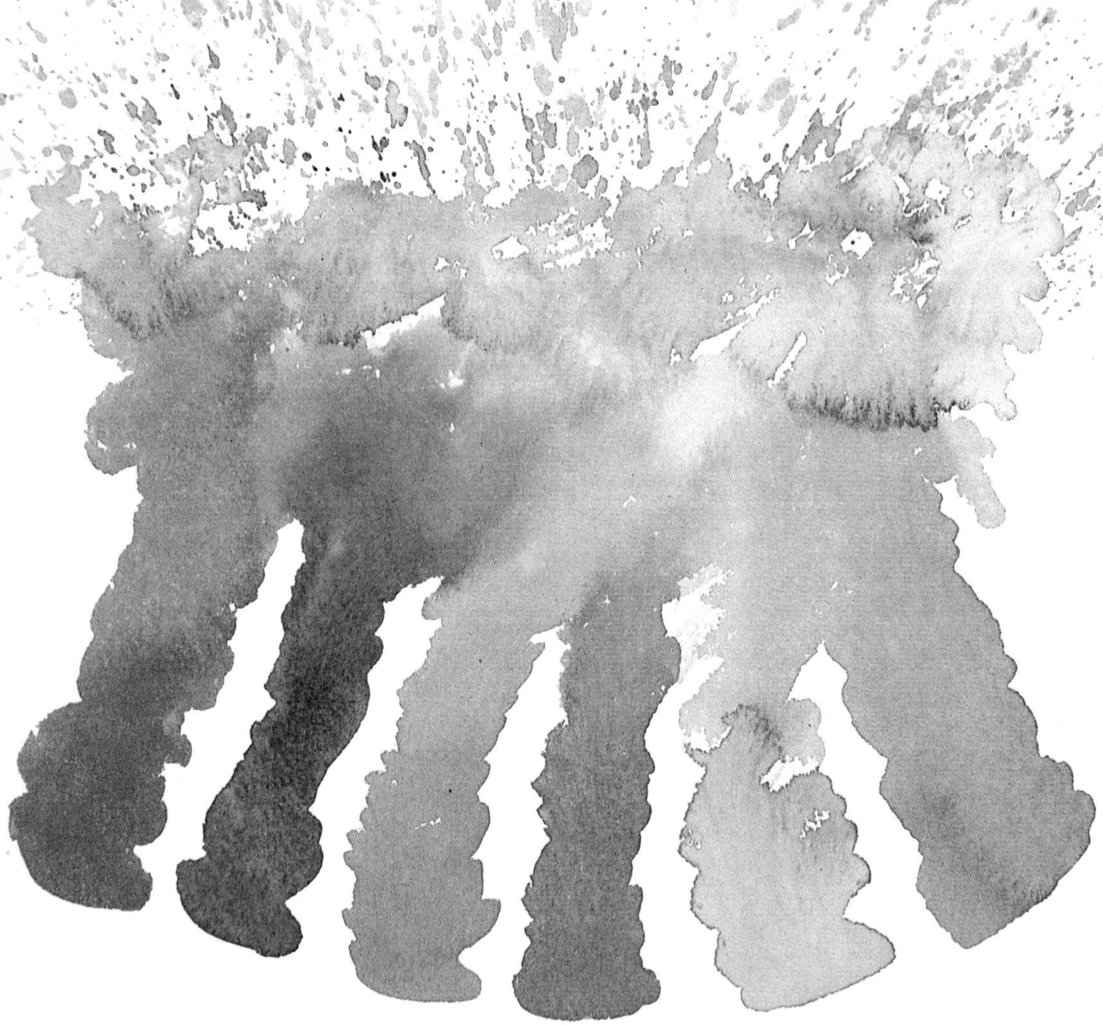

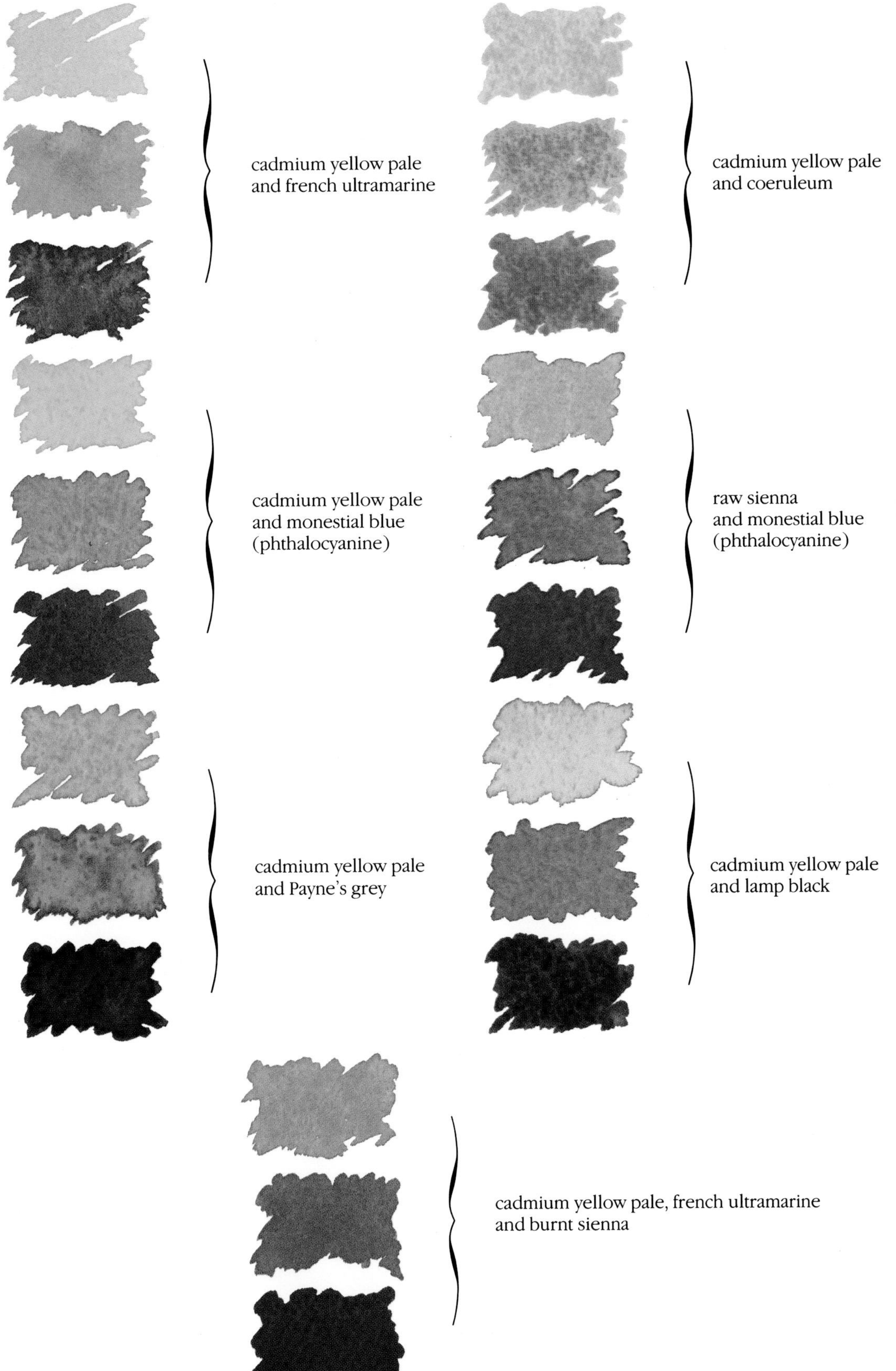
cadmium yellow pale
and french ultramarine
cadmium yellow pale
and coeruleum
cadmium yellow pale
and monestial blue
(phthalocyanine)
raw sienna
and monestial blue
(phthalocyanine)
cadmium yellow pale
and Payne's grey
cadmium yellow pale
and lamp black
cadmium yellow pale, french ultramarine
and burnt sienna

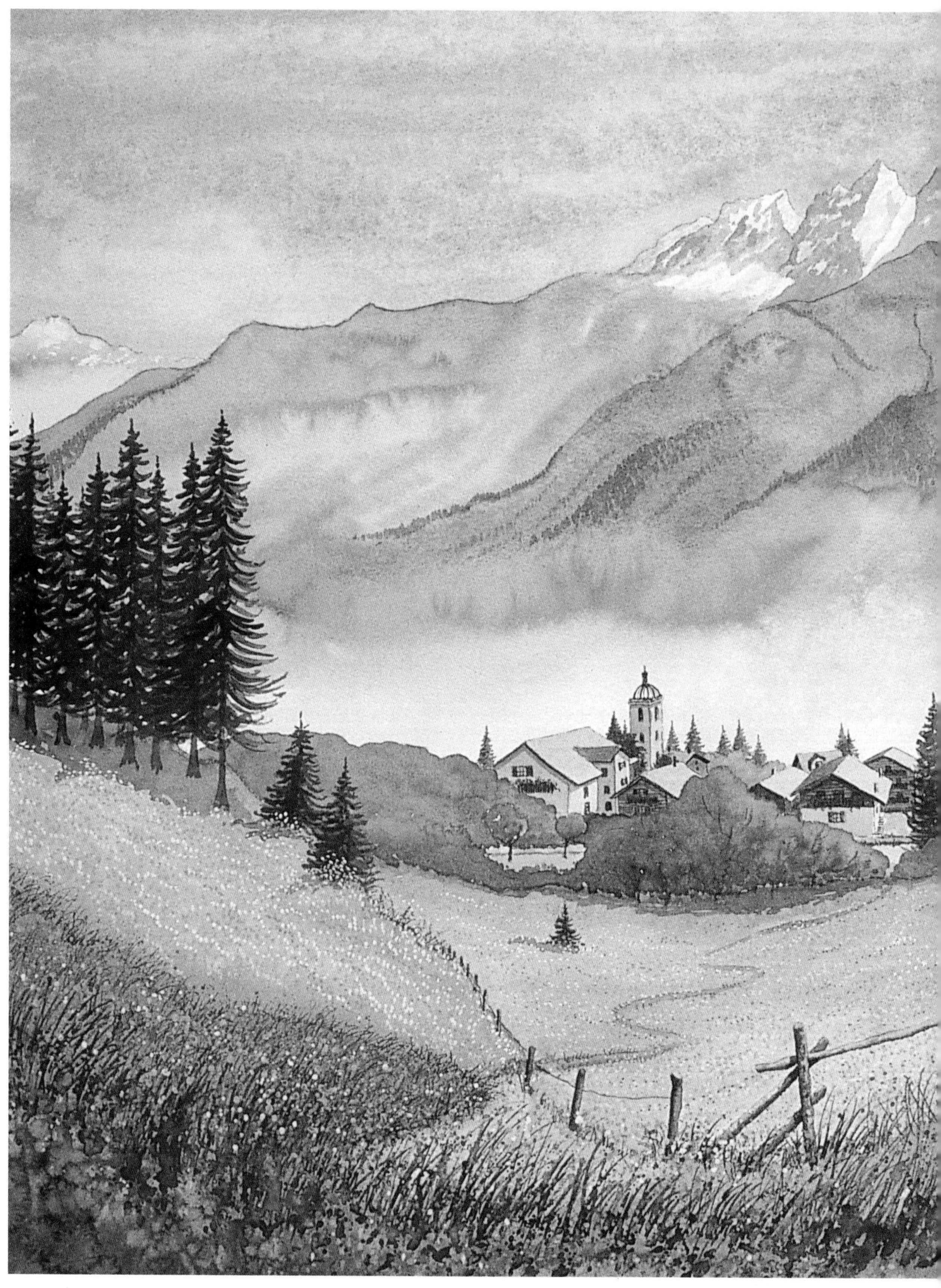

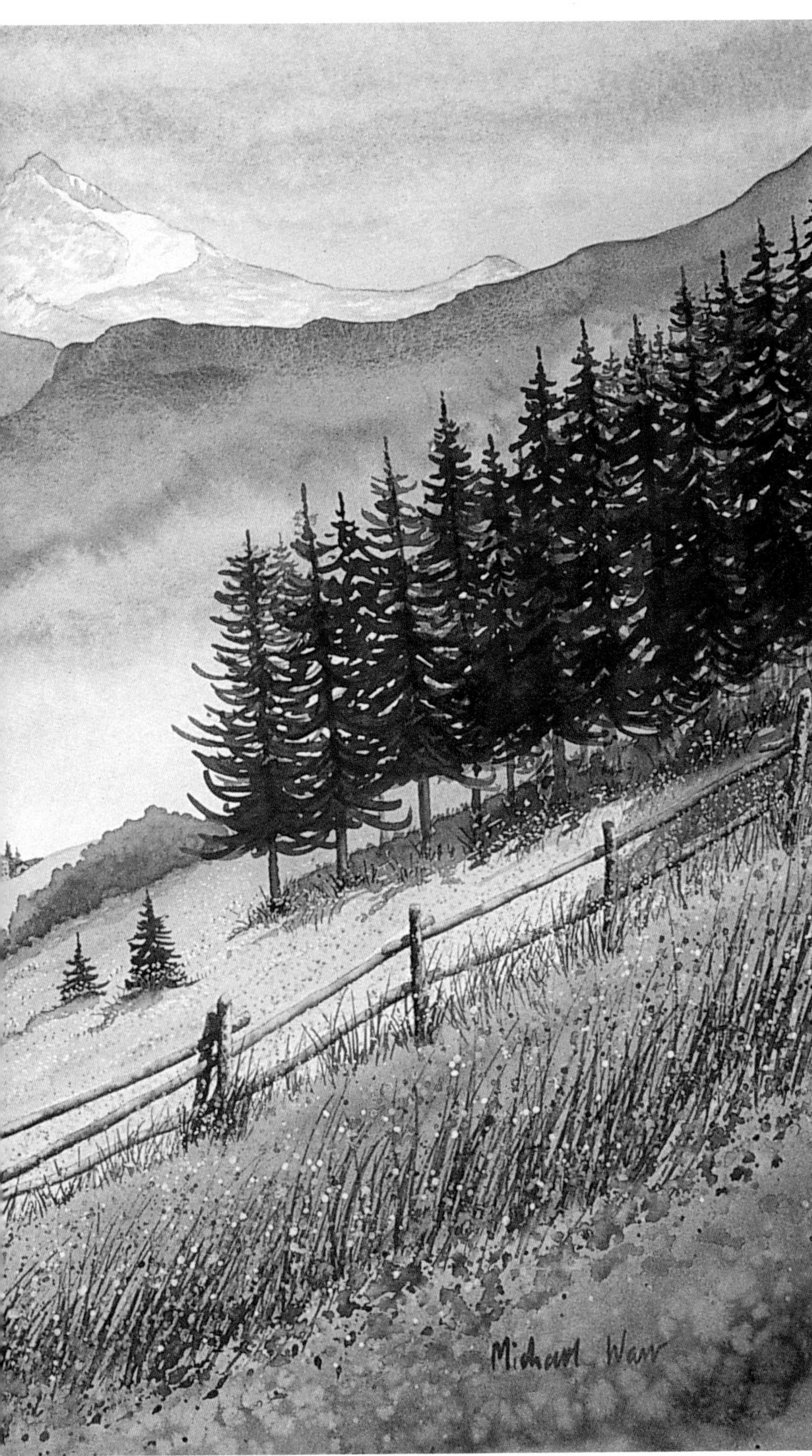

Champéry and Dents Du Midi
This painting contains muted greens as well as stronger ones of the pine trees. Raw sienna and Payne's grey as well as raw sienna mixed with french ultramarine form the basic greens in this painting. Note how the colour is weak behind the village, creating a misty look; this effect enables the buildings to be seen very clearly. Dark greens are various mixtures of Payne's grey, french ultramarine, raw sienna and cadmium yellow pale. Even the fence-posts contain muted grey-greens

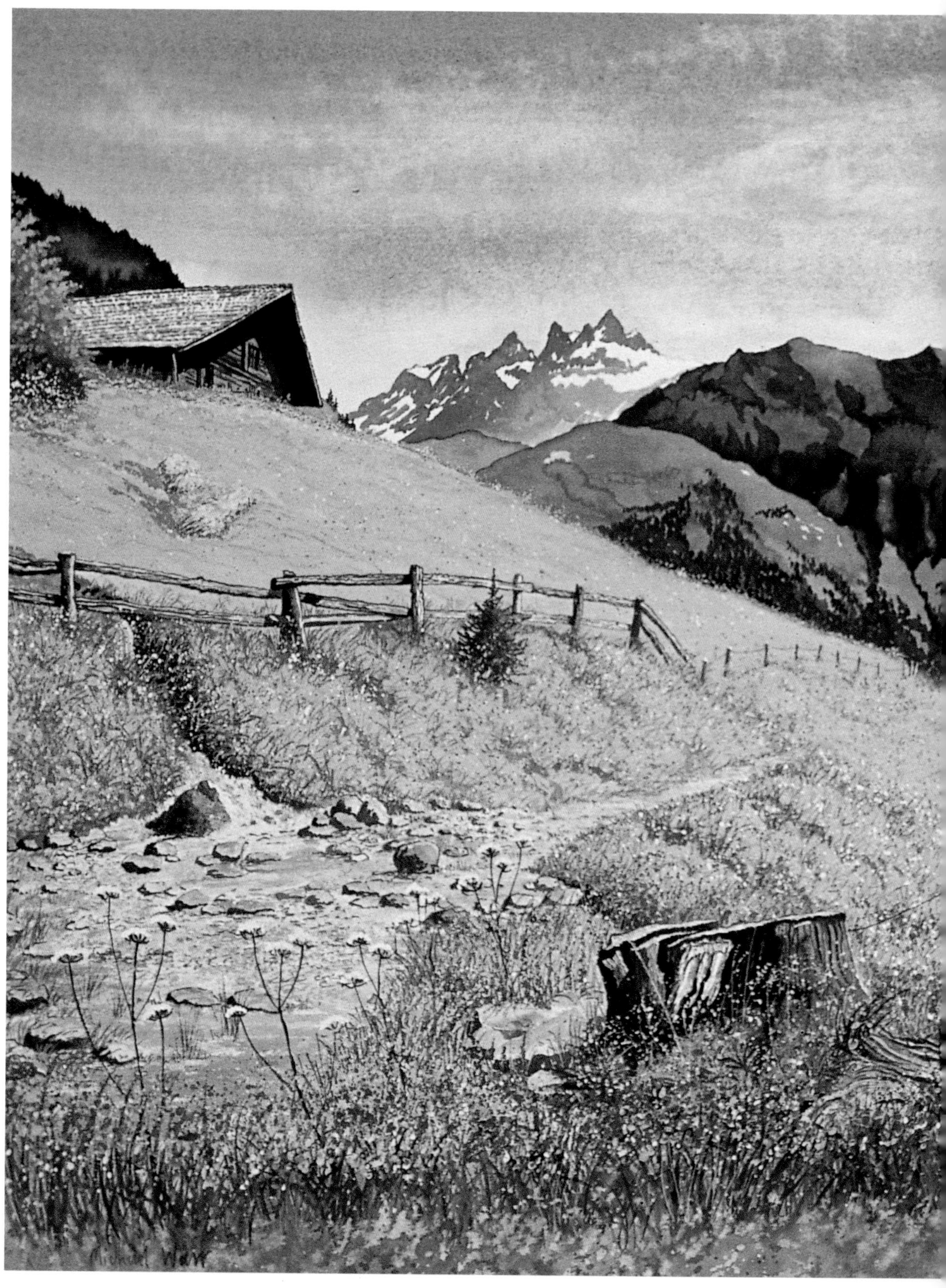

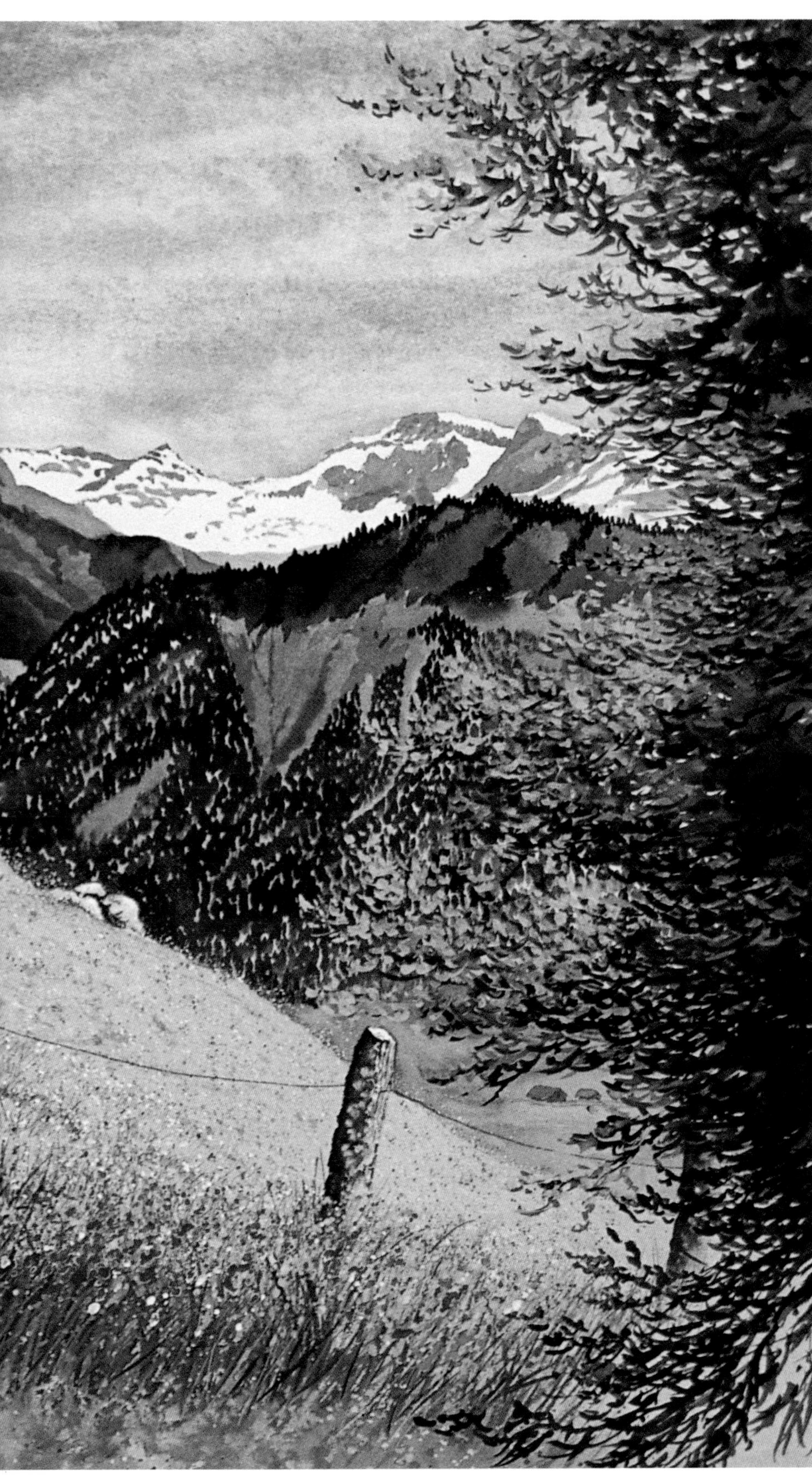

Colourful Pathway (Near Champéry)
An interesting combination of the blues and greens discussed is illustrated in this colourful painting. The sky is produced with a mixture of coeruleum and monestial blue painted directly on to white paper. This is exposed by blotting off with kitchen towelling, creating interesting, wispy clouds. French ultramarine and a touch of crimson alizarin produce shadows on the distant mountains. The nearer mountains are stronger versions of this mixture, but the lower slopes of muted green are french ultramarine mixed with raw sienna. Lush yellow-green for the large expanse of meadow is produced by mixing a small amount of french ultramarine to a great deal of cadmium yellow pale. Combinations of this mixture are also used for the trees. Rather more french ultramarine is introduced on the far right, where the tree is in shadow

Features in the Landscape

In order to include detail in landscape paintings it is necessary to observe the smaller subjects – for example, wild flowers, grasses, shrubs, etc. There is no better way to observe these subjects than by drawing or painting them. A comprehensive collection of studies can be kept in a sketchbook and used at any time for inclusion in paintings. Sometimes we are looking for ways of improving a composition or searching for foreground material; a wealth of information stored in a sketchbook is invaluable. Every opportunity should be taken to record details of the landscape; I cannot over-stress the importance of this exercise as it paves the way to producing well-observed, meaningful landscape paintings.

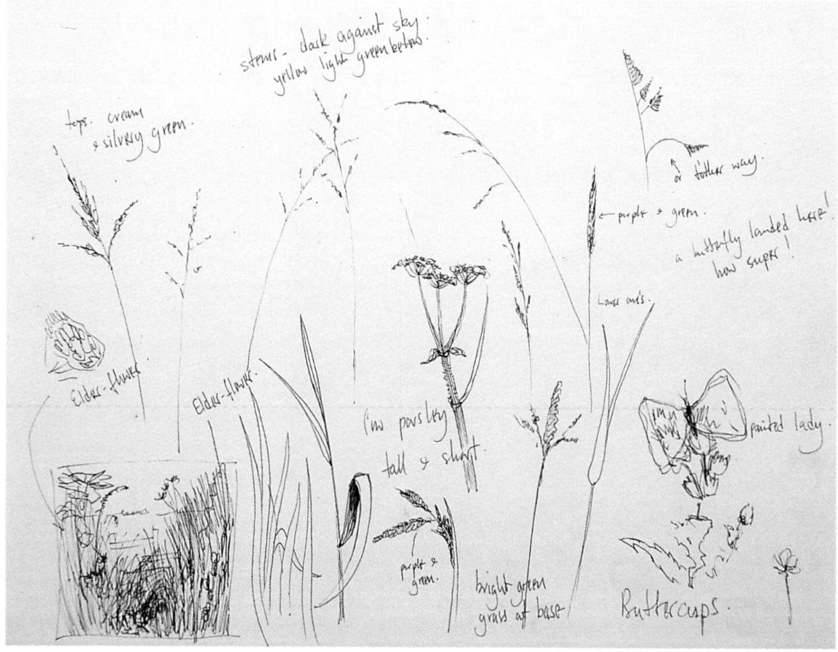

A page of an A3 sketchbook filled with sketches of grasses and plants found on a canal bank. Some written notes accompany the visual notes which are recorded with a fibre-tip pen. An idea for a composition begins to form (bottom left)

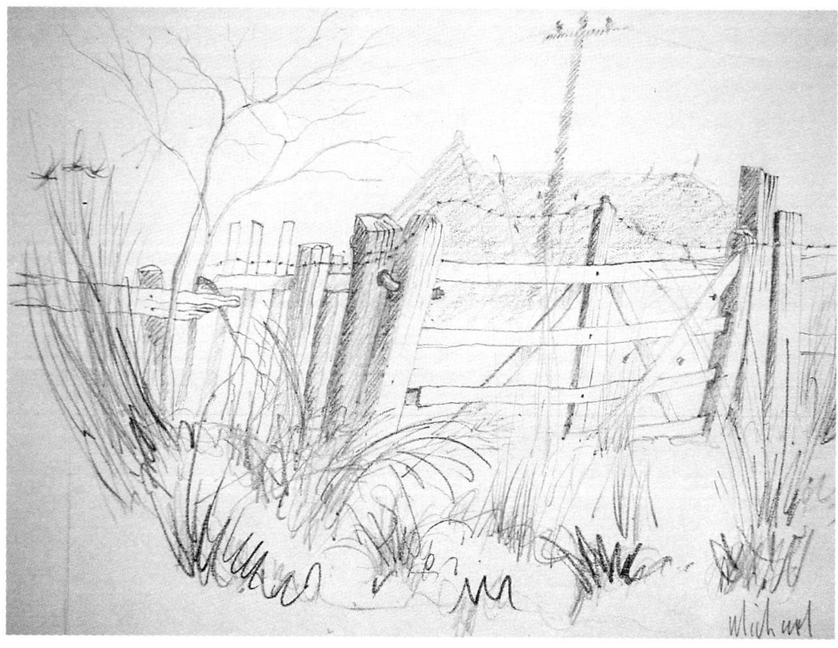

Old gates are often found in landscapes; this one provides an ideal subject for a sketch in graphite pencil. Note that the building and telegraph-pole behind are excellent background material

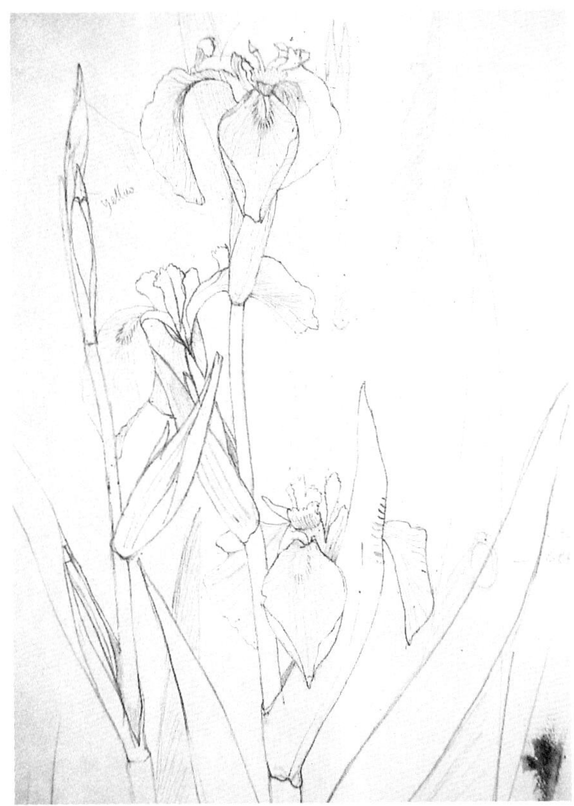

Wild iris recorded in pencil; attention is given to detail on the petals in the form of veins and sepals, etc. Many blooms may appear in a landscape, or two or three blooms could become main subjects in a painting

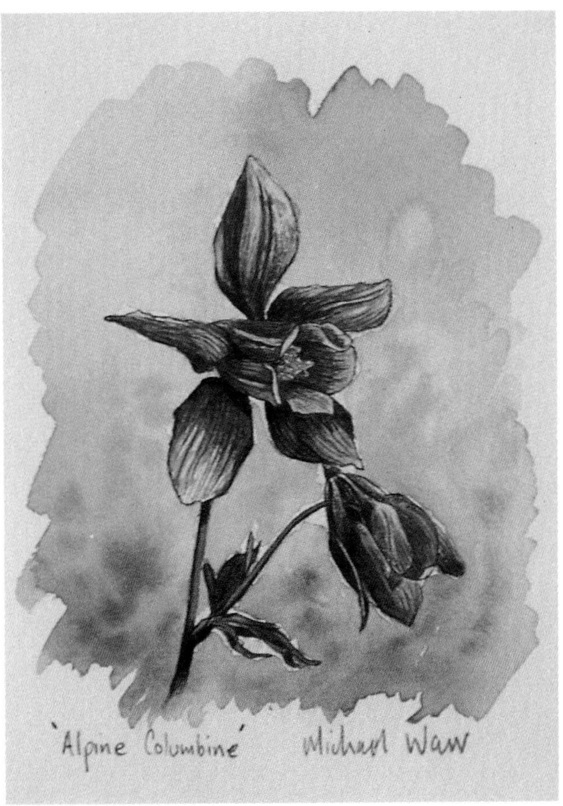

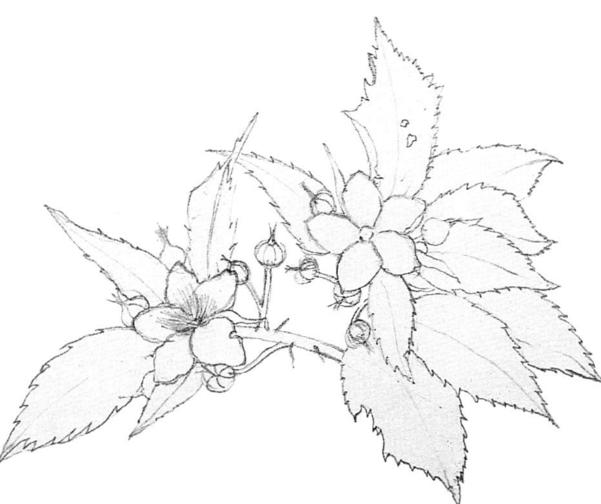

Above: A careful study in graphite pencil of blackberry blossom

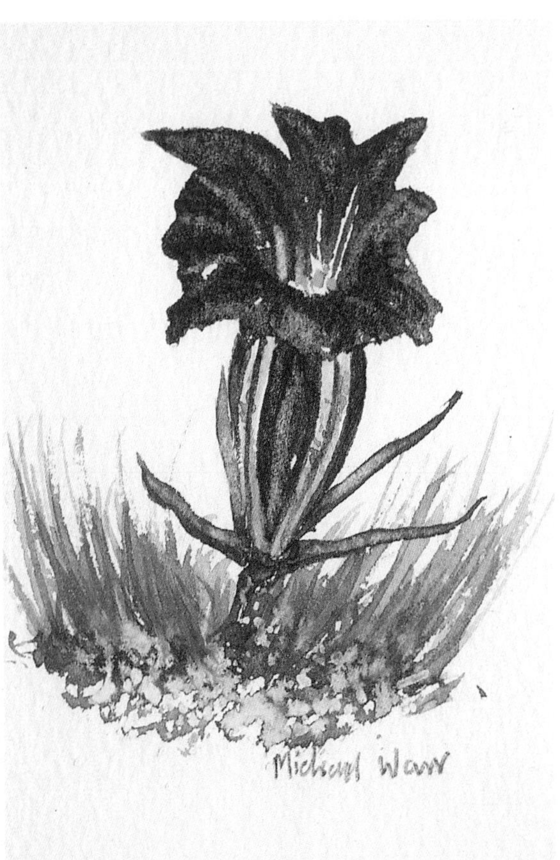

Above and below right: Mountainous regions contain myriads of alpine flowers. Making close-up studies of them leads to a better understanding of the mass. These examples were produced on location using a small watercolour box and telescopic sable brush

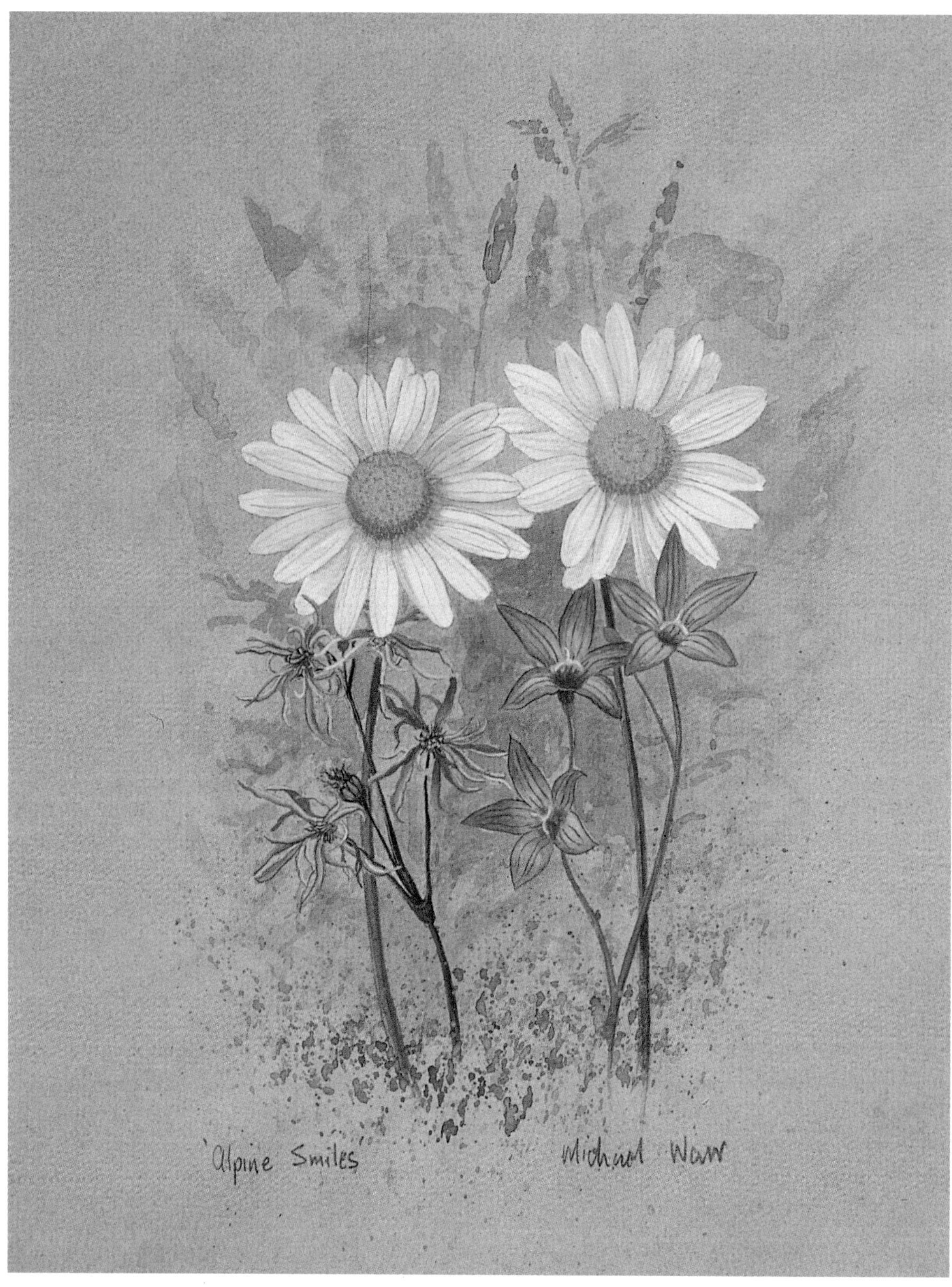

This painting of oxeye daises shows the use of gouache on tinted paper. This study was made in the studio under controlled conditions

In this small watercolour painting there is a combination of wild flowers, a building with weathered and ageing textures, trees which are knifed out, and light and shade – in short, a small corner of landscape containing a wealth of subject matter

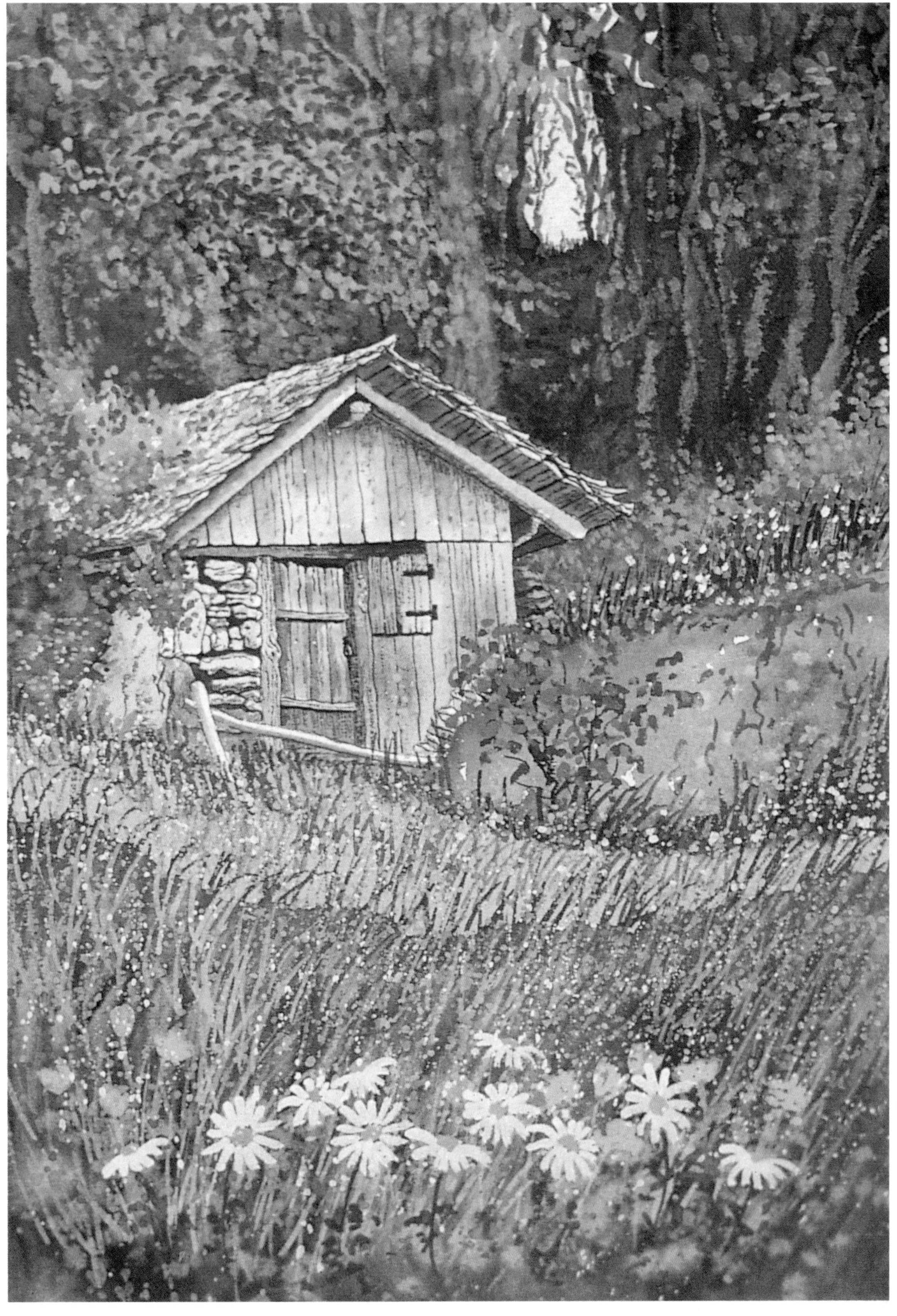

Trees

Trees usually feature in landscape paintings in one form or another, whether they are stunted specimens in a desert, giants in a rain forest or cultivated trees in a city street or park – trees always seem to be there.

As different species of trees have differing characteristics, these should be observed and recorded in order to make paintings credible; there is nothing worse in a landscape painting than the 'lollipop syndrome' – I am sure that you have seen a green ball on a stick in a picture at some time.

The overall shapes of trees vary tremendously and by studying their underlying structure – that is, the shapes and directions of their branches – these differences will become apparent. In the case of deciduous trees, if this exercise is carried out in winter, clues can be obtained as to how the summertime leaves are supported. Some knowledge of this can be extremely helpful in determining the overall shape of a tree.

Look also at the differing colours of branches and trunks between the species of trees; these may vary from grey-green, silver grey, dark grey, through to red-browns. The colours of leaves are extremely different as are the colours between coniferous or evergreens. Their range extends from bright yellow-green to dark blue-green. If information of this kind is recorded in a sketchbook, it will be found to be helpful during the production of landscape paintings. Tree shapes and colours in a painting need to look realistic and natural in their setting.

Further information regarding the painting of trees is to be found in Chapter 5

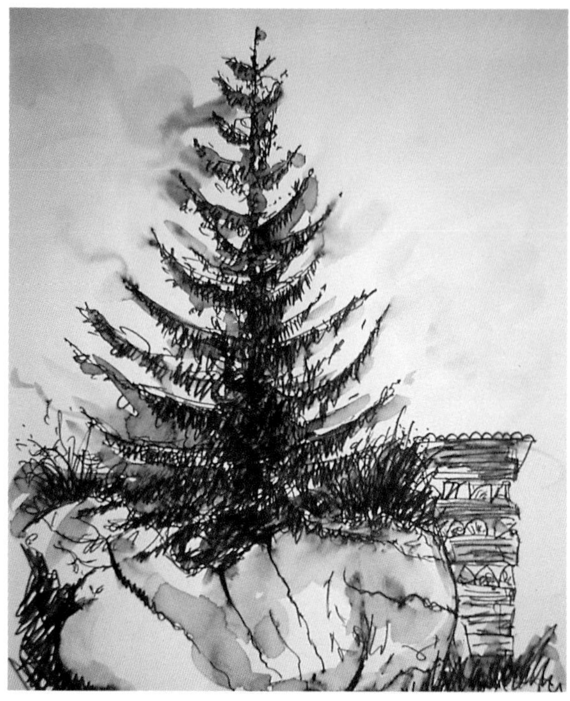

Pine trees seem to have the ability to exist in very little soil. Incredibly this one is growing out of a rock. A water-soluble fibre-tip pen was used to produce this drawing

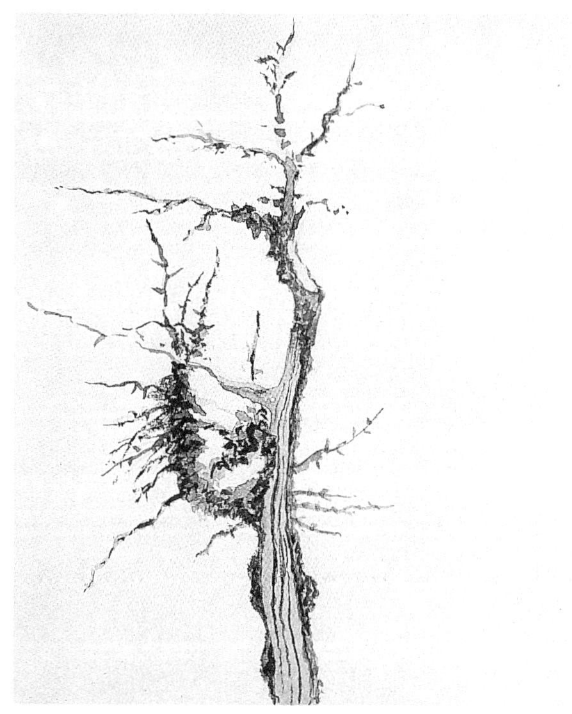

Pine trees at high altitudes have a hard life battling against the elements. This is the remains of such a tree, which has seen better days. Nevertheless, it became an important foreground subject in a recent painting of a mountain range

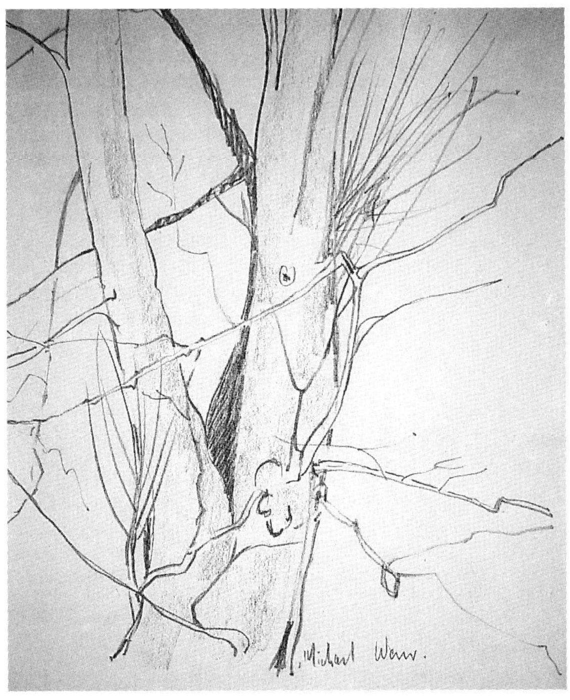

A pencil-drawing of the trunk of a beech tree. Studies of this type are very useful for detailed information in a painting

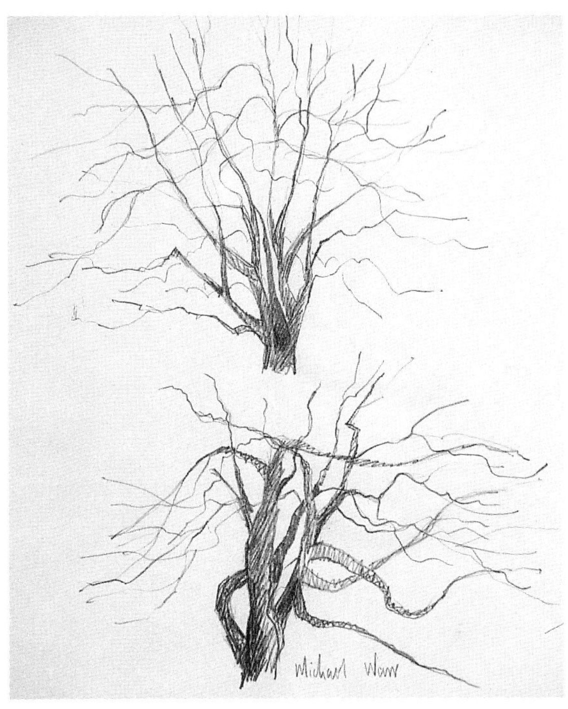

Two studies in graphite pencil which record the twisted antics of hawthorn bushes. Seeing them in winter enables a greater understanding of their contorted structures

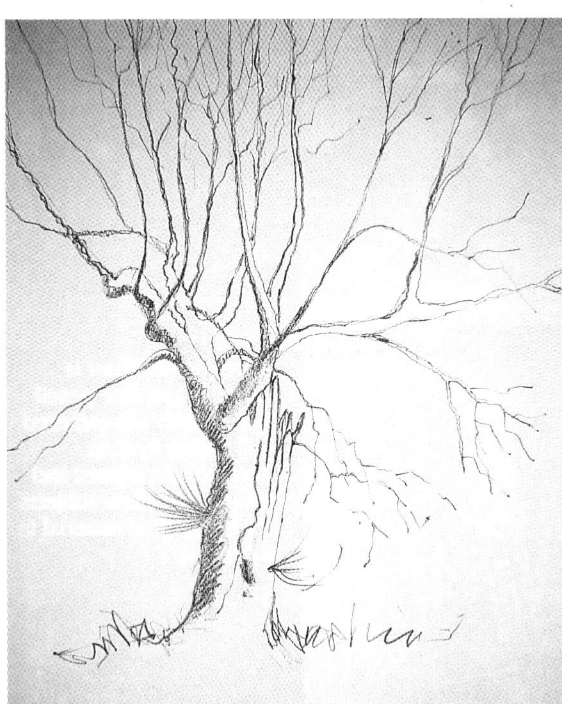

An old split willow is studied and drawn for the same reason

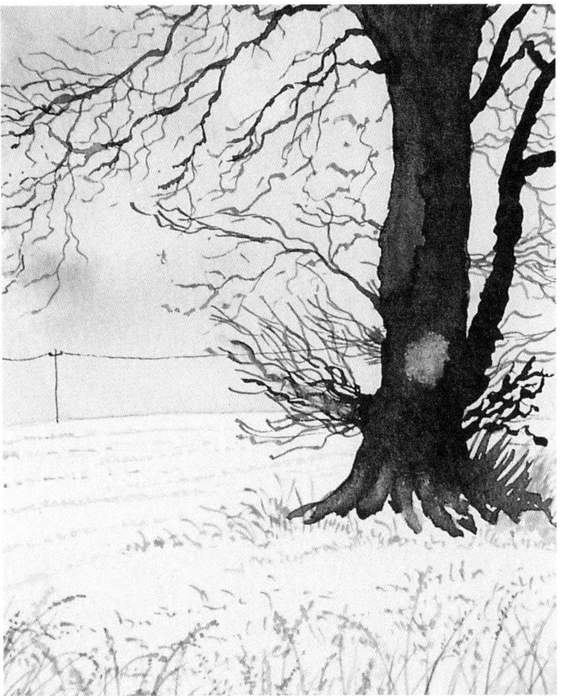

A tree in winter provides the main subject for a painting. Mixtures of french ultramarine and light red are the ingredients for the textured tree-trunk and branches. Note how a distant telegraph-pole echoes the vertical feeling of the composition

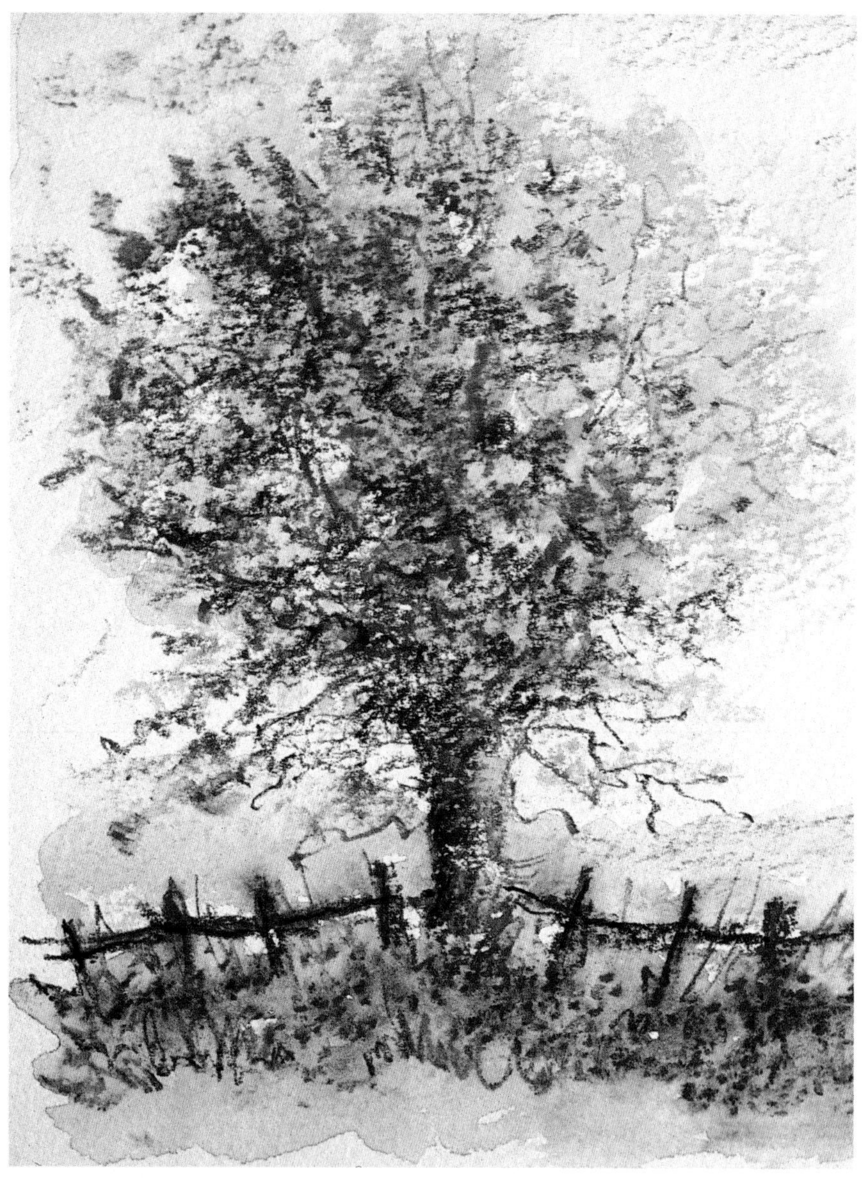

A study of a summer tree produced with Caran d'Ache water-soluble crayons. Colour is applied on to a dry paper surface and then softened with a wet brush. Dark tones on the left of the tree are added when lighter colours are completely dry. This technique can be used to aid an ailing watercolour painting

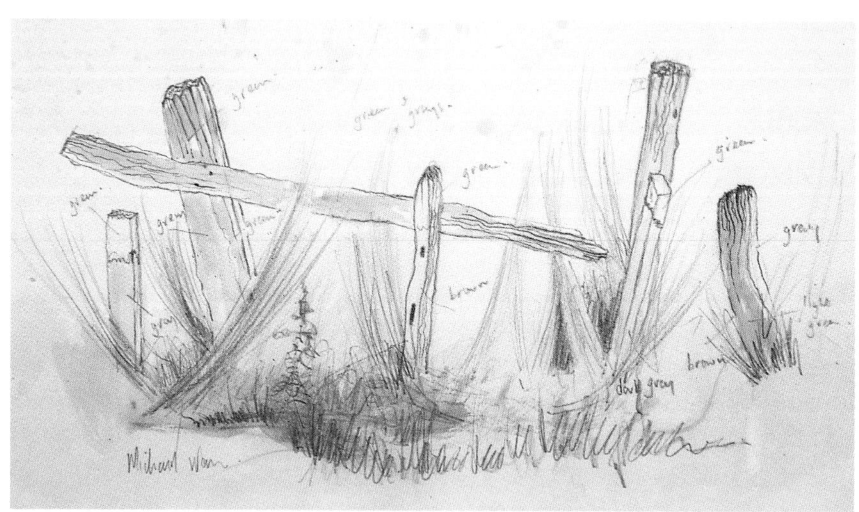

A little watercolour is added to graphite pencil in this study of weathered and ageing fencing. Textures are created and provide excellent subjects for foreground material in a painting

Textures

Landscape textures are fascinating; they provide us with a wide range of shapes and colours and deserve a great deal of attention. Subjects to look out for may include the bark of trees, wood grain in fences and posts, rocks, ploughed fields, etc. Studies of landscape textures, in the form of drawings and colour sketches, can be stored in a sketchbook for future reference. Wooden posts and fences are useful as compositional aids and also as foreground material. They can be introduced into many landscape situations; their textural qualities add life and credibility to paintings, and they are a rich source of inspiration.

Soil, stones and rocks offer interesting textures; they form the sub-structure of the landscape. If we remove the plant life, these subjects are what we are left with. The geological differences to be found from one area to another offer us a fantastic diversity of colour and texture with regard to soil and rock; some are hard, others are soft; some are red, others are yellow. These changes can be a real feast for the artist. Very often, buildings are constructed from local materials; it may be wood, stone or both. It is important to look at the texture of the materials because often it is the colour and texture of a building which identifies it with a certain region. If this visual information is recorded accurately, it can help to make your paintings more convincing. Buildings which are constructed from local materials often appear as an integral part of the landscape, almost as if they have grown out of the soil.

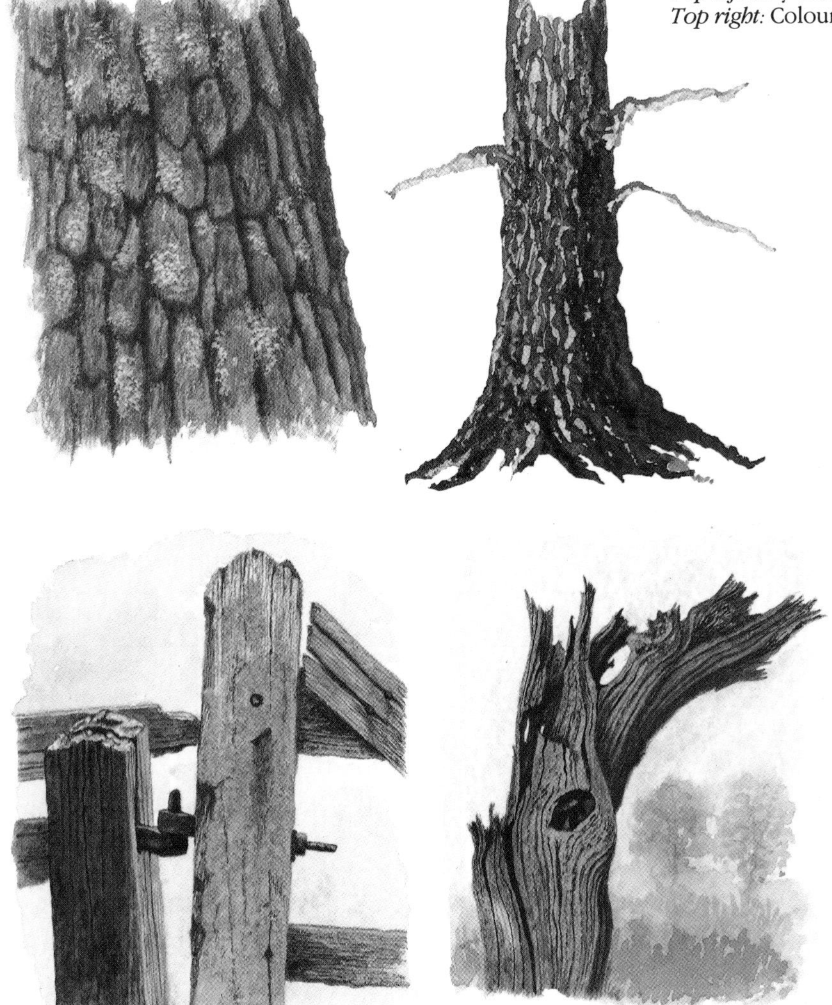

Two methods of creating tree-bark textures. *Top left:* Dry-brushing colour on top of a wash. *Top right:* Colour lifted off with a painting knife

Two examples of lichen growing on wood. *Bottom left:* A mixture of cadmium yellow pale, french ultramarine and white gouache is dry-brushed on to a gate-post, while (*bottom right*) the same mixture is applied to an old decaying tree-stump

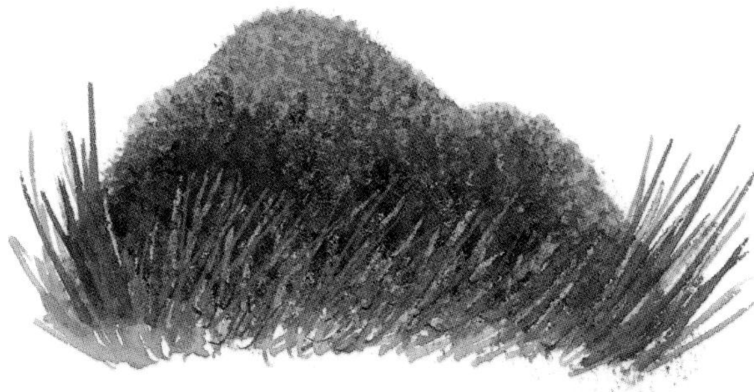

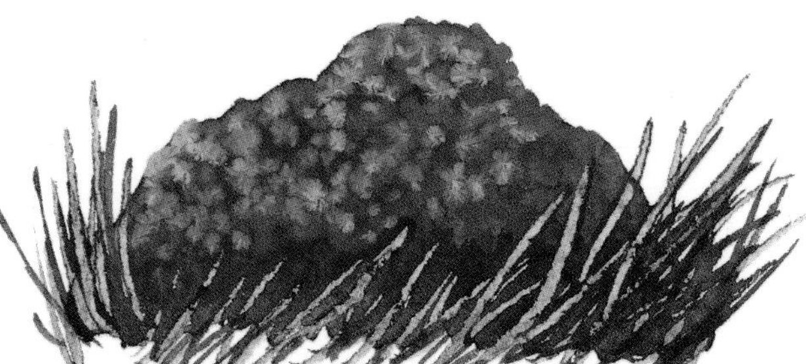

Left: A rock created by applying colour with a sponge
Right: To produce this moss-covered rock, gouache is fed into damp watercolour

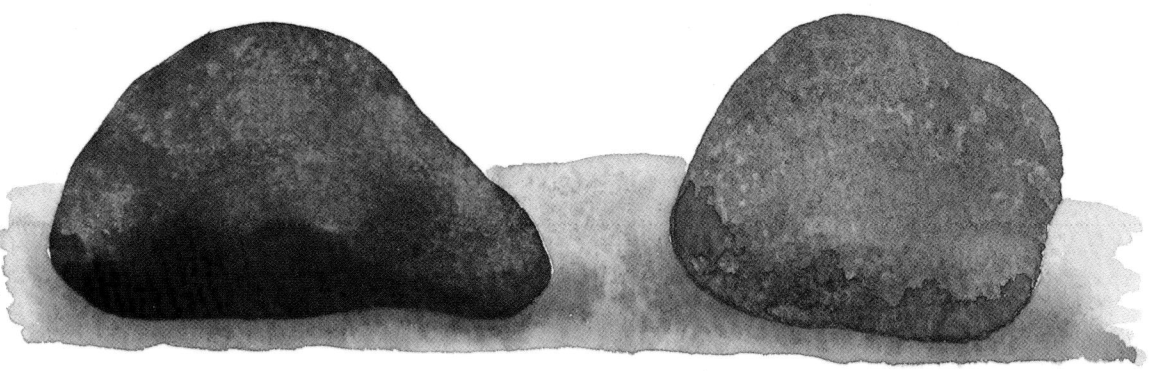

Two smooth rocks in a dry riverbed are formed by painting the shapes and then removing the colour with a thirsty sponge

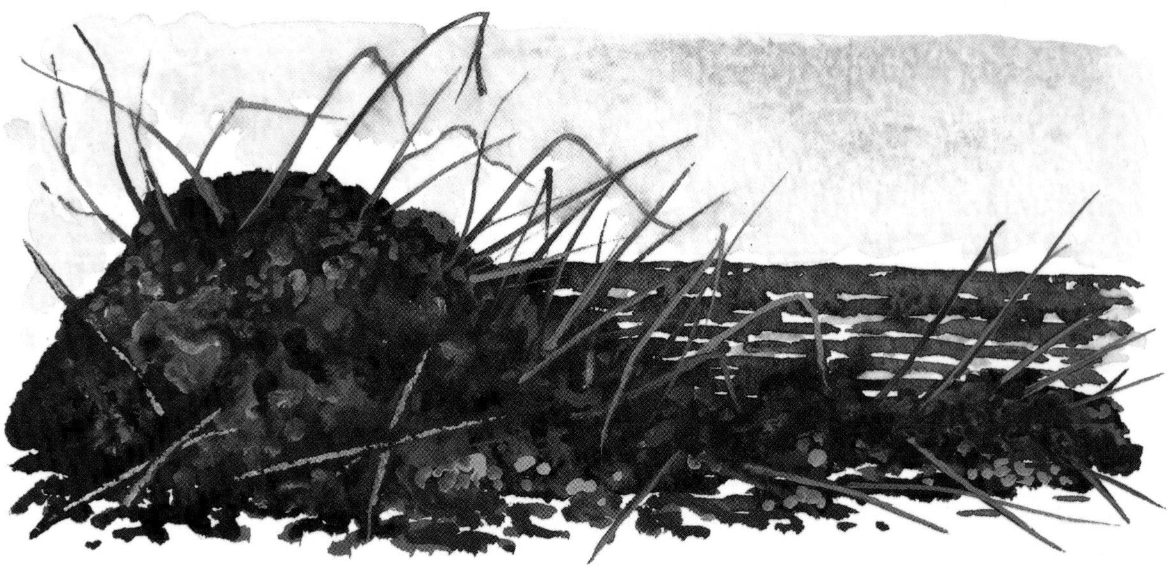

A clod of earth in the corner of a ploughed field after rain, depicted by feeding gouache into damp watercolour. Some of the stubble is produced with a painting knife

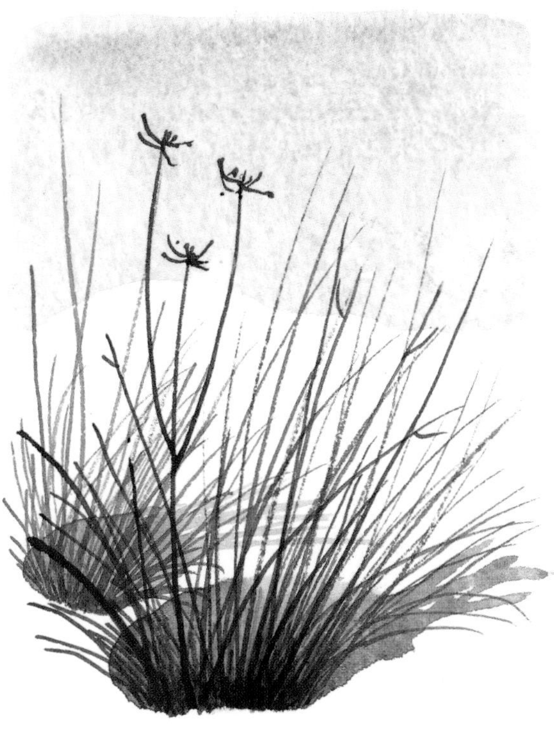

Stems and grasses growing out of 'holes' in the snow. A mixture of crimson alizarin and french ultramarine is used to depict the melting holes. Warmer coloured stems and grasses are painted with raw and burnt sienna

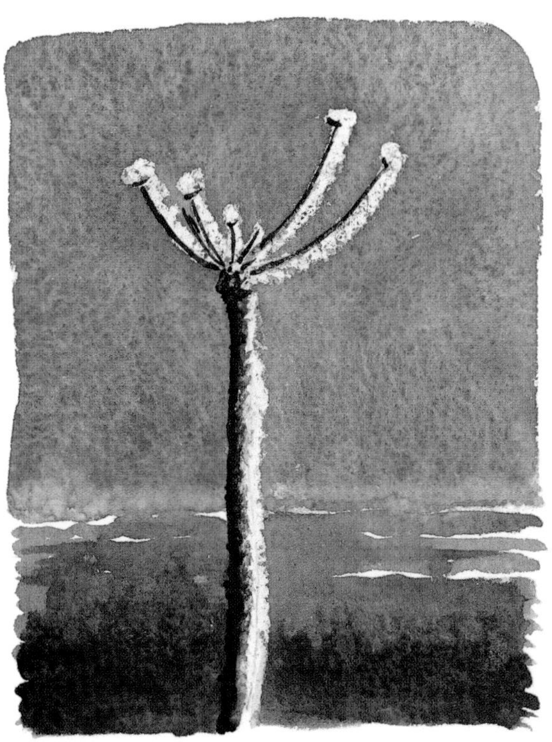

Hoar-frost clinging to a cow parsley (Queen Anne's lace) stem is created by using wax resist

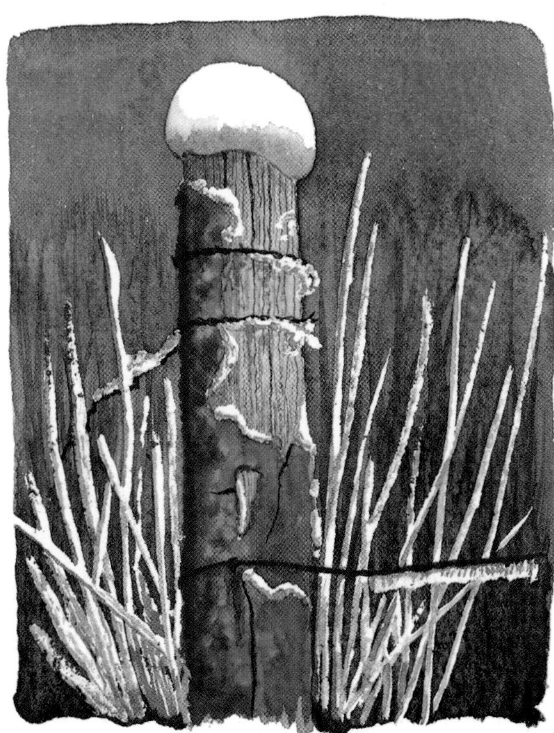

The snow-cap on top of the post is painted around with sky colour, but masking fluid is used for the remaining white shapes

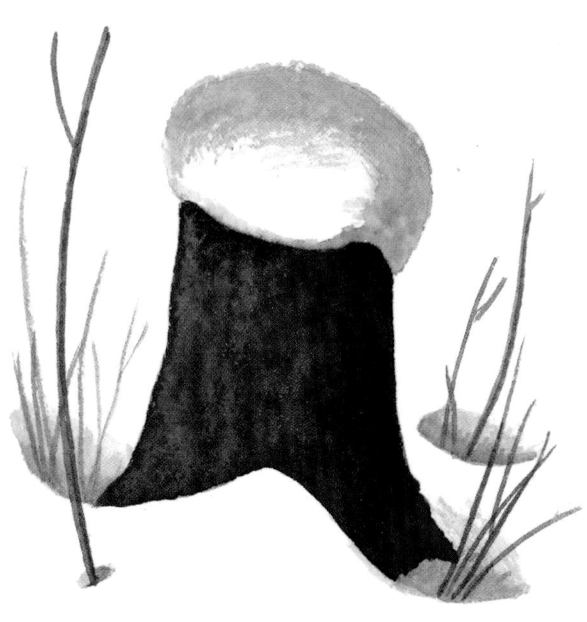

A mixture of monestial blue (phthalocyanine) and crimson alizarin forms a large snow-cap on an old tree-stump

Step-by-Step Demonstrations

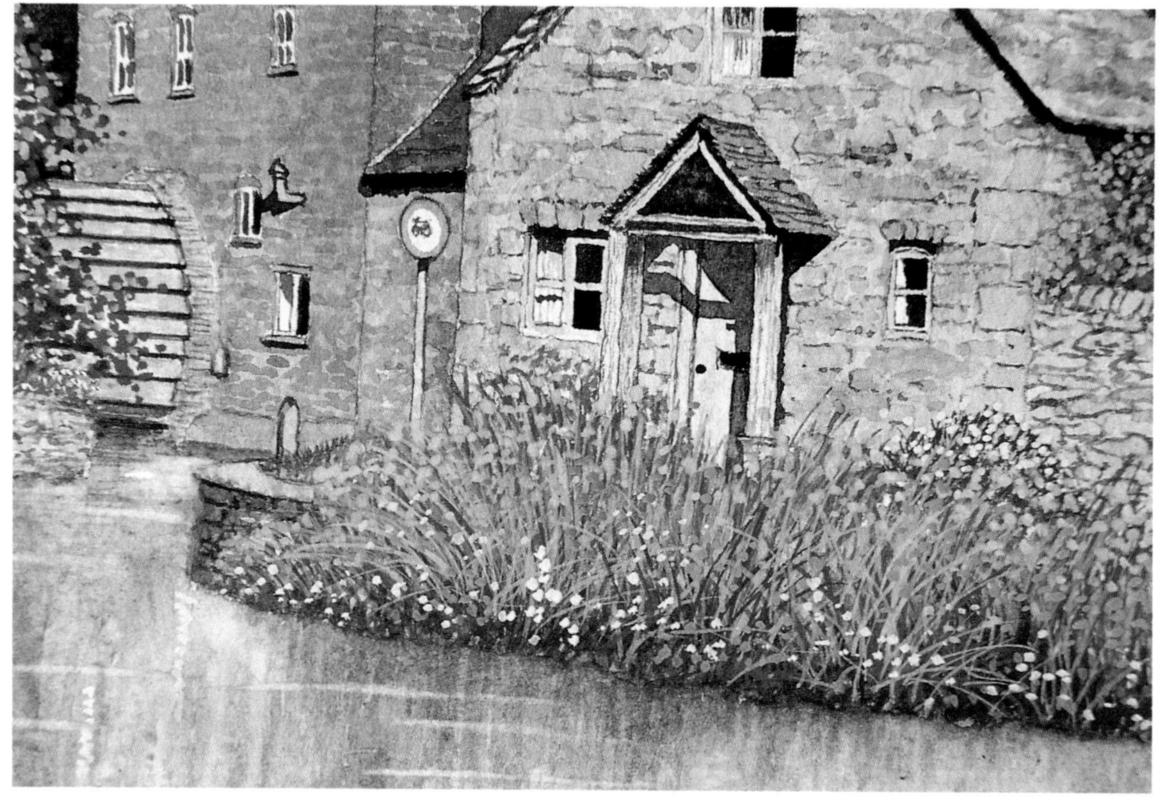

Lower Slaughter Mill (detail)

Pioneertown

Pioneertown is an amazing place. It is located in Yucca Valley, California, and, as its name suggests, has survived since the West's pioneering days. Fortunately, it is not just another ghost town visited by tourists at weekends, but people have chosen to make the livery stable, sheriff's office and the 'Palace' saloon into their homes. The main street still exists in the form of hard-packed desert sand which creates a large cloud of dust as you drive along it. 'Pappy and Harriet's' Palace Saloon Restaurant has been used as a film set on many occasions, because it has retained its old saloon atmosphere. The legendary Roy Rogers has been on location in the past, and as I was fortunate enough to meet him prior to visiting Pioneertown, my time spent there was all the more interesting. It seemed rather fitting to dedicate a painting to the 'King of the Cowboys' and this quiet corner seemed to conjure up memories from times gone by. There is an eerie presence of long-forgotten heroes here; something special and nostalgic!

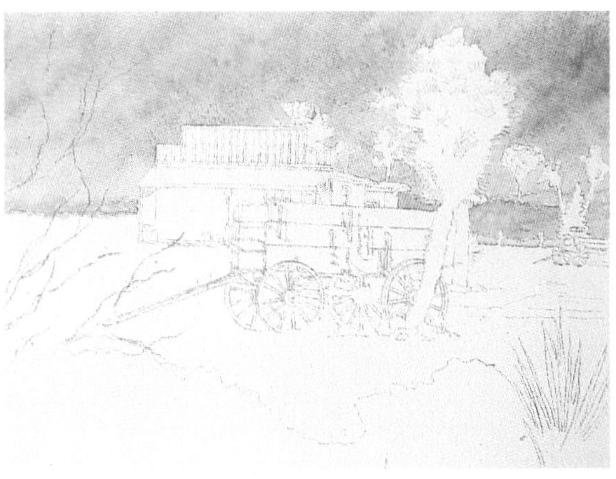

Stage 1 There is no visible sky in this picture, only the base of foothills form the background; but they act as a useful foil for the main subjects in the painting. An out-of-focus effect seemed in order here. It is possible that a background like this could take over and swamp the main subjects, so a soft overall textural effect is desirable. A wash of clear water is applied to the area around the building and trees with a no 12 round pointed Dalon. As this dries, mixtures of Payne's grey, french ultramarine, cadmium yellow pale, raw sienna and white gouache are added with a no 6 round pointed sable. As the paint dries, granulation occurs, creating an appropriate texture

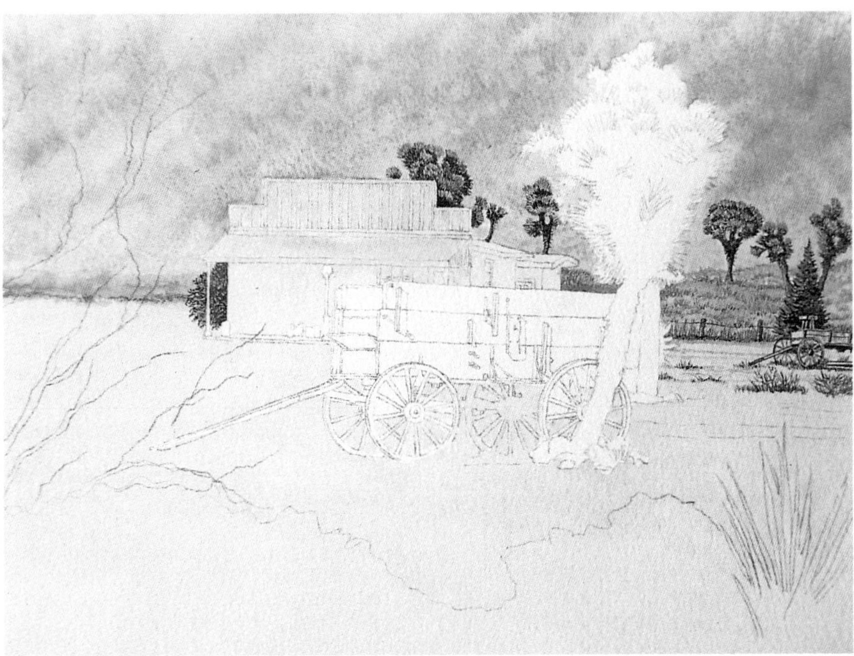

Stage 2

Stage 2 A wash of raw sienna is applied to the middle ground and foreground areas with a no 12 round pointed Dalon. This is done to create the gritty sand feel to the ground. Distant Joshua trees are painted with mixtures of french ultramarine and cadmium yellow pale for the light areas, while the darker tones consist of Payne's grey, cadmium yellow pale and warm sepia, which are also used for the trunks. A small fir tree is painted with the same greens. The distant waggon on the right is depicted with a no 1 round pointed sable and warm sepia mixed with Payne's grey. Initial light washes, consisting of raw sienna, Payne's grey and warm sepia, are applied to the building with a no 3 round pointed sable. A small brush is used to ensure accuracy

Stage 3

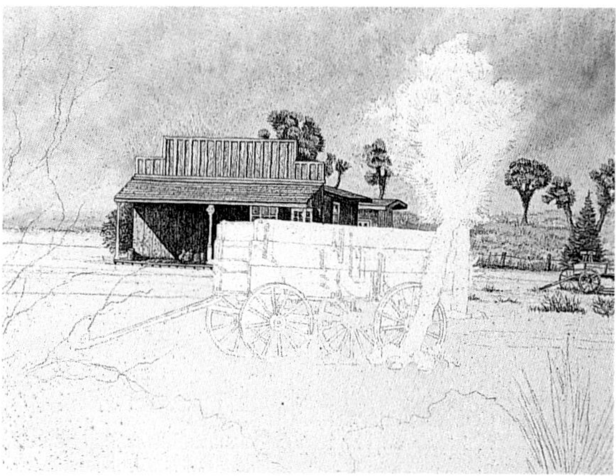

Stage 3 Detail in the buildings is next on the agenda. The dark colour of the buildings behind the waggon will help to define it later on. These dark tones are a mixture of warm sepia and neutral tint; a little detail is included – that is, a door and a window. The larger building is detailed with a no 00 round pointed sable, warm sepia and Payne's grey. Some dilute green is added to suggest weather-staining of the timber. A cast shadow on the front porch is painted with a no 2 round pointed sable and warm sepia mixed with neutral tint; the bright sunlit area is depicted with a wash of raw sienna and burnt sienna. The porch support posts remain unpainted; they are white, so white paper is left exposed, apart from the shadow at the tops which is a mixture of crimson alizarin and french ultramarine

Stage 4

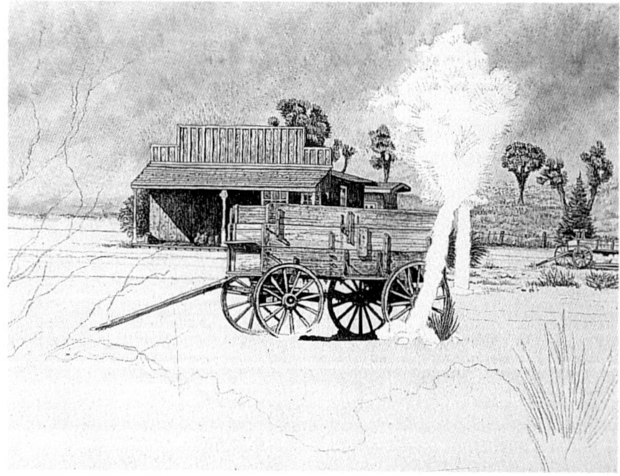

Stage 4 A very dilute wash of raw sienna with a touch of Payne's grey is applied to the waggon. When this is completely dry, detailing begins. A no 00 round pointed sable and warm sepia mixed with a neutral tint describes the lines, small features and wood-grain. The rear far wheel is very dark and entirely in shadow. A mixture of warm sepia and neutral tint is used to depict this. Rusty metal parts, including the rims of the wheels, are painted with mixtures of burnt sienna and warm sepia

Stage 5

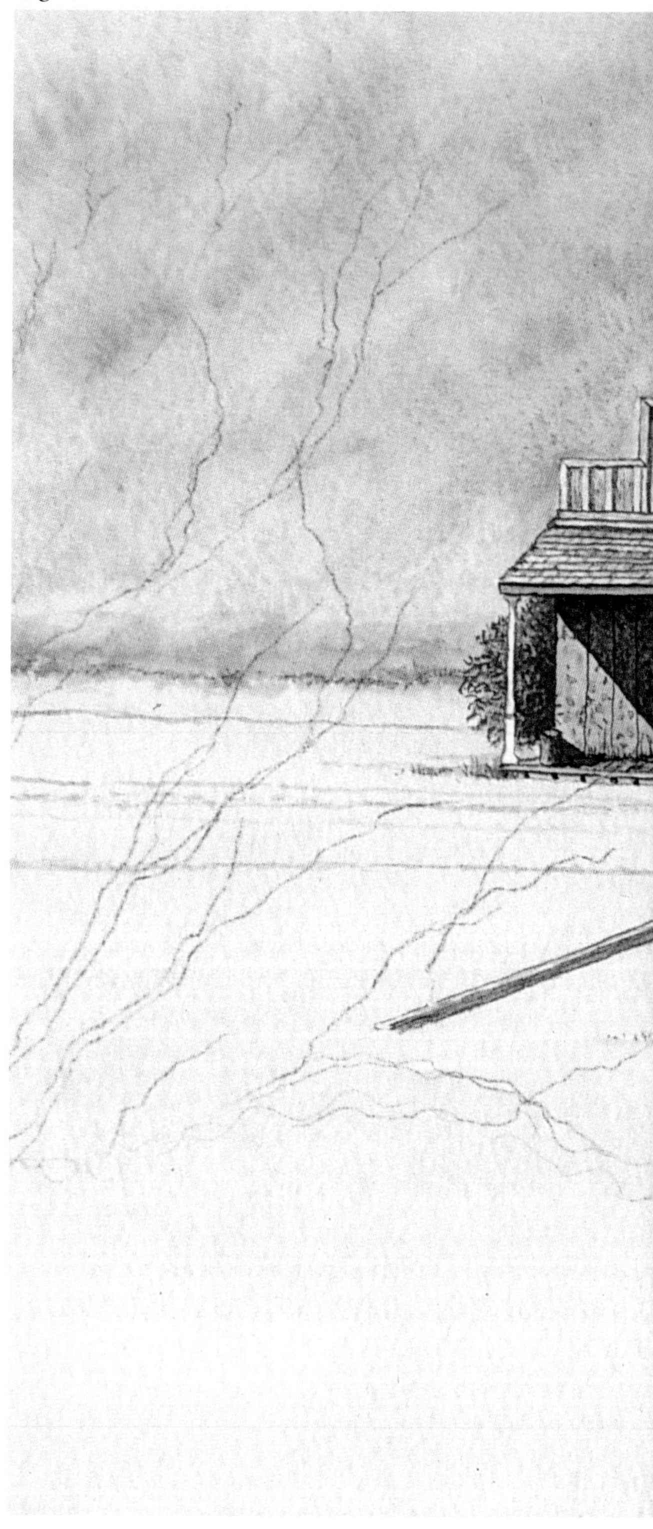

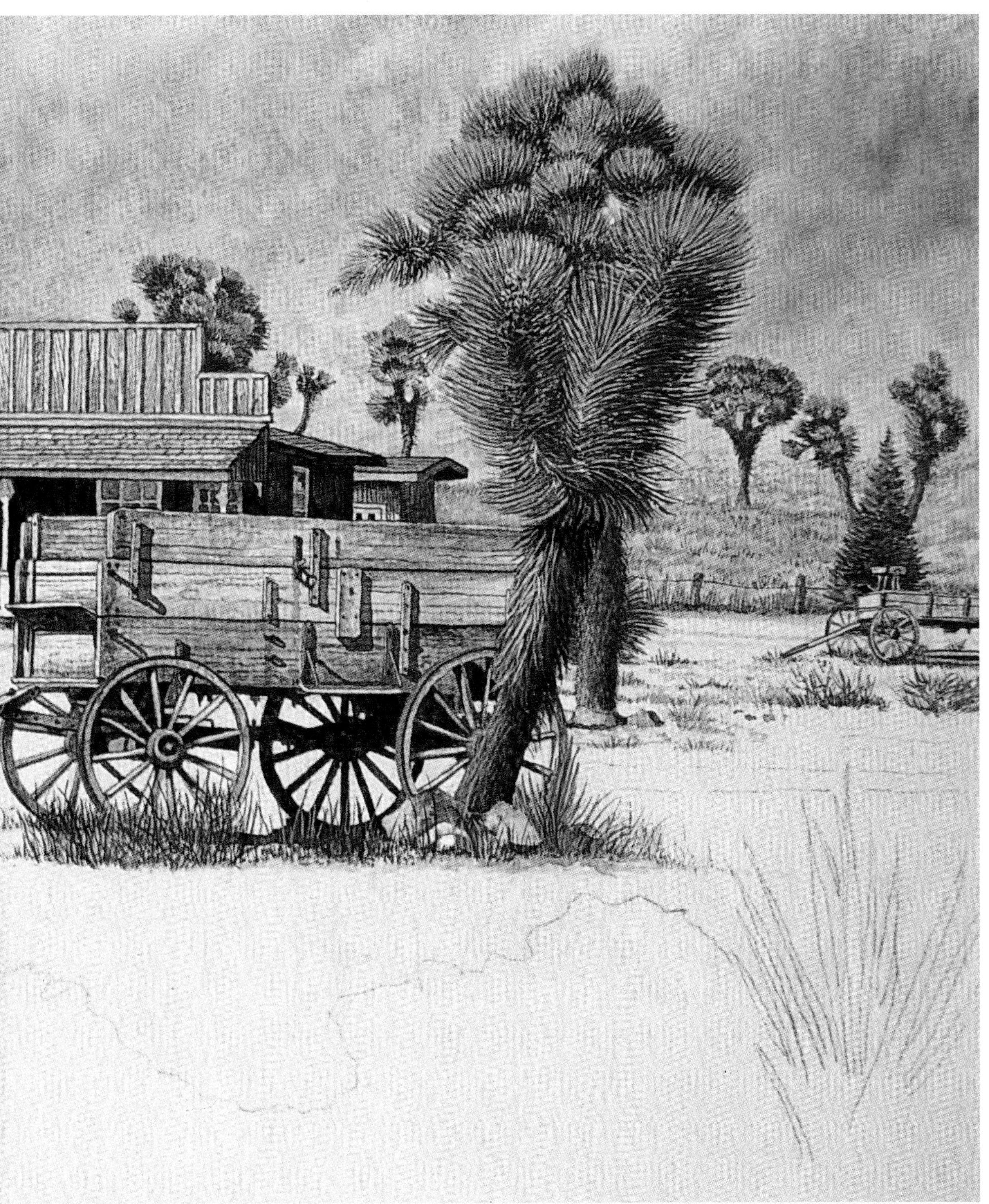

Stage 5 The spikes of the Joshua trees are painted with a no 00 round pointed sable and mixtures of cadmium yellow pale with Payne's grey; the latter is used extensively in areas of very dark tone. Raw sienna mixed with burnt sienna depicts spikes which are dying off. Highlights are added with touches of cadmium yellow pale and white gouache. The trunks are painted with mixtures of Payne's grey, raw sienna and white gouache. Note that the grey spikes are much lighter on the sunlit side. Large stones around the base are added as well as some dry grasses. The waggon-wheels disappear into these, providing it with a firm base

Stage 6 Cast shadows are indicated on the ground with a mixture of french ultramarine and crimson alizarin. Other horizontal 'lines', suggesting tracks, are painted with raw sienna, and some ground vegetation is also added. Plants are introduced into the foreground with mixtures of Payne's grey, cadmium yellow pale, french ultramarine and white gouache using a no 1 round pointed sable. The yucca on the right is a mixture of french ultramarine and cadmium yellow pale. Branches entering the picture far left are painted with mixtures of warm sepia, Payne's grey and white gouache. They help to form a natural frame for the view beyond. Finally, light coloured grasses are painted into the immediate foreground with a no 00 round pointed sable and mixtures of raw sienna, burnt sienna and white gouache, providing a dry, brittle feeling

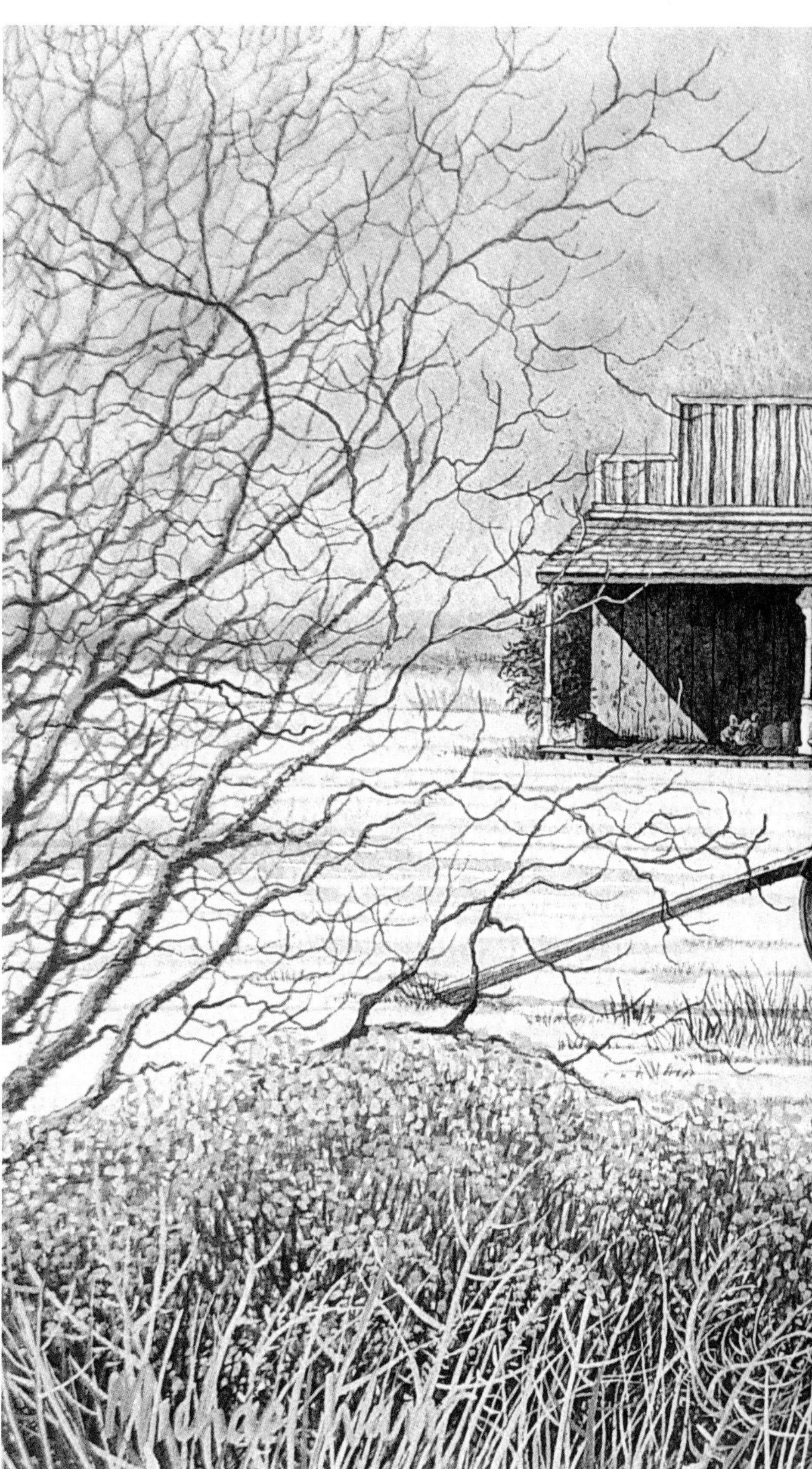

Colours Used
Payne's grey french ultramarine cadmium yellow pale raw sienna warm sepia neutral tint burnt sienna crimson alizarin white gouache

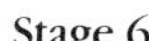

Stage 6

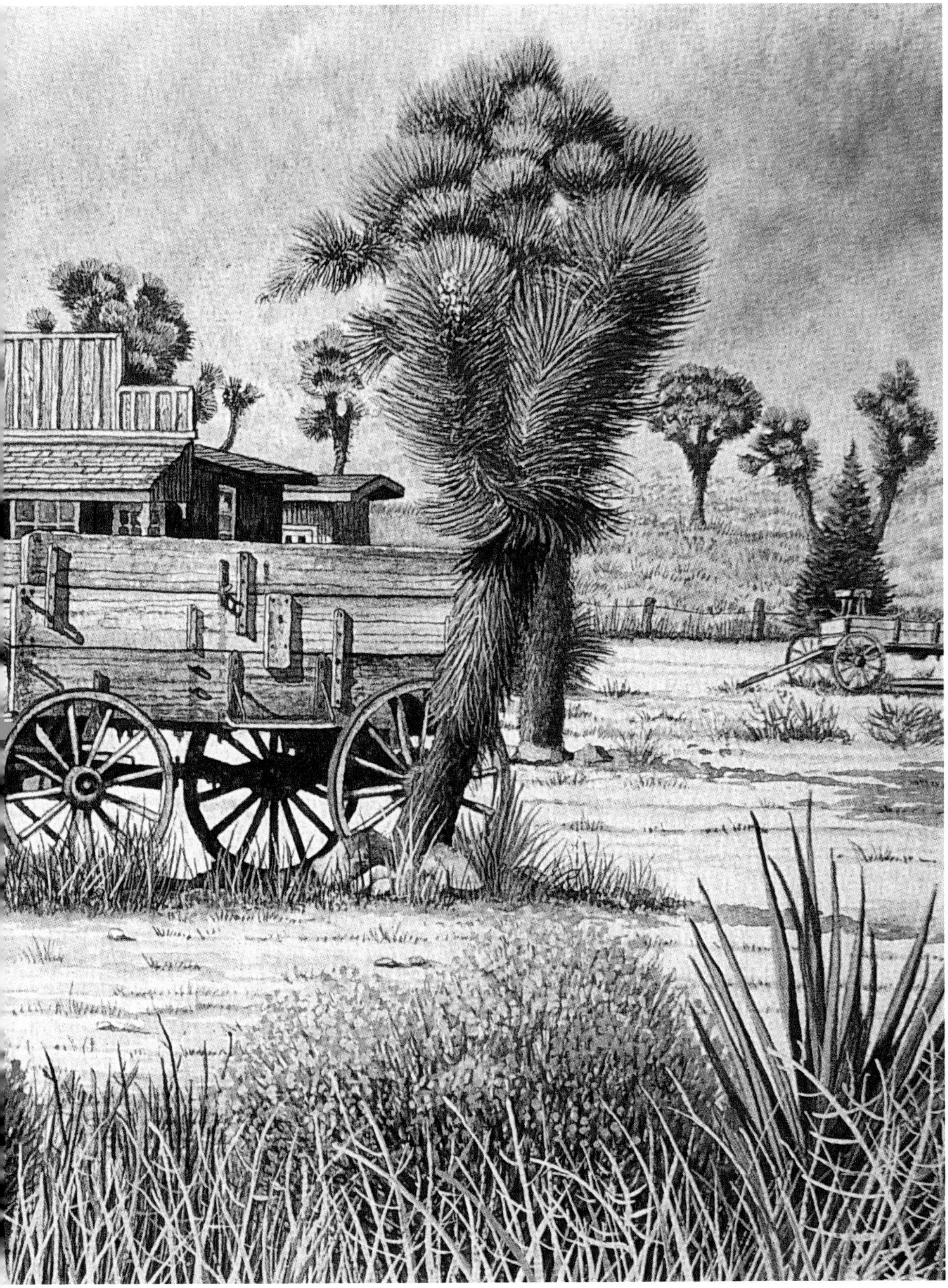

California Desert

Colours Used

raw sienna
coeruleum
french ultramarine
crimson alizarin
burnt sienna
warm sepia
cadmium yellow pale
white gouache

Travelling to Palm Springs from the Pacific coast makes an interesting journey. The road via San Juan Capistrano winds its way through hilly countryside and on to Sun City, Hemet, and then into desert mountains. In the main, colours are subtle and harmonious as rock and plant life interact with one another, creating a palette of warm hues. Sunlight forms ever-changing, interesting shadows in the desert and on the distant mountains. These ingredients inspired me to make a painting of this scene situated on the edge of the Coachella Valley, near Palm Springs. The San Jacinto Mountains (left) and the San Bernadino Mountains (in the distance, right) complete with fresh snow, form a perfect backdrop to an array of interesting desert subjects, and a splash of bright colour from the early flowering plants adds panache.

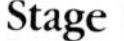

Stage 1

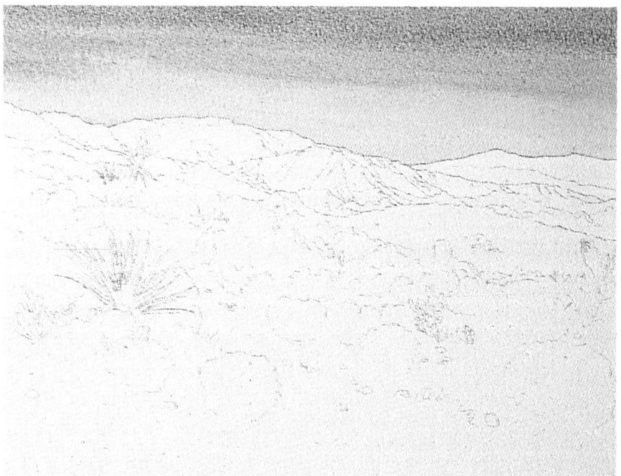

Stage 1 After drawing the mountains, the desert plants are drawn in lightly and loosely to suggest a general idea for reasons of perspective. Drawn detail in the middleground and foreground is kept to a minimum.

A wash of dilute raw sienna is painted into the sky directly above the mountains with a no 6 round pointed sable, producing a warm glow radiating from the desert. While this initial wash is still damp, a mixture of coeruleum and french ultramarine is applied with a no 12 round pointed Dalon. A no 6 brush is used to paint around the mountains to assist in maintaining accuracy; there is snow on the mountain tops and it is important to retain the white of the paper at this stage

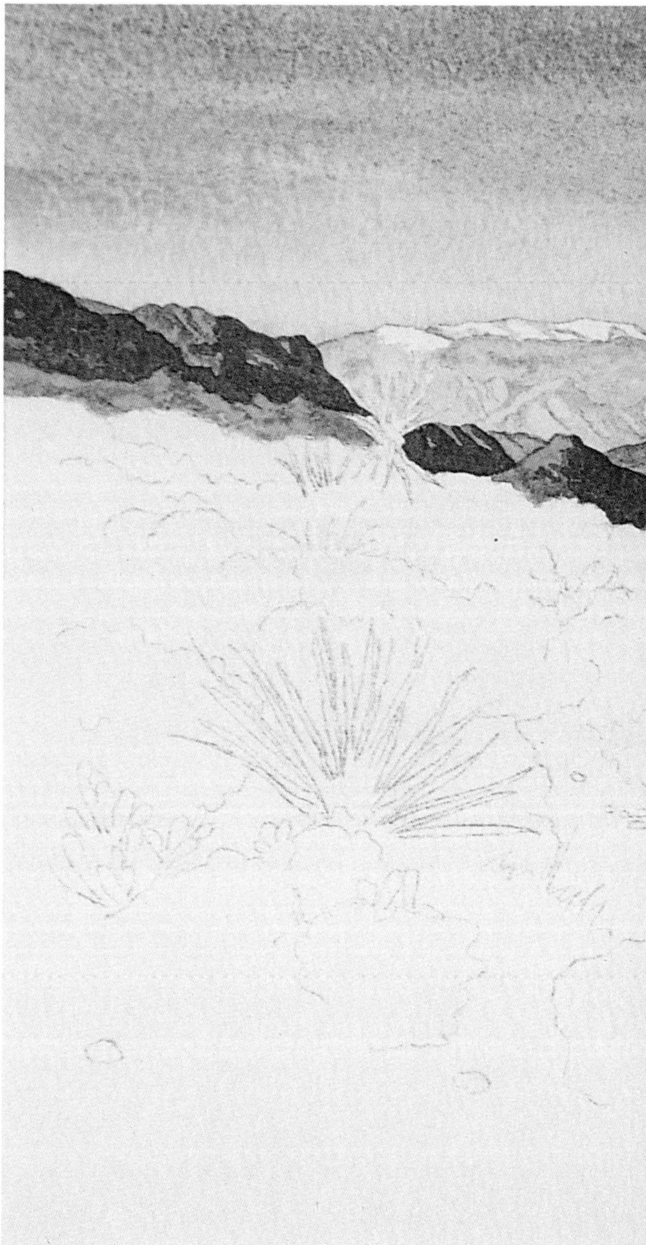

Stage 3

Stage 2

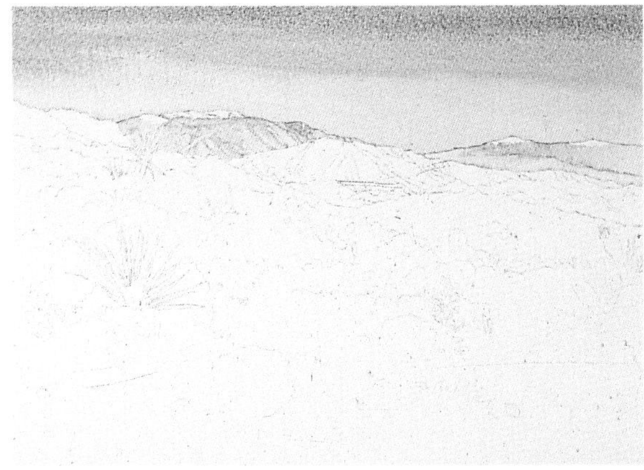

Stage 2 A no 3 round pointed sable and a mixture of coeruleum, french ultramarine and crimson alizarin is used for the distant mountains. Detail is introduced into the mountains with a no 1 round pointed sable and stronger versions of the same colours

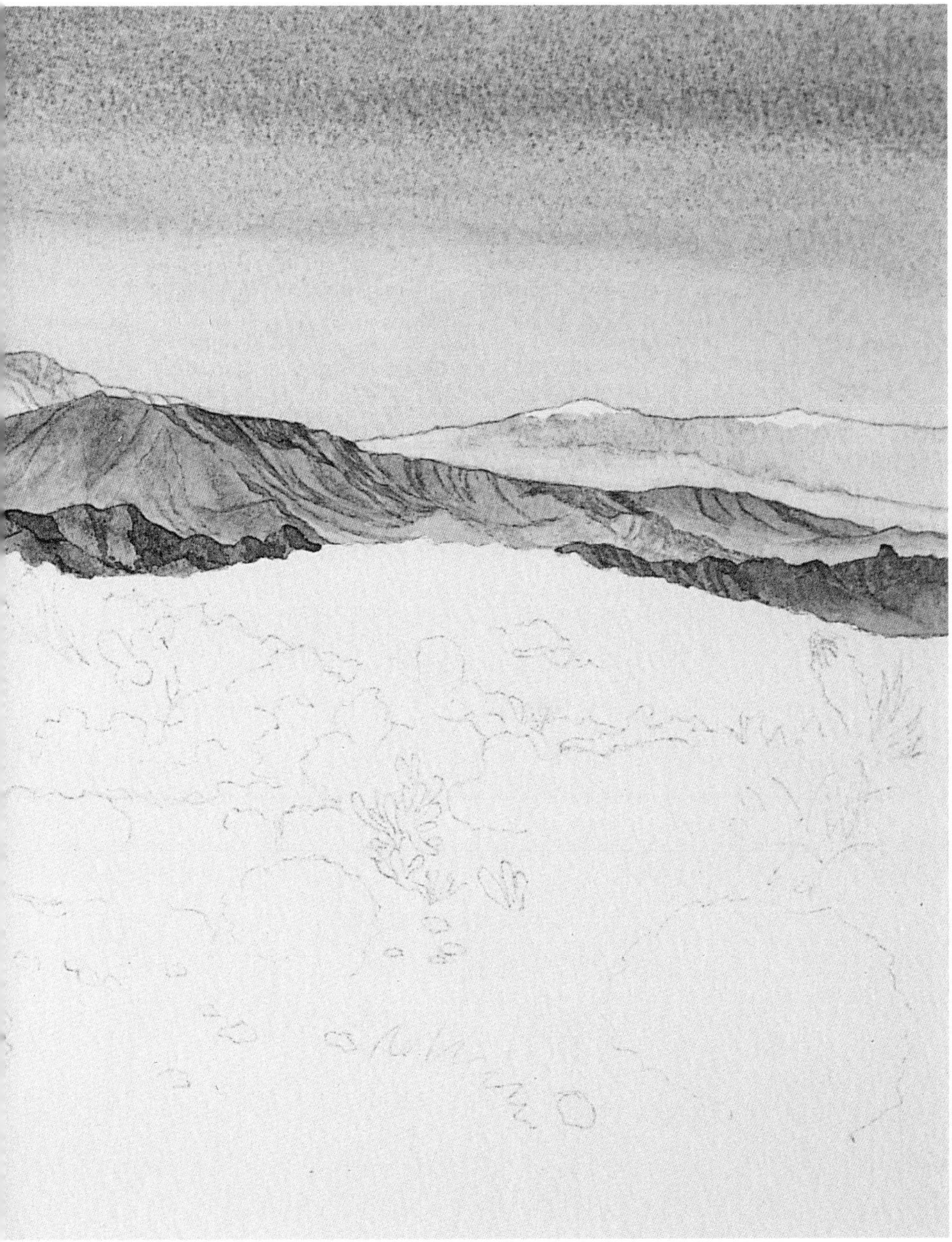

Stage 3 Mixtures of coeruleum and burnt sienna are used for the lower, middle range of mountains. A touch of crimson alizarin is added and all of the work is carried out with a no 1 round pointed sable. The closer hills are painted with stronger versions of the same colours, but with the addition of warm sepia

Stage 4

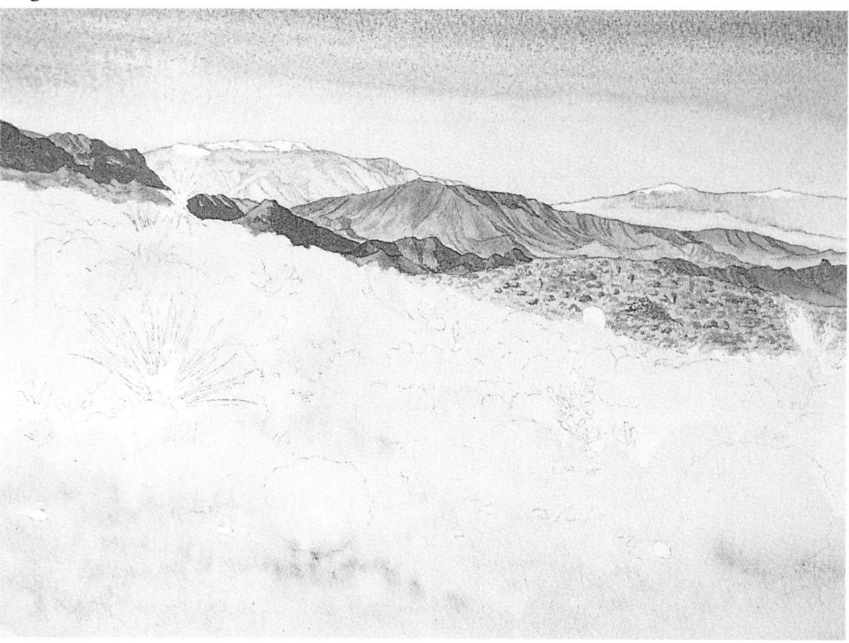

Stage 4 A wash of raw sienna with a touch of warm sepia is applied to the whole of the desert floor area with a no 12 round pointed Dalon. This is done to suggest an overall effect of sand. Note that one or two of the plants are left unpainted at this stage. Warm sepia is fed into the foreground area to suggest texture in readiness for plant life. The area of desert directly in front of the mountains is detailed with distant desert plants. A thirsty brush removes colour from some of the pebbles in the immediate foreground

Stage 5 It is time to begin the desert vegetation, and in the middle ground – that is, the line in the picture between the mountains and desert – is the best place to start. A horizontal approach is necessary to make the vegetation appear convincing as it moves across the desert floor. Working across the painting with a no 1 round pointed sable and mixtures of light browns and silver-greens begins to set the scene. Raw sienna, burnt sienna and light greys depict the 'brittle' feeling of the desert plants – the desert is extremely arid. Work on this area requires patience as the various plants are built up individually. Dark tones in the form of shadows help to separate the shapes of the plants by creating good contrasts

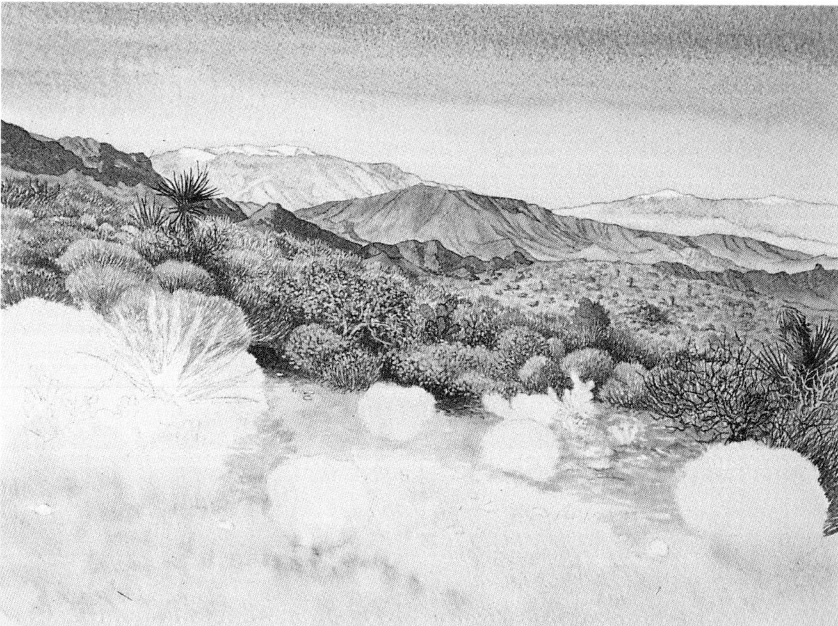

Stage 5

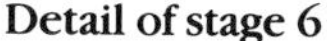

Detail of stage 6

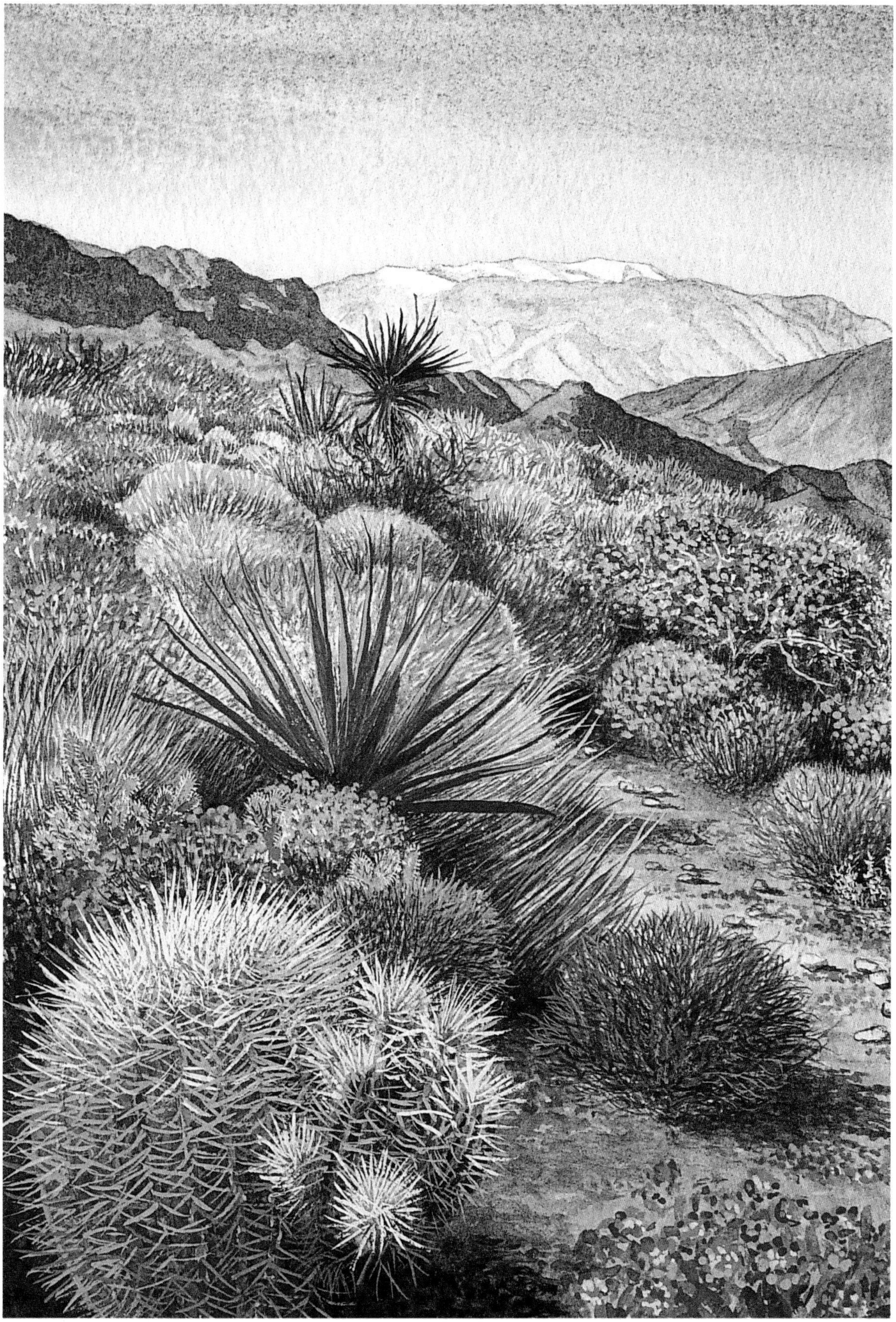

Stage 6

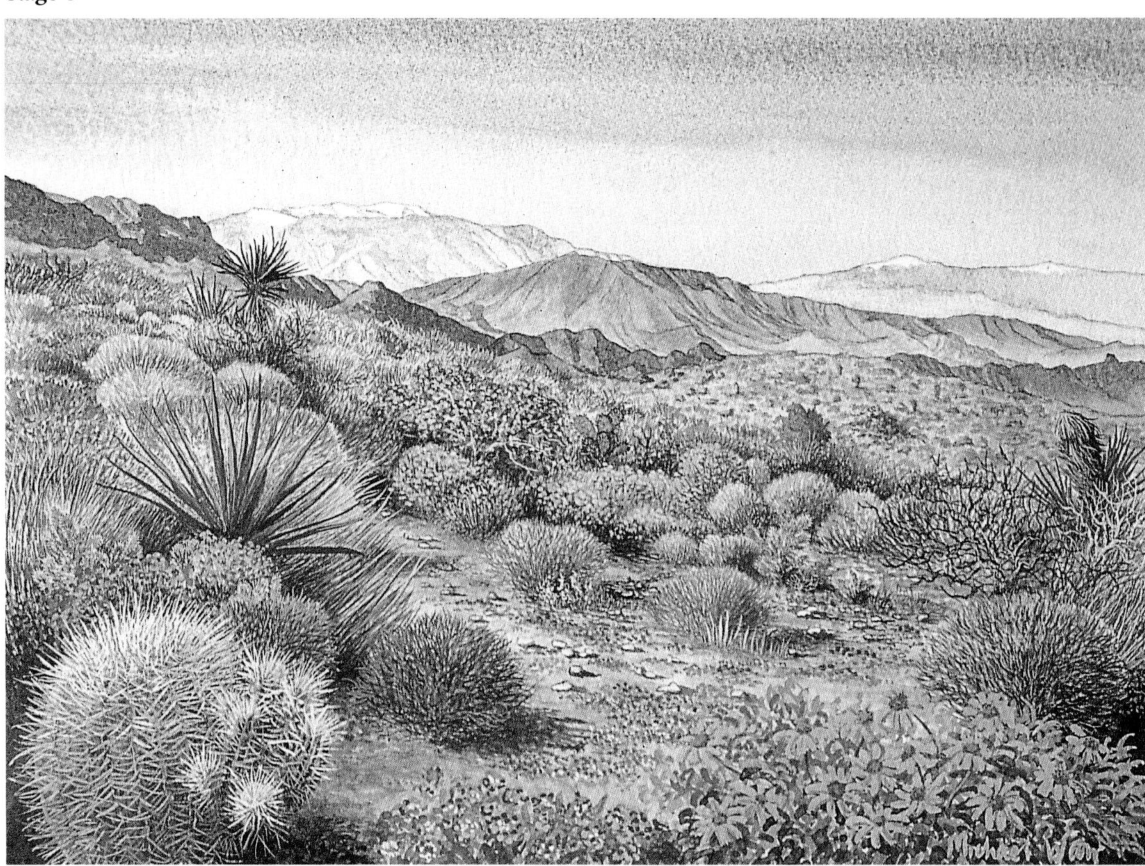

Stage 6 Work continues on the desert plants and a little more raw sienna is introduced into the foreground area of the desert floor. Mixtures of french ultramarine and cadmium yellow pale are used for the green spikes of a yucca plant on the left. Small purple flowers on the ground are a mixture of crimson alizarin and white gouache. The yellow brittle-bush (foreground right) consists of mixtures of cadmium yellow pale and raw sienna; the silver-green leaves are french ultramarine, cadmium yellow pale and white gouache. A large Barell cactus on the extreme left is painted with mixtures of french ultramarine, cadmium yellow pale and burnt sienna. The spikes are painted with a no 1 round pointed sable and white gouache tinted with raw sienna and burnt sienna

Approach to the Eighteenth

The Belfry golf complex is the home of the British Professional Golfers Association which organises the biennial Ryder Cup match between Europe and the United States; every four years the competition is played in Britain. The Belfry was awarded the match in 1985 and again in 1989. Within the complex is the Brabazon course and it is the approach to the eighteenth green which is particularly interesting, because behind the green stands an historic building which includes a bell-tower that gives its name to the complex. Past occupants include monks and farmers, and it was even a famous nightclub at one time. Now it is an hotel. The buildings stretch delightfully across the landscape, creating an almost stage-set effect. It was an autumn afternoon when the sketches were made for this painting. The complexity of the subject meant that detailed drawings of the buildings were necessary, as well as the green itself. Cast shadows drifted across the ground creating interesting patterns, while two keen golfers putted to the best of their ability. Bullrushes (cat's-tails) in the foreground provided an excellent 'entrance' to all of this, and trees on the left and right created a natural framework to the composition.

Stage 1

Stage 1 After completing the drawing, a wash of dilute raw sienna is applied with a no 20 round pointed Dalon. This is also washed over the water, which later will be exposed as other colour is applied, to create highlights. When the initial wash is bone-dry, with the painting upside-down and tilted, mixtures of french ultramarine and monestial (phthalocyanine) blue are washed on; these washes are applied very dilute directly above the buildings, with a stronger application high in the sky. While these washes remain damp, areas are blotted with tissue, exposing warm coloured clouds. After allowing the blue washes to dry, mixtures of light red and french ultramarine are applied to depict darker clouds. A mixture of raw sienna and light red above the buildings is used to convey distance

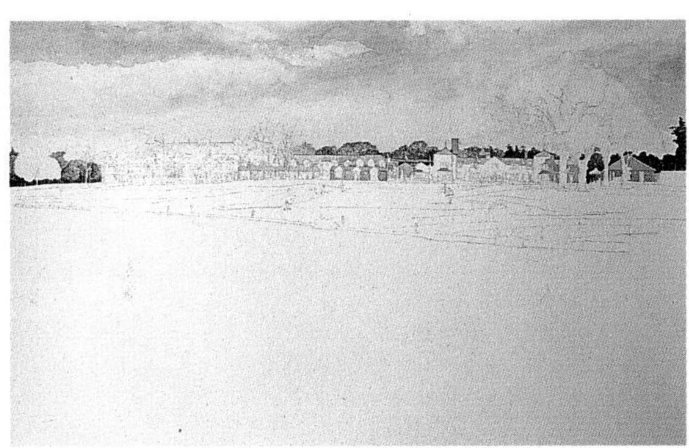

Stage 2

Stage 2 It is time to look at the distant trees and buildings. The buildings are quite complex and it is essential to work slowly, looking at the architectural structures piece by piece. Work begins, moving from right to left, across the buildings in an attempt to complete a 'strip' across the painting. In order to paint detail in the buildings, it is necessary to rest my hand on the paper, so it is a good idea to use a piece of paper to lean on, keeping the work clean. The background trees are painted with nos 0 and 2 round pointed sables and mixtures of raw sienna, crimson alizarin, light red and cadmium yellow pale, but the green trees (Scots pines) are painted with a mixture of cadmium yellow pale and french ultramarine. Grey roofs of the buildings are painted with Payne's grey and crimson alizarin; the tiled central roof is a mixture of crimson alizarin and french ultramarine. Green is introduced because moss is growing here and there. Ridges of the roofs are painted in the form of lines with a no 00 round pointed sable. Warm red-brick colours in the walls are mixtures of raw sienna and crimson alizarin; shadows will be included at a later stage

Stage 3

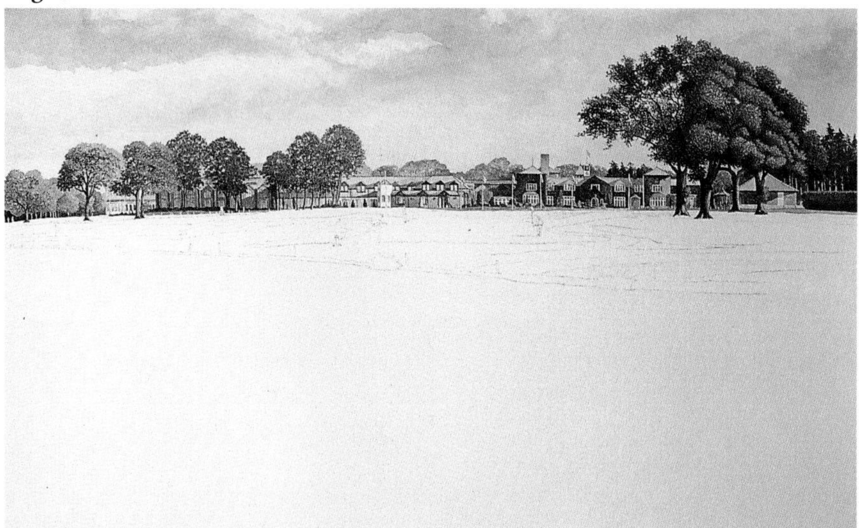

Colours Used

french ultramarine
monestial (phthalocyanine)
light red
raw sienna
crimson alizarin
cadmium yellow pale
Payne's grey
burnt sienna
warm sepia
coeruleum
white gouache

Stage 3 Work continues on the buildings; the white building on the extreme left is created simply by leaving the white of the paper. Windows are added with dark tones and a no 00 round pointed sable; the small gazebo on the right is painted with a mixture of light red, warm sepia and a no 0 round pointed sable. Dark window-panes are painted with Payne's grey. The ivy-clad walls are a stippled version of french ultramarine, cadmium yellow pale and a touch of burnt sienna. A no 2 round pointed sable is used. Cast shadows on the roofs are a less diluted form of Payne's grey and crimson alizarin, while the cast shadows on the warm brick walls are washed in with warm sepia. The buildings are completed and the evergreen trees which stand in front are introduced by using a no 0 round pointed sable and cadmium yellow pale mixed with french ultramarine. Tall trees directly in front of the buildings are added; their trunks are a mixture of raw sienna and Payne's grey, while the foliage consists of crimson alizarin, raw sienna and cadmium yellow pale. Larger oak trees on the extreme left and even larger ones on the extreme right (both sets of trees assist the composition by framing the picture) are painted; the tree-trunks and branches are mixtures of raw sienna and Payne's grey, while the foliage contains greens which are mixtures of french ultramarine and cadmium yellow pale, plus warmer autumnal colours consisting of raw sienna, burnt sienna, crimson alizarin, warm sepia and cadmium yellow pale

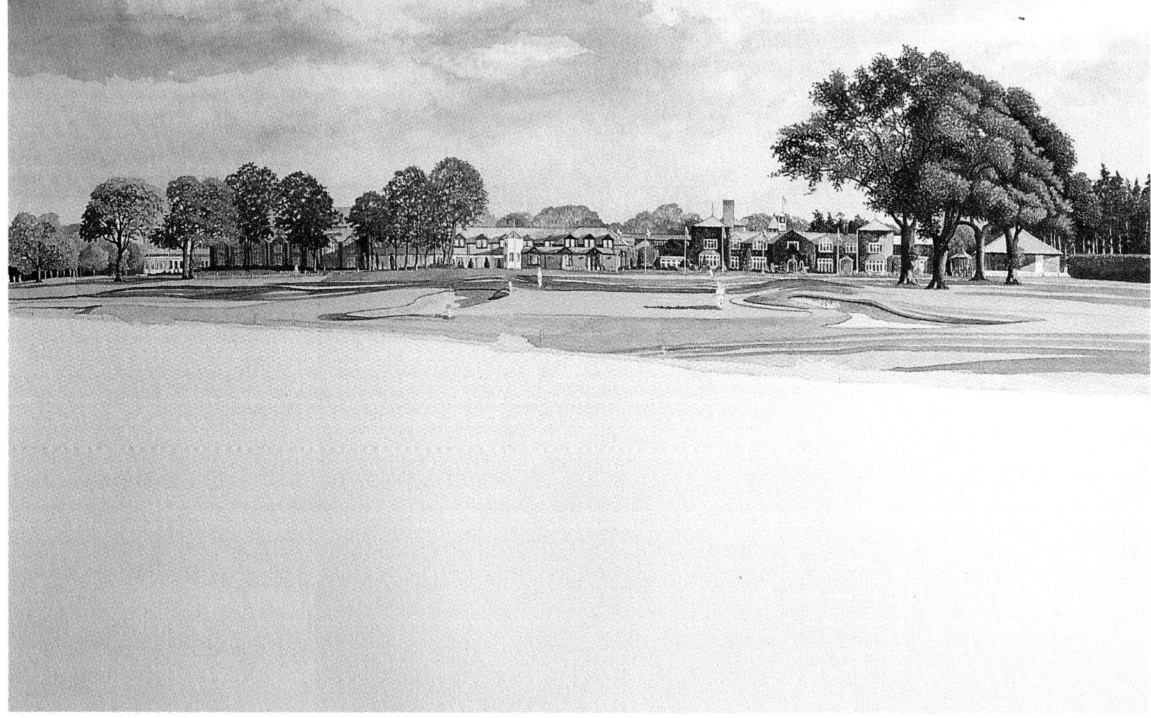

Stage 4

Stage 5

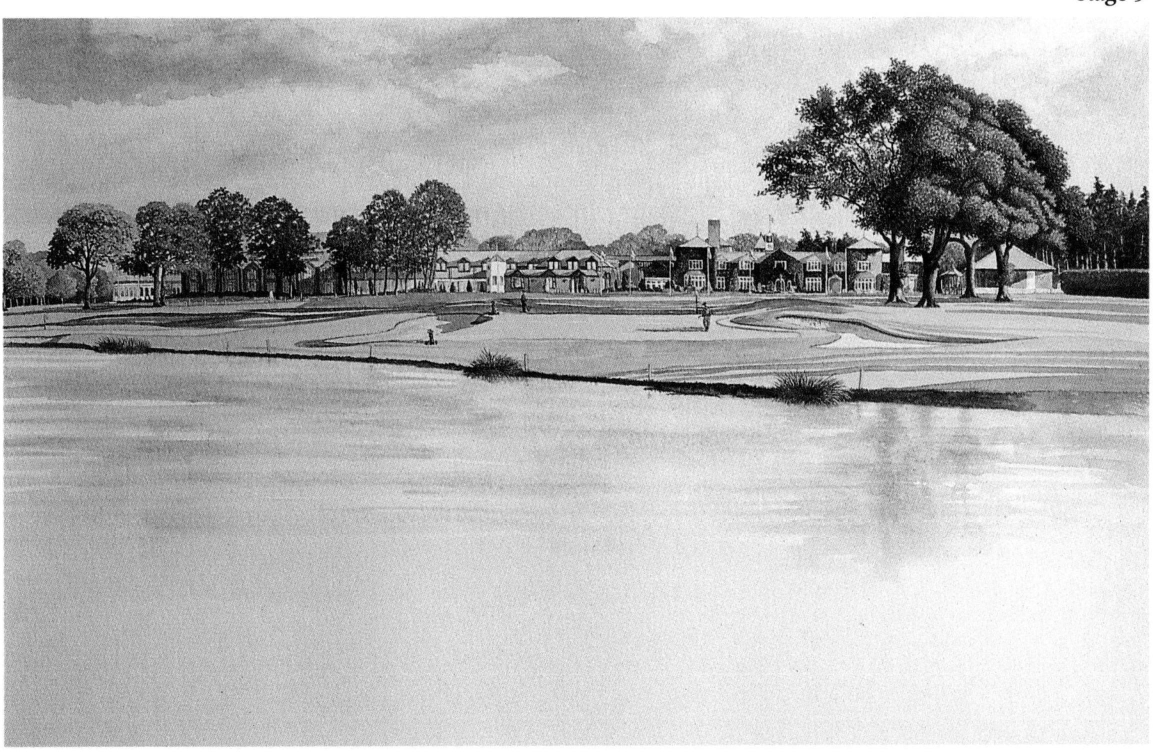

Stage 4 The greens and bunkers are ready for attention. Washes of cadmium yellow pale and french ultramarine are prepared in differing strengths. Because the green and surrounding areas are cut at varying lengths – the green itself is virtually shaved – many shades of green rather than only one are seen. If washes of differing shades are already prepared, you can quickly paint the complete area rather than pause to mix various colours as they are required. Textural qualities are not needed here as the grass is very short – a 'flat' appearance is more convincing. A dilute wash of green is applied and allowed to dry thoroughly; other washes are then added until the desired effect is obtained. Cast shadows are finally painted by adding more french ultramarine to the mixtures. All of the preceding washes are applied with a no 6 round pointed sable and a no 12 round pointed Dalon. Shadows in the bunkers are formed with a mixture of french ultramarine and crimson alizarin. It is necessary to retain clean washes in this area and therefore it is essential to be direct with the application of paint and to avoid 'fiddling' with the colour, as this temptation would lead to the underlying wash being picked up, leading to a muddy appearance

Stage 5 The golf trolleys, figures and flags on the green are painted with a no 1 round pointed sable, as are the posts at the water's edge. The bank surrounding the water is depicted with mixtures of warm sepia and french ultramarine. In order to convey their spiky appearance, the reeds are painted with a no 00 round pointed sable. Colourwise, they are 'dry', so burnt sienna is added to a green made from mixtures of cadmium yellow pale and french ultramarine. A pause is often necessary in a very detailed landscape – somewhere for the eye to rest. It seemed logical to use the water for this purpose; a large flat expanse is ideal. An unfussy area here will allow the foreground detail to be seen clearly. The water is treated in a simple fashion; a no 20 round pointed Dalon is used to apply a large sweeping wash comprising mixtures of dilute coeruleum, french ultramarine and crimson alizarin. Areas of light underlying colour remain exposed to convey highlights. The only suggested reflections are those of the large right-hand trees

Stage 6 A wash of cadmium yellow pale and french ultramarine is applied to the immediate foreground with a no 20 round pointed Dalon; raw sienna and burnt sienna are also added. When the wash is damp rather than very wet, white gouache tinted with raw sienna is fed in with a no 6 round pointed sable. It spreads naturally, forming a texture which will be incorporated later on. A no 2 round pointed sable is used to depict reeds and dry vegetation. Mixtures of raw sienna, burnt sienna and existing greens blend together during this process. When the paint is dry, a no 6 round pointed sable suggests the leaves of bullrushes (cat's-tails). White gouache mixed with a blue-green produces the desired colour. Small shrubs are also introduced; Payne's grey is used for the branches, while cadmium yellow pale, french ultramarine and warm sepia are used for the leaves. Stems are added to support the seed-heads of the bullrushes and when these are dry the actual heads are painted with a mixture of burnt sienna and warm sepia. A little cadmium yellow pale is dry-brushed on to the lighter sides. After darkening the base of the stems all across the painting, paint is dribbled, flicked and spattered below them, creating an overall texture and allowing the eye to enter the picture gently. Meanwhile, overhead, a flock of birds is indicated. To sum up, the bullrushes act as a link between the two sides of the lake. Notice that they break through the bank on the far side, as does a shrub on the extreme right. Compositionally, the eye travels from the shrub, up through the large oak trees, along the birds and tree-tops, returning down through the trees on the left and the bullrushes. It is then led into the picture again, taking in all the points of interest

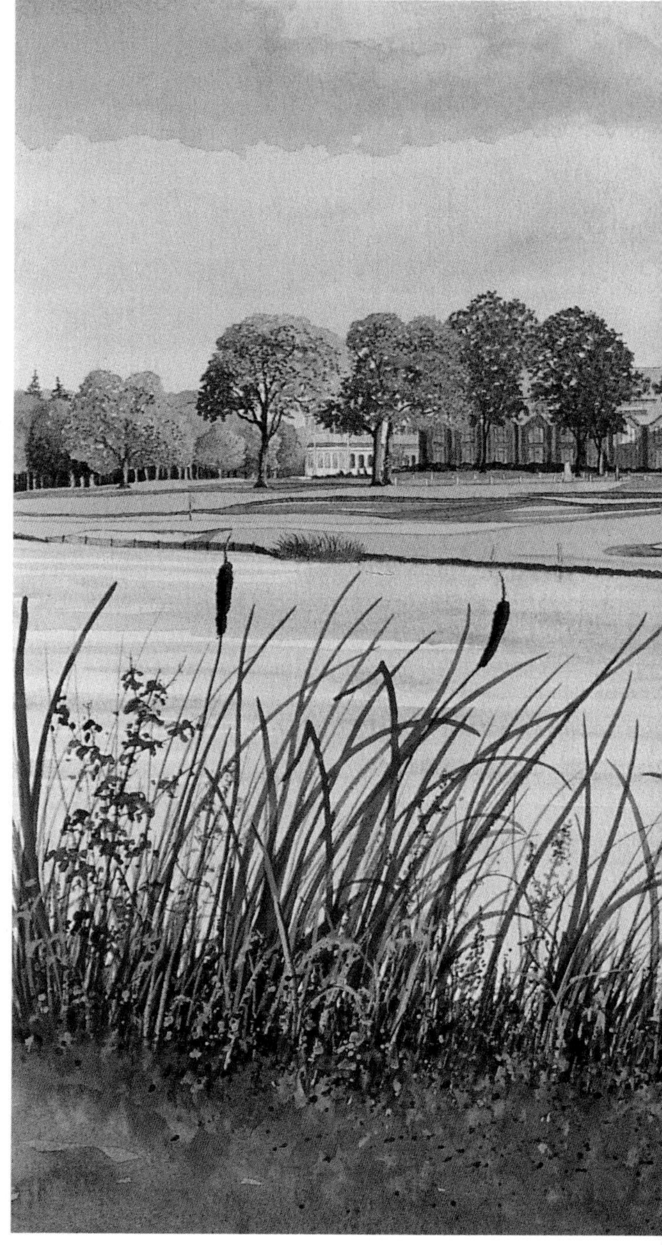

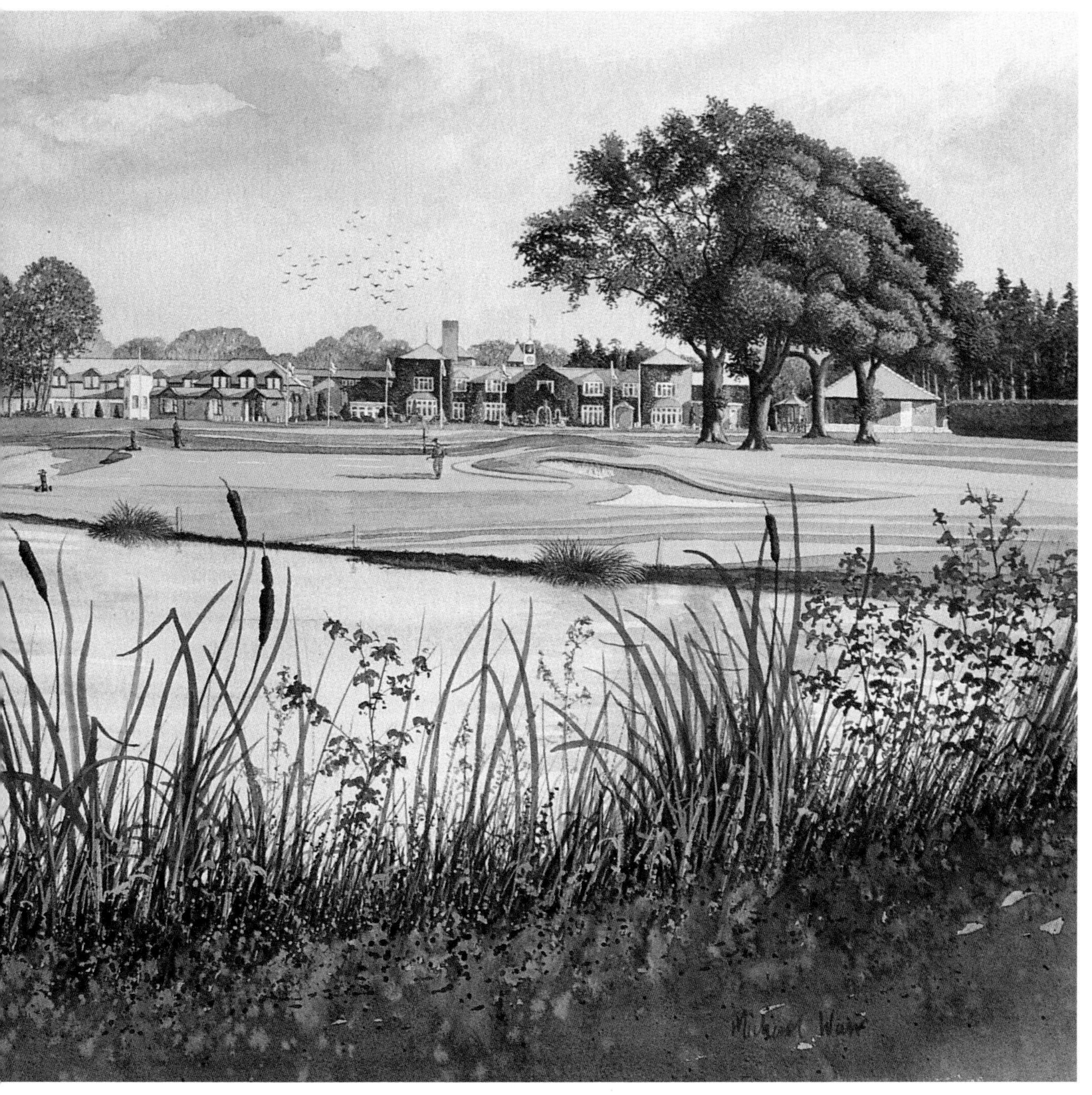

Stage 6

Nettle Hill Farm

Seen against an uncluttered sky, the buildings of Nettle Hill Farm form an interesting play of angles; walls and roof-tops play one another off in a display of rural architecture. Seen from this low viewpoint, the strong, crisp shapes are well defined against the sky. Side-lighting from the sun produces tonal contrasts in the buildings, bringing them to life and adding even more interest to them. The buildings are over two hundred years old and derive their warm colours from hand-made bricks which were made on site. Some of the angles may appear to be a little odd, but when the buildings were constructed, levels were not taken; they simply follow the contour of the ground.

The large barn on the extreme left was my studio for ten years. It served me well, providing much inspiration over the years. The large windows and north-facing roof-lights were excellent. The reason for the name of the farm soon became apparent – there were stinging nettles all over the place during summertime. The construction of this painting is divided into four parts: (1) a simple sky to enable (2) complex buildings to be seen clearly; (3) a simple meadow in order that (4) the foreground subjects (fence, flowers, etc) can be clearly seen. This technique is useful, as it allows detail to be seen and is not confusing.

Stage 1

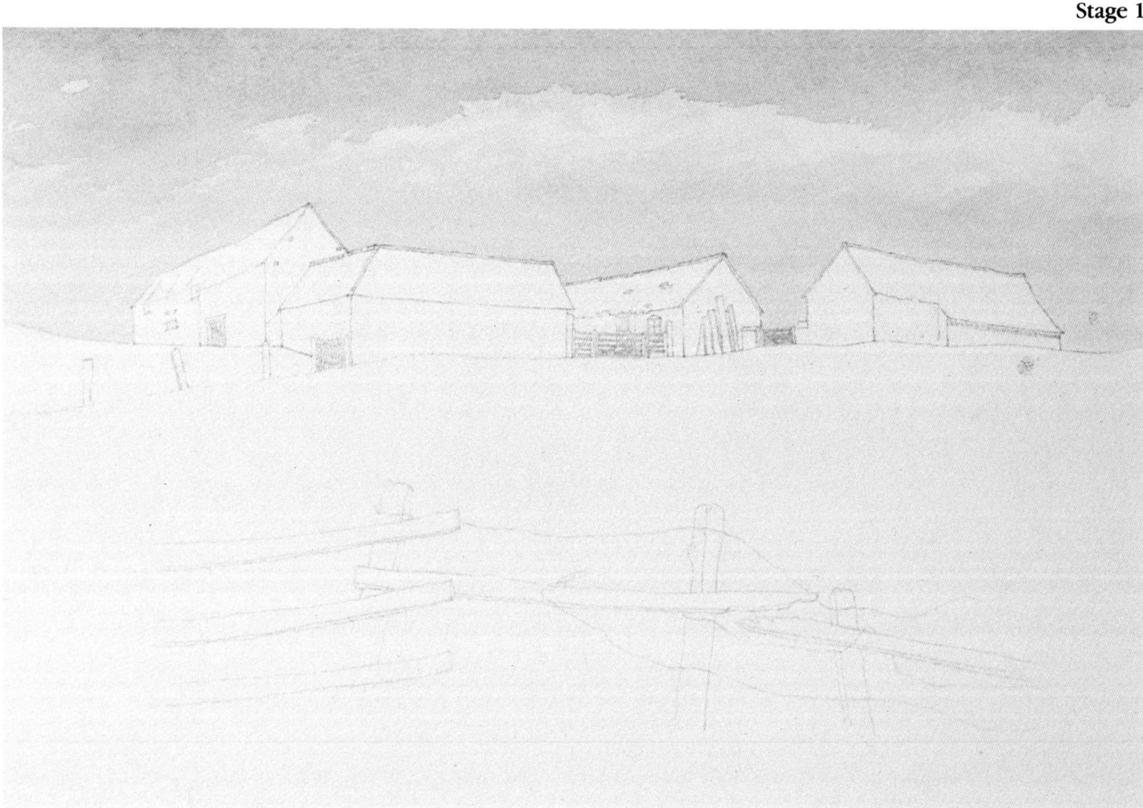

Stage 1 With a no 18 round pointed Dalon, a wash of very dilute burnt sienna is applied to the sky. Before it dries, some colour is lifted out with tissue in order to suggest clouds. When the first wash is bone dry, the painting is turned upside-down and tilted away so that a wash of coeruleum mixed with french ultramarine can be painted around the buildings, which have been drawn in carefully. Some areas are left unpainted, exposing the underlying wash, which creates cloud shapes. The sky remains fairly simple, allowing the buildings to be sharply defined later on. The initial burnt sienna wash adds warmth and relates, in colour, to the buildings

Stage 2

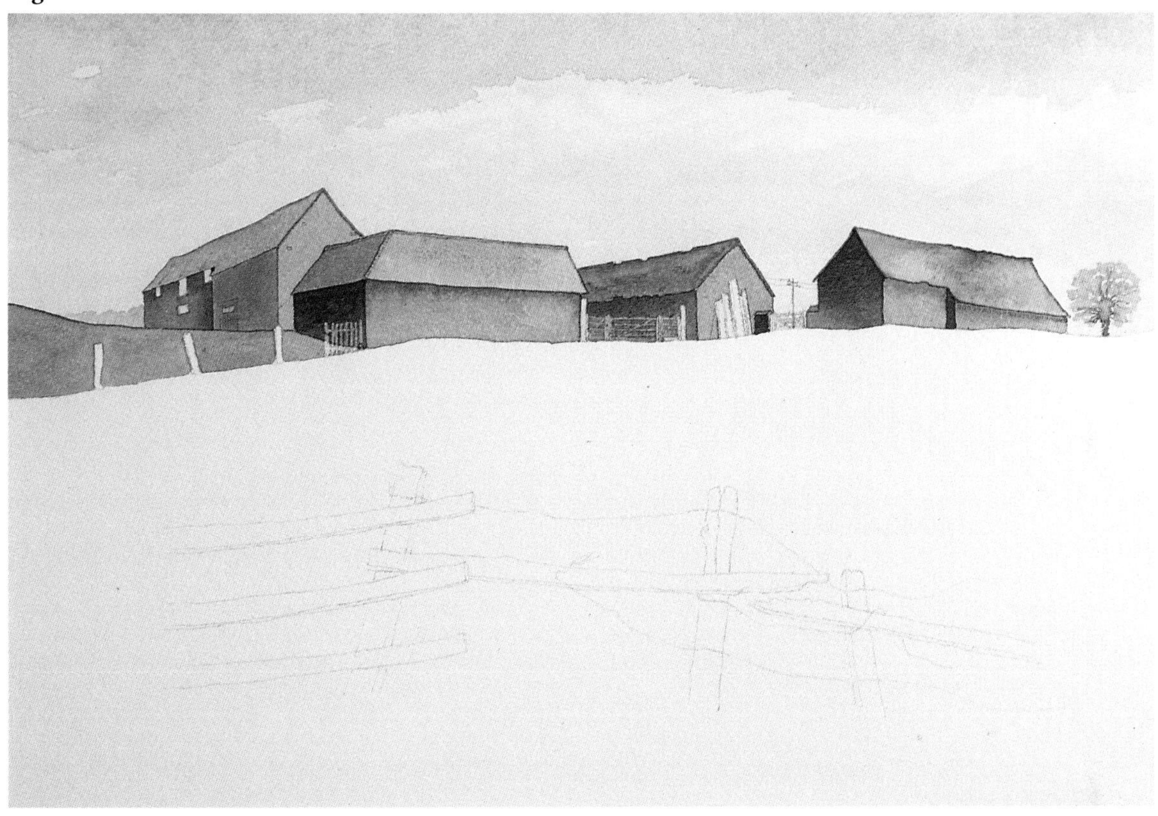

Stage 2 The painting is tilted away in order to allow washes applied over roof areas to 'rush' towards the ridges, forming edges. Some painters try to avoid such edges, but I find them to be extremely useful in this situation. Lighter sides of the roof-tops are initially painted with washes of light red, crimson alizarin and a little raw sienna. The darker sides are painted with washes of light red mixed with french ultramarine. Masking fluid is applied to the large central gates and the 'garden' gate on the left. By good fortune, these are white and provide good contrast against the buildings beyond. When the masking fluid is dry, walls are washed in with a mixture of light red and raw sienna for the lighter sides, while warm sepia and french ultramarine are added to this for the darker sides. The granulating effect caused by mixing these colours together creates desirable textures, suggesting tiles and bricks. A small paddock to the left of the buildings is painted with a mixture of french ultramarine, cadmium yellow pale and a touch of burnt sienna. This area remains a simple wash because later it will form the background to detail which will need to be clearly defined

Colours Used

burnt sienna
french ultramarine
coeruleum
light red
crimson alizarin
raw sienna
cadmium yellow pale
warm sepia
Payne's grey
white gouache

Stage 3

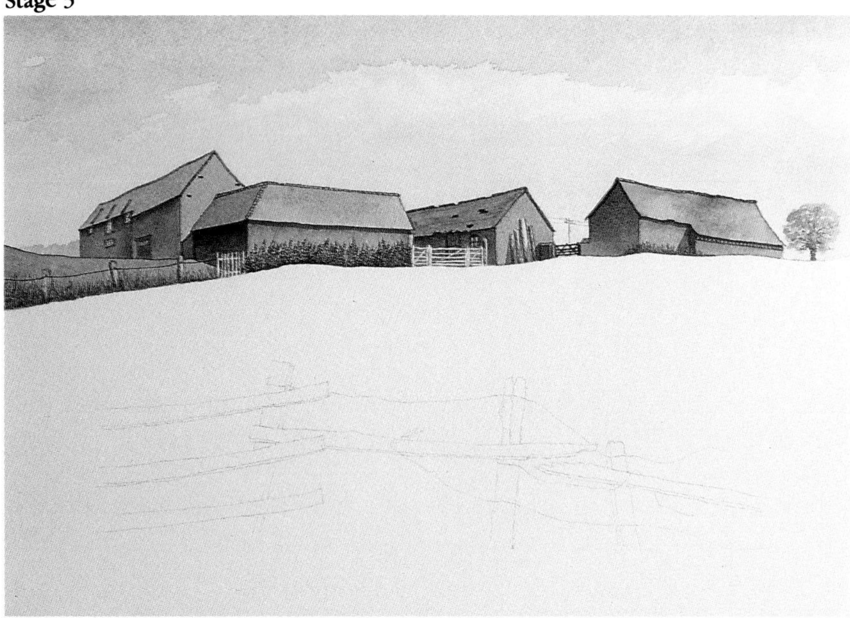

Stage 3 Initial washes of the buildings are completely dry and it is time to look at details. A no 00 round pointed sable is used to define such features as ridge tiles, doors and windows; dark left-over colour remaining on the palette is suitable for this purpose. Masking fluid is removed from the gates, enabling them to be seen against the darker tones of the buildings. Detail is added with a touch of Payne's grey and a no 00 round pointed sable. The nettles and grasses immediately in front of the buildings are painted with a no 00 round pointed sable and french ultramarine, mixed with cadmium yellow pale

Stage 4 With the painting tilted away, a strong wash of cadmium yellow pale mixed with french ultramarine is applied with a no 20 round pointed Dalon. The tilting action causes the paint to 'rush' upwards in the picture, producing an 'edge' at the top of the field, which is very satisfactory. Because the foreground fence is very light in parts, I felt that it was better to paint around this, leaving the white of the paper. Mixtures of the existing green and raw sienna with burnt sienna are introduced at the bottom of the picture to form textures from which vegetation can grow later on. As the wash dries, interesting natural shapes appear, which in this case are useful. Although the wash representing the field needs to be reasonably flat (it will act as an excellent foil for the foreground details), some texture is required and this is provided by granulation at the top of the field

Stage 4

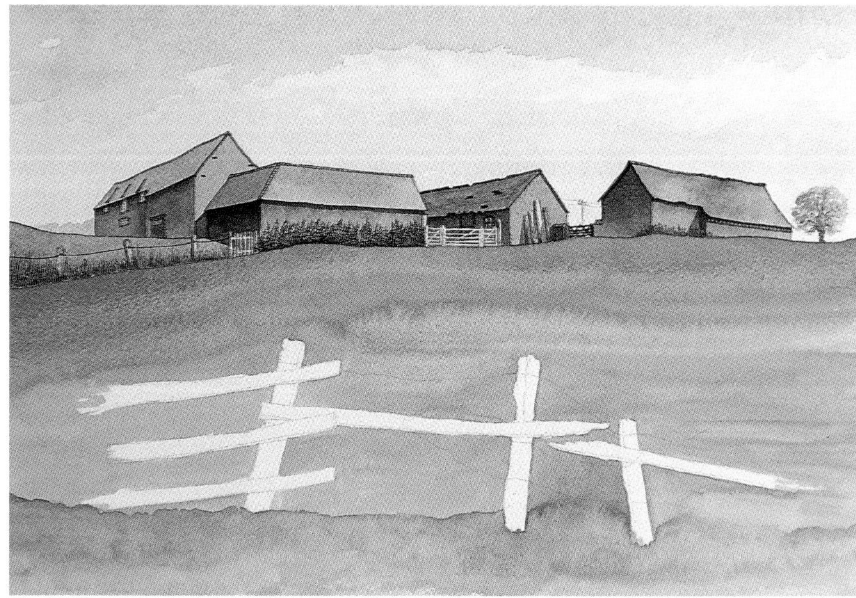

Stage 5

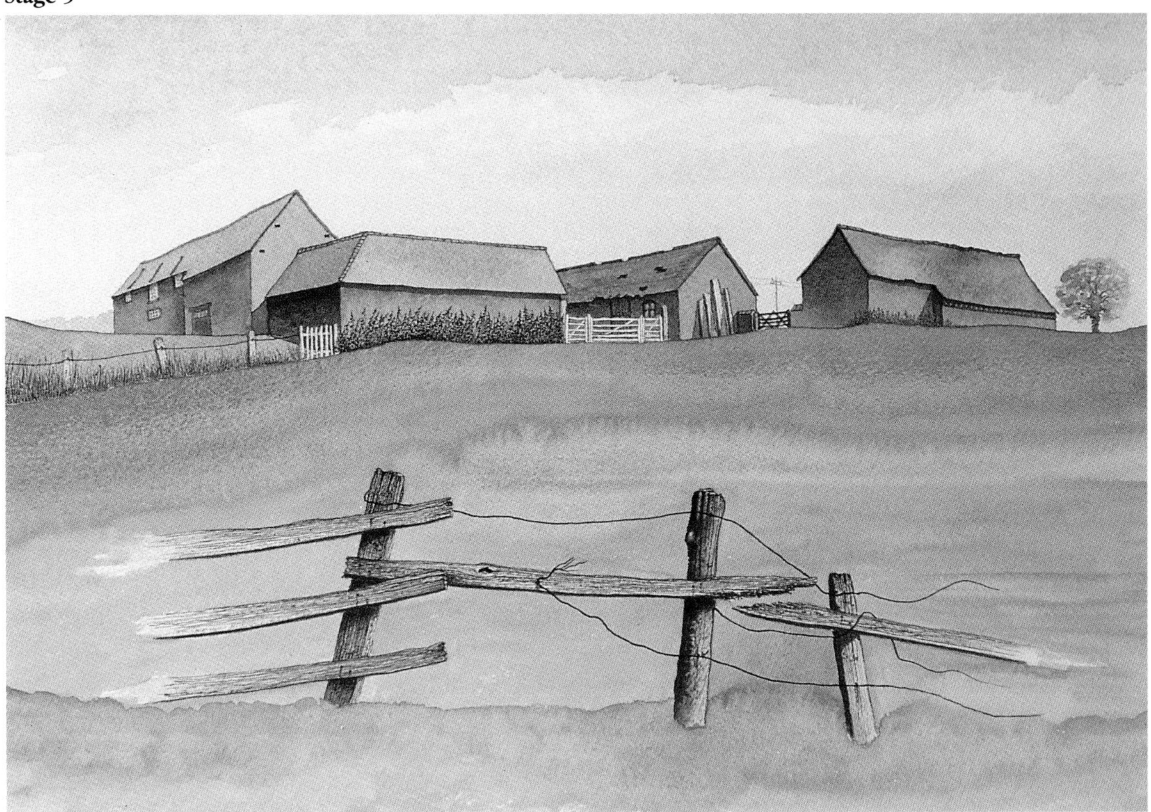

Stage 5 A weak wash of raw sienna mixed with Payne's grey is brushed on to the upright fence-posts and as this dries a stronger version of this mixture is fed into the existing damp wash, particularly on the left side of the round post (the light source is from the right). Wood-grain and splits are painted into the upright posts with a no 00 round pointed sable and a mixture of Payne's grey and warm sepia. When the uprights are dry, the cross-bars are painted in a similar way. Wire, which straggles the fence, is painted with Payne's grey mixed with warm sepia and a no 00 round pointed sable. Burnt sienna mixed with warm sepia is used for staples where the wire remains attached to posts and cross-bars. A weaker version suggests rust stains on the wood. Colour at the top of the round upright post is lifted with a thirsty brush and blotted away. Finally, colour is dry-brushed on to lighter parts of the post, suggesting texture

Stage 6

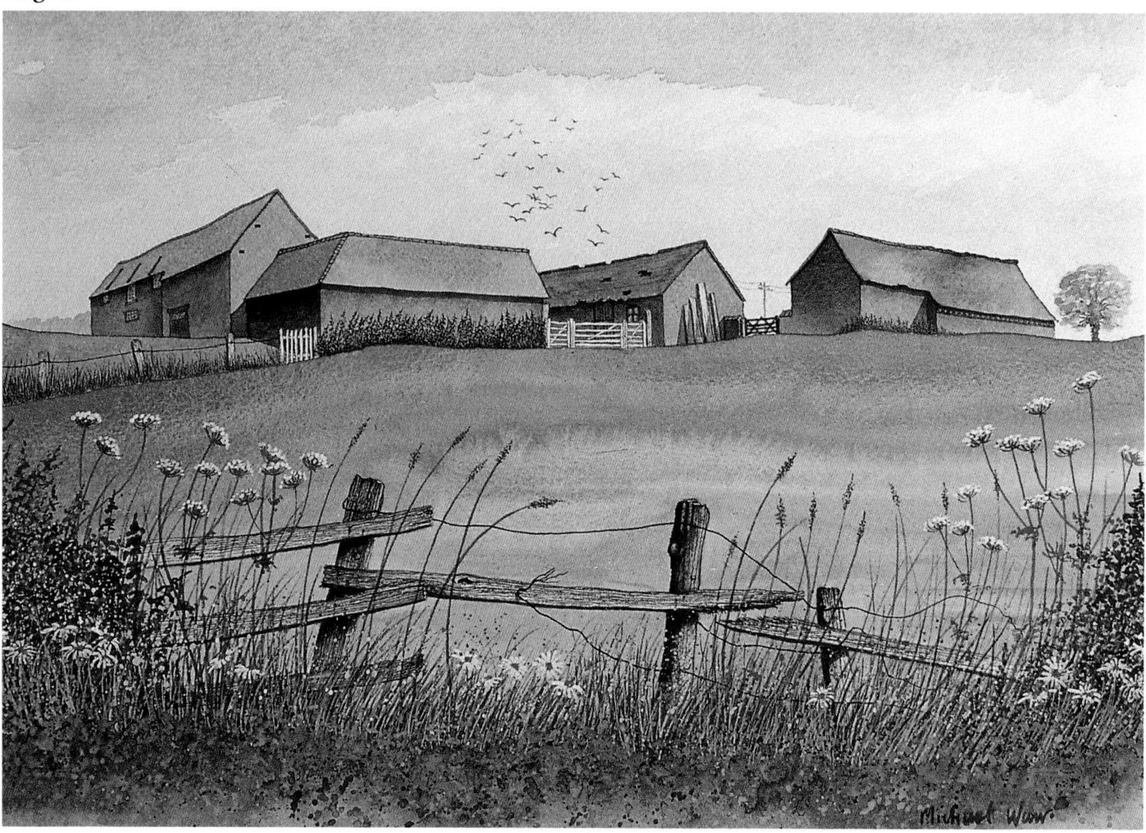

Stage 6 Areas on either side of the fence comprise dense vegetation, allowing the wooden cross-bars to disappear. Mixtures of cadmium yellow pale and french ultramarine are applied with a no 2 round pointed sable, depicting rose bay willow herb leaves, grasses and cow parsley (Queen Anne's lace) stems. Tall plants help the composition, linking the foreground with the field beyond. It is important to lose the bottoms of the posts in undergrowth; the grass colours are applied with the addition of white gouache, ensuring good covering power. Seed-heads of taller grasses are touched in with burnt sienna, while the cow parsley heads are strong white gouache tinted green. Flowers of the rose bay willow herb are produced with a mixture of crimson alizarin and white gouache. Ox-eye daisies are painted with strong white gouache; this is also flicked here and there, as are strong versions of cadmium yellow pale. More colour is spattered at the bottom, creating texture. Finally, when the area is dry, french ultramarine mixed with white gouache is flicked on to suggest speedwell

Lower Slaughter Mill

The village of Lower Slaughter is peacefully situated in Gloucestershire. It is quaint and unhurried, as you would expect from an Old English setting, with a narrow river meandering through it. Such beauty attracts tourists from all over the world, but mainly at weekends. On Monday mornings it is a haven for artists.

Having had the privilege of organising painting holidays in Lower Slaughter on numerous occasions, many hours have been spent looking at the village with like-minded people. There is no better way to spend a warm summer evening than discussing the day's painting activities with enthusiastic students over supper, and watching the sunset.

The mill, complete with an overshot waterwheel, has stood at the far end of the village for at least two hundred years. Originally, it was used to grind flour and, to this day, it houses a bakery. The building appeals as a painting subject because of an interesting combination in its structure; the main part is built of local limestone (as are all of the dwellings in Lower Slaughter), but the tall chimney is constructed with red bricks, probably imported from the neighbouring county of Warwickshire. Limestone would not withstand the constant fumes given off by coal. Perspectively speaking, there are some challenging angles to cope with, both from the mill and its surrounding cottages. Textures of brick and limestone with a collection of interesting angles provide a painter's feast. As a bonus, some of these features are reflected, too.

Colours Used

coeruleum
raw sienna
burnt sienna
Payne's grey
french ultramarine
cadmium yellow pale
warm sepia
neutral tint
white gouache

Stage 1

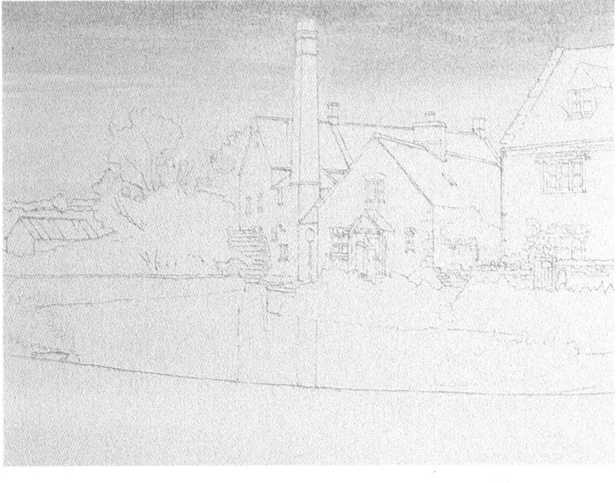

Stage 1 A clear blue sky provides the backdrop for this picturesque subject. The outline of the buildings can be seen clearly on a beautiful summer's day. Coeruleum and a no 16 round pointed Dalon are used to paint the sky. Turn the picture upside-down and tilt it towards yourself to paint carefully around the buildings. Dilute colour is applied directly above the buildings, while a stronger version is used for the higher part of the sky

Stage 2

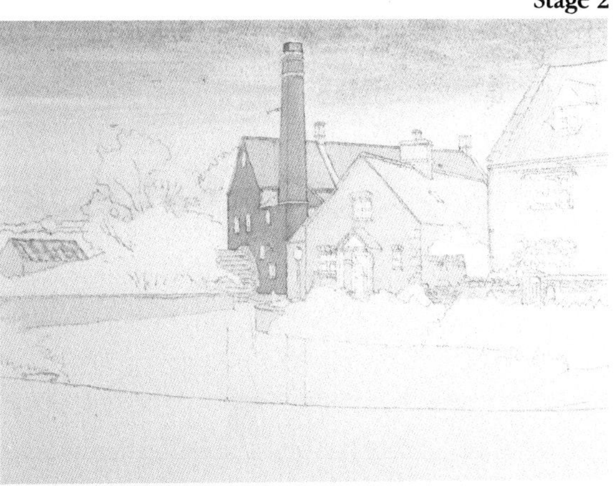

Stage 2 Washes are applied to the buildings, in a mixture of raw sienna and burnt sienna for the brickwork areas and raw sienna mixed with Payne's grey for the remaining cottages. Blue bricks at the top of the chimney are a mixture of french ultramarine and Payne's grey. All of these washes are applied with a no 3 round pointed sable. Any architectural details will be included at a later stage – at the moment I am just feeling my way into the group of buildings

Stage 3

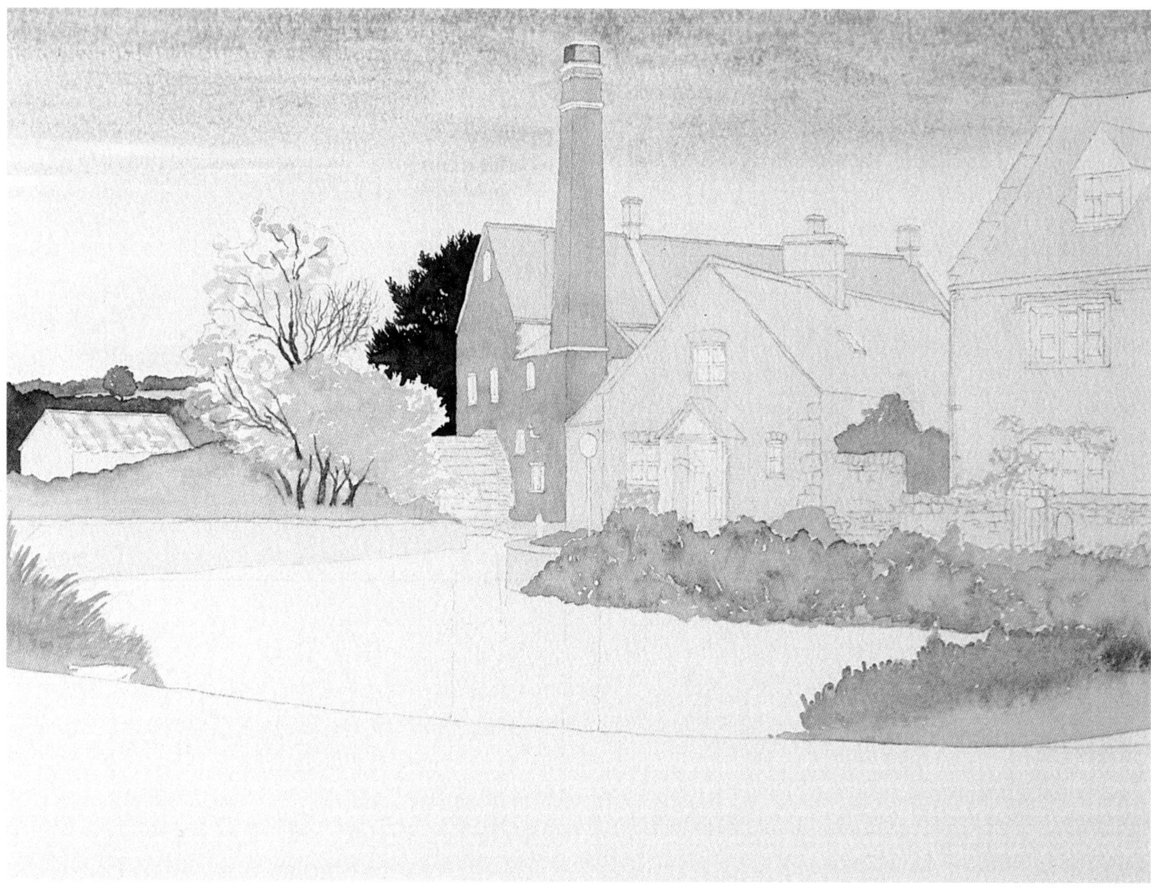

Stage 3 Trees and vegetation behind and around the buildings are washed in – there is no detail yet, only indications of the green areas. A no 3 round pointed sable is used with varying mixtures of cadmium yellow pale, french ultramarine and burnt sienna. Notice that the yew tree directly behind the mill is very dark in tone

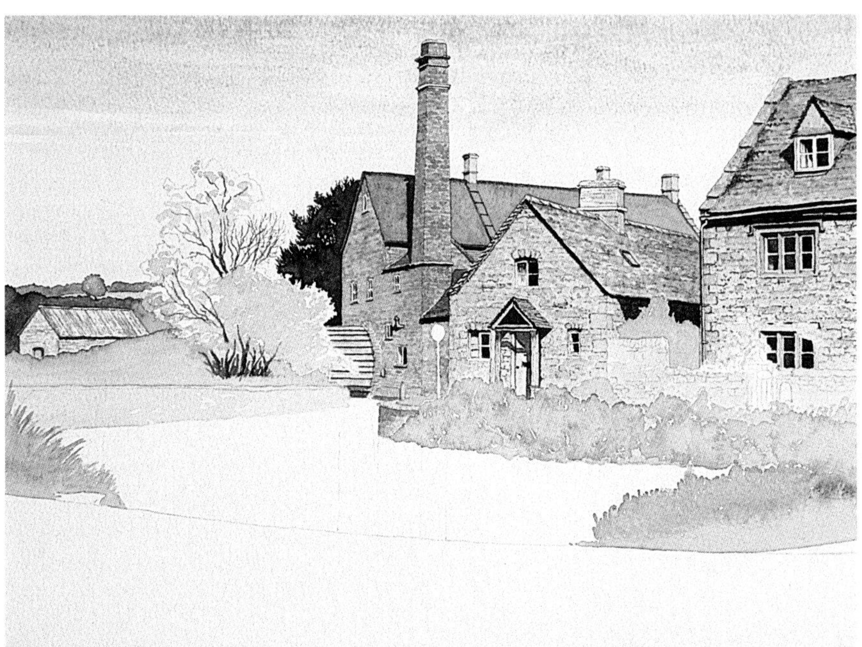

Stage 4

Stage 4 Detail in the buildings is next on the agenda. Mixtures of raw sienna and Payne's grey with white gouache are used to depict the texture of Cotswold stone, which includes lichen and natural erosion. The same technique is used to paint the split stone-roof tiles. Mullions around the windows of the cottage on the extreme right are painted with neat raw sienna. A no 3 round pointed sable is used initially, followed by a no 1 round pointed sable, which picks out the stonework joints with a mixture of warm sepia and Payne's grey. Some detail is painted into the brickwork of the tall chimney. Do not over-emphasise the detail, but merely suggest an overall brick-like texture. Dark tones in the windows are painted with mixtures of warm sepia and a neutral tint. Cast shadows are also painted with the same mixtures

---

Stage 5 Work continues by completing the small walls, and foliage is added to the wall of the cottage on the right, with mixtures of french ultramarine and cadmium yellow pale. The trees are painted with french ultramarine, cadmium yellow pale, Payne's grey and white gouache. Grasses and wild flowers are built up on the water's edge, comprising mixtures of french ultramarine, cadmium yellow pale, warm sepia and white gouache. Bright colours are spotted in with a no 2 round pointed sable to suggest blooms of flowers

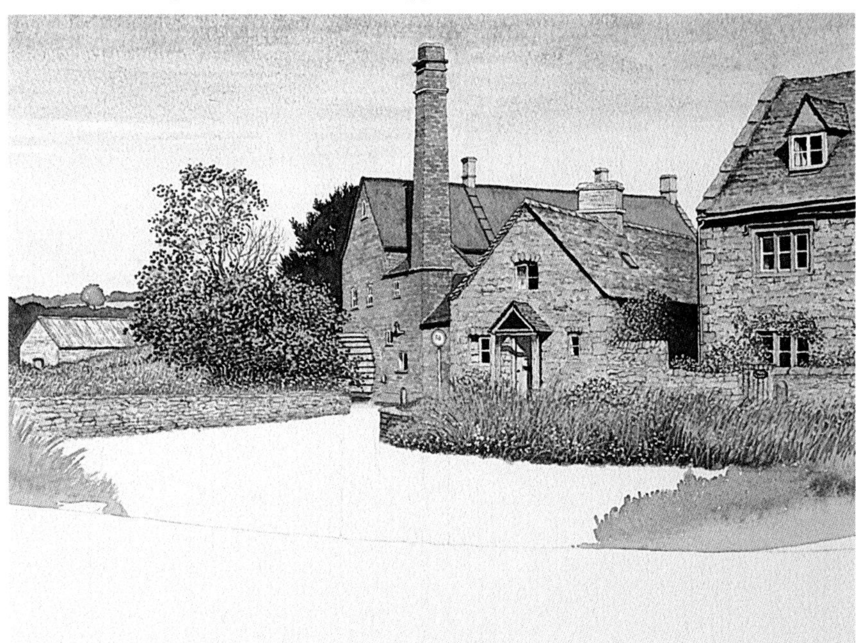

Stage 5

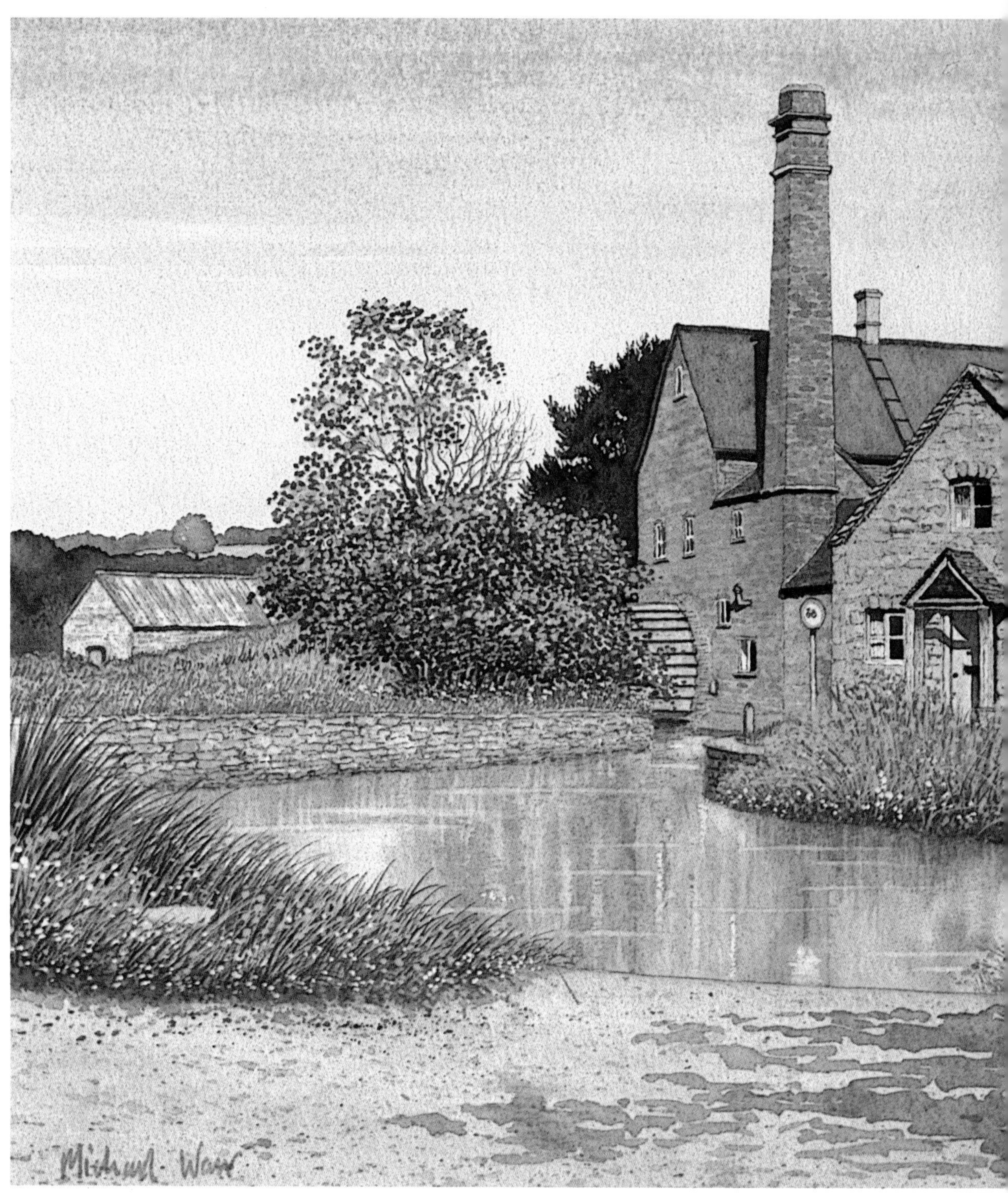

Stage 6

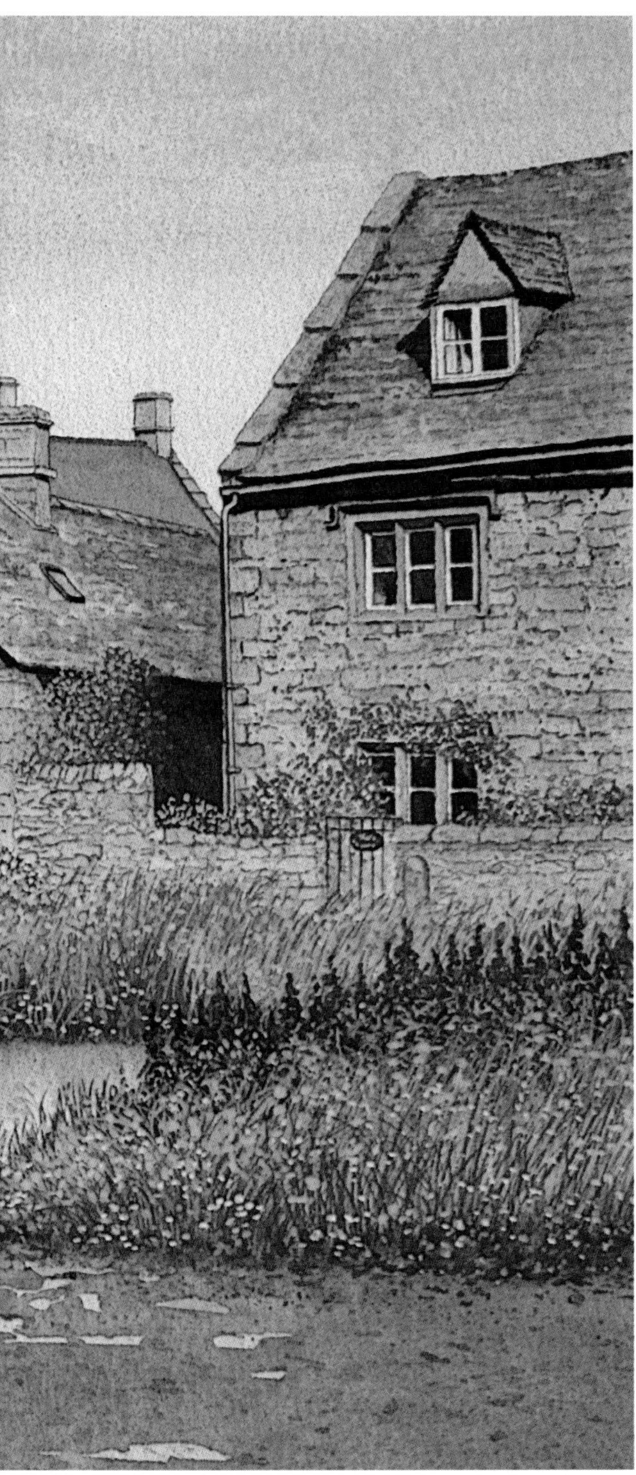

Stage 6 The whole of the water area is dampened with a wash of clear water and as this dries, colours are fed into the damp wash with a no 6 round pointed sable. Water reflections are a combination of vertical shapes versus horizontal shapes; it is a question of creating a horizontal feel to the surface of fairly still water, while the reflected shapes appear to be entering the water vertically. Wetting the area prior to painting enables the reflected shapes to merge slightly so that hard edges are not formed. One or two are acceptable to give some definition, but on the whole it is better if a flowing effect is achieved. When the water is dry, a wash of raw sienna is applied to the road. As it dries, Payne's grey is fed into the wash to create a texture. A cast shadow of french ultramarine mixed with crimson alizarin is added when the initial wash is dry. Both of these washes are applied with a no 16 round pointed Dalon. The verges on either side are then detailed with a no 1 round pointed sable combined with mixtures of cadmium yellow pale, french ultramarine, Payne's grey and white gouache. Wild flowers are depicted with dots of colour and finally the road is spattered with colour to take away the pristine appearance. Note how the texture and colour of the roadway echoes that of the buildings

Summer Vines, Féchy

I was first introduced to Féchy wine by a waiter in central Switzerland. It is described as dry, lively, fine and elegant, and to me it tasted very good. It seemed a good idea to go to the French-speaking region on the shores of Lake Geneva to discover the village where this wonderful wine is produced. From the Berner Oberland, Féchy is approached by travelling along the shore of Lake Geneva – a fantastic journey with high mountains on either side. The area in which Féchy stands is known as La Côte – an abundant wine-growing area of French Switzerland. My first view of Féchy was not disappointing; there was something very medieval about it. A church with a group of buildings on a ridge, surrounded by vines made a delightful subject to paint. It came as a complete surprise and immediately inspired me. There seemed to be all the ingredients for a detailed landscape painting, right down to a Swiss flag flying. The Swiss are very patriotic and the flag gave the picture a touch of bright colour. Perspective also played an important part; the rows of vines were very challenging. I began work immediately.

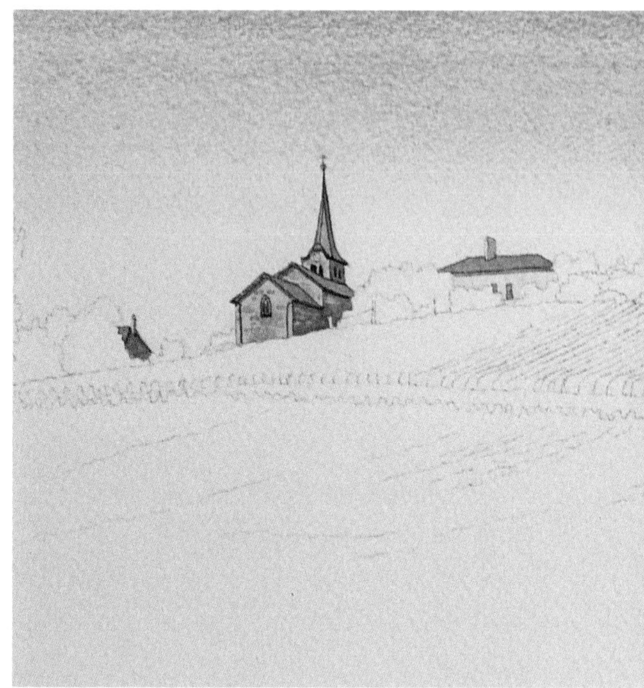

Stage 1 (below) Because the vines are planted in rows, attention is given to perspective, so careful drawing is necessary. The rows run at differing angles, creating a pattern-work of shapes, which produce a great deal of interest in the picture. There is so much similar colour in the greens of the vines that the differing shapes help to define certain areas. The lines of vines lead the eye towards the buildings – a good compositional aid.

Work beings on the sky, which is cloudless, enabling the buildings to be well defined. A no 18 round pointed Dalon is used to apply a wash of coeruleum mixed with french ultramarine. The sky is lighter near the horizon, and here, a touch of crimson alizarin is added to a dilute mixture of french ultramarine and coeruleum

Stage 1

Stage 2

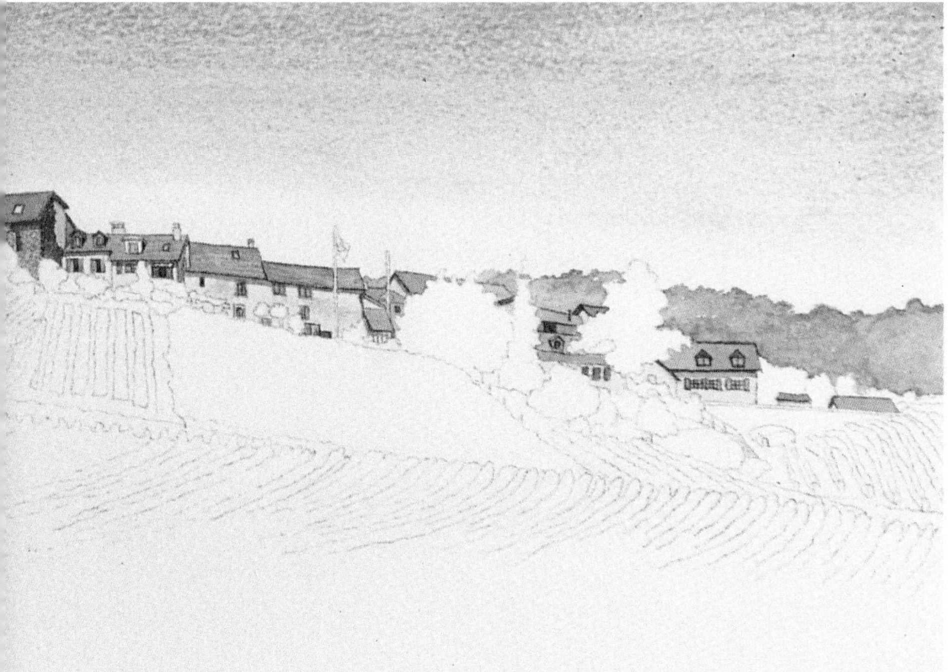

Colours Used

french ultramarine
coeruleum
crimson alizarin
raw sienna
burnt sienna
Payne's grey
cadmium yellow pale
warm sepia
white gouache

Stage 2 The roof-tops are initially painted with mixtures of crimson alizarin, raw sienna and burnt sienna. Roofs in the central area possess texture caused by lichen growth. White gouache mixed with a touch of raw sienna is introduced into the existing damp wash to suggest texture. A no 0 round pointed sable is used for the roof-tops. Because the roofs are similar in colour, they form an interesting curve against the sky. The church is a mixture of raw sienna and Payne's grey; because the walls of the houses are rendered and painted, these are depicted with a no 0 round pointed sable and a weak wash of raw sienna. Shadows on the buildings are produced with a mixture of crimson alizarin and french ultramarine. Detail on the buildings is added with a no 00 round pointed sable. Ivy growing on the central house is a mixture of cadmium yellow pale and french ultramarine; distant trees are painted with a dilute wash of cadmium yellow pale and a large amount of french ultramarine

---

Stage 3 A no 2 round pointed sable and mixtures of cadmium yellow pale, raw sienna, french ultramarine and warm sepia are used to paint the trees in front of, and around the buildings. Care is taken to ensure that the shading is on the left side of each shape. This action conveys sunlight and gives shape and form to the trees. The red-orange roof-tops look very warm with the greens added because complementary colours are working together. The Swiss flag is added, producing a bright touch of colour against the sky

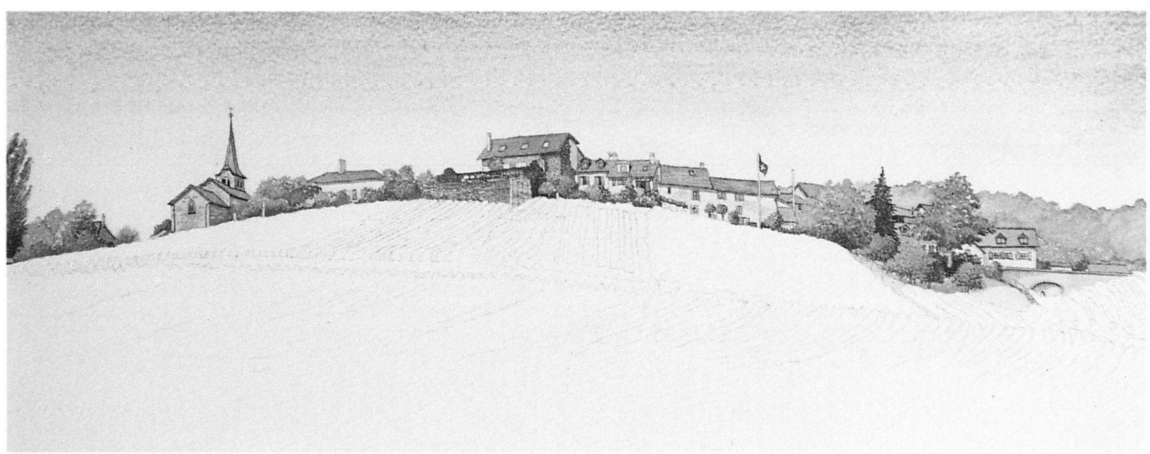

Stage 3

Stage 4 The areas of soil exposed between the vines are painted with mixtures of raw sienna and Payne's grey with a no 1 round pointed sable. A retaining wall which divides the vineyard is painted with the same colours. Detail in the wall is depicted with a no 00 round pointed sable

Stage 5 (right) Now is the time to deal with the vines. The darker areas are observed, and in the main, form rows. Working from left to right, these are painted with a strong mixture of french ultramarine and cadmium yellow pale, using a no 2 round pointed sable. Paint for the lighter areas is stippled with a no 2 round pointed sable. White paper shows through here and there, creating a glinting effect that suggests highlights

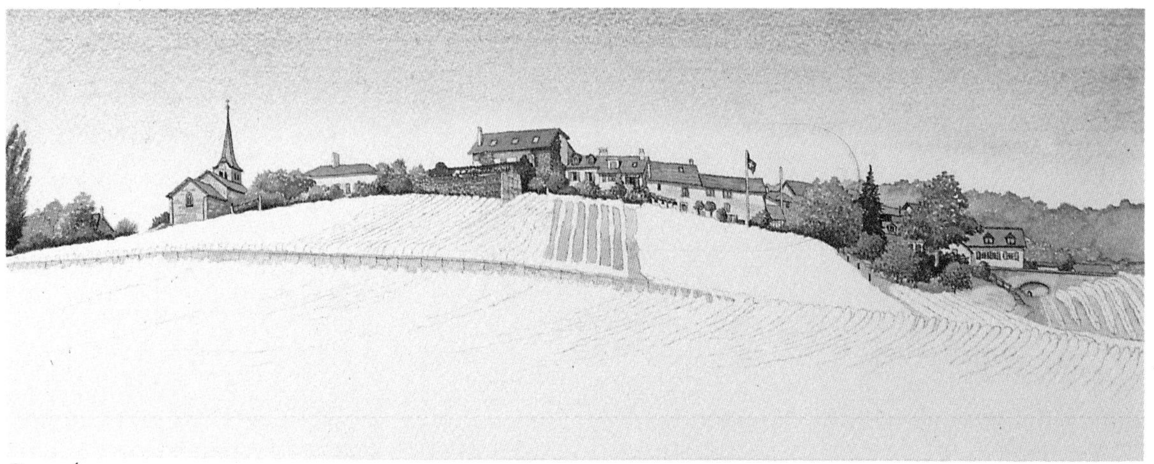

Stage 4

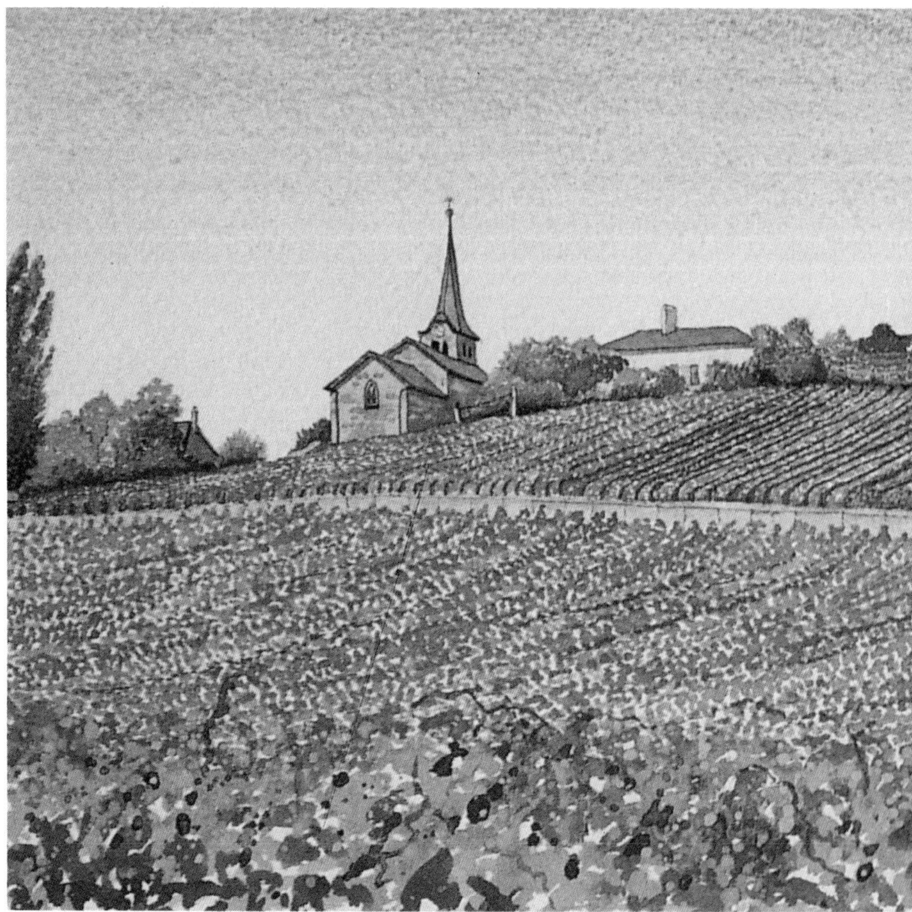

Stage 6

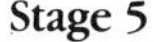

Stage 5

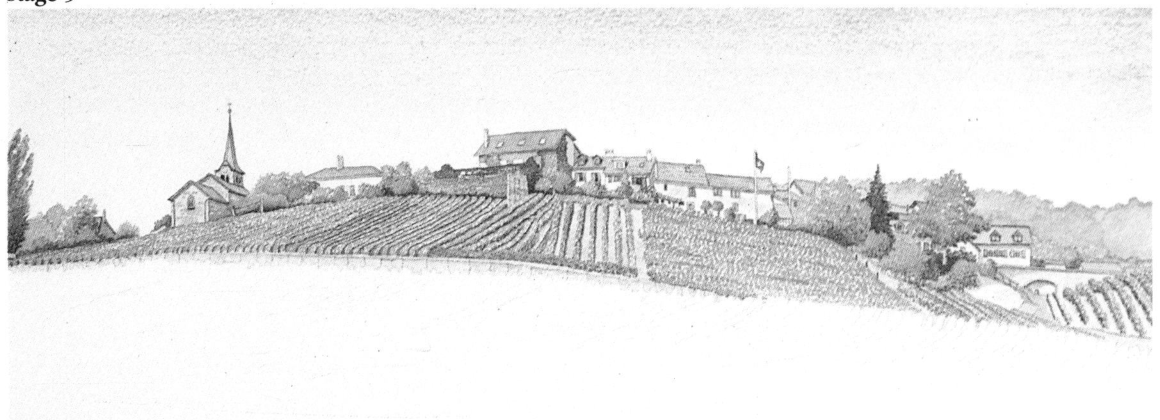

Stage 6 Vines in front of the retaining wall are now considered. Shadow areas are painted first, working from left to right. When these are dry, lighter parts are stippled with a no 2 round pointed sable and mixtures of french ultramarine and cadmium yellow pale. Note that stippling is not random but follows the rows of the vines. There is a gradual change to larger out-of-focus leaves in the immediate foreground. French ultramarine, cadmium yellow pale and white gouache are used to create an overall texture. Finally, these colours and a no 3 round pointed sable complete the picture with some flicking and spattering.

There are strong compositional features in this painting. The eye is swept through the out-of-focus foreground vines which lead off to the right, up through the area towards the buildings, along the roof-tops and church spire. It is brought down again through the poplar trees on the left, and is drawn into the picture once again by the various rows of vines leading to the buildings, enabling detail to be explored. The spire, flag-poles and pine tree act as vertical 'exclamation marks' in a horizontally orientated picture

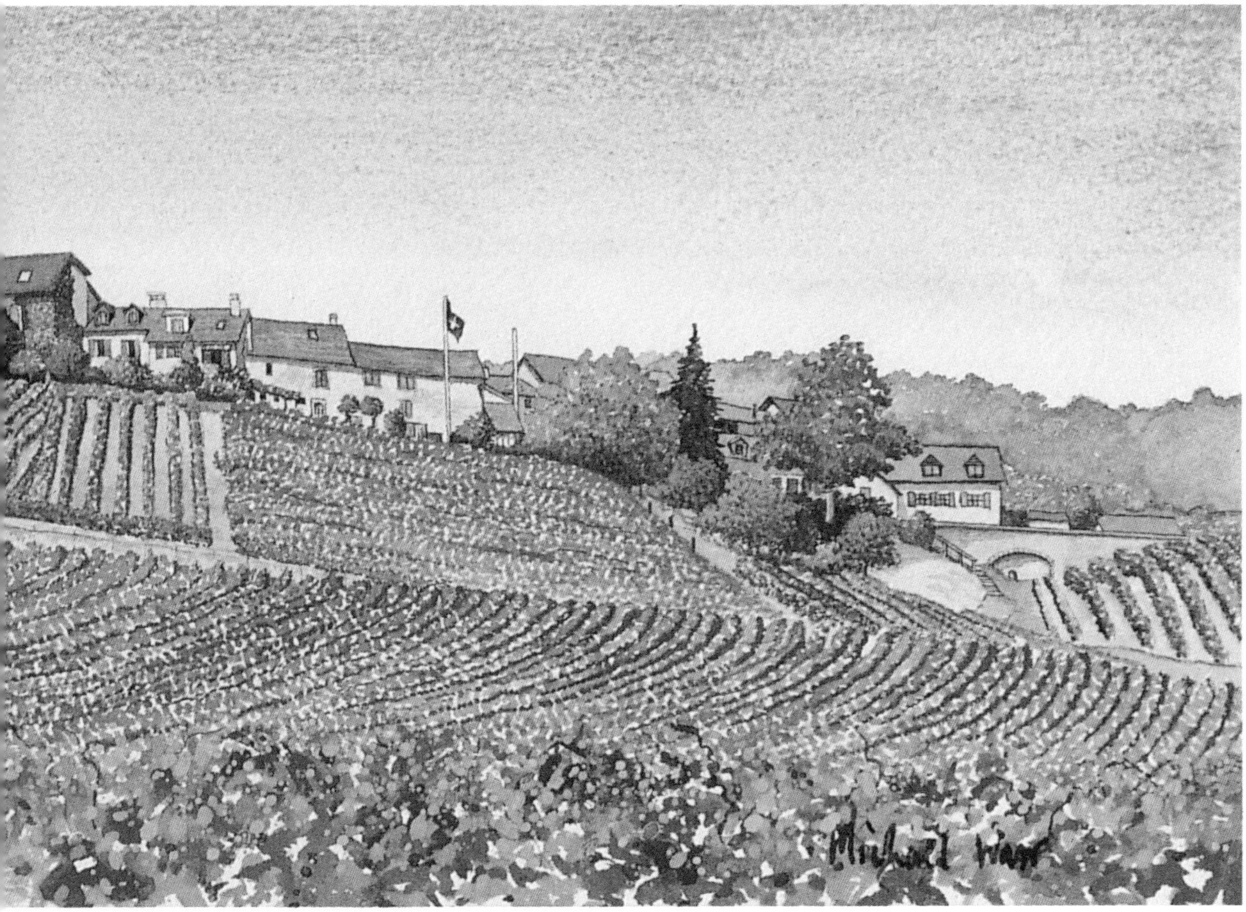

Palm Canyon

Palm Canyon is a delightful area – an oasis of peace and tranquillity. Situated in the desert near Palm Springs, California, it provided a home for the ancestors of the Agua Caliente Cahuilla Indians for many centuries. As I stood in the canyon it became clear why it served as a beautiful home to them – it has everything: rushing cool water, shade from the ever-present sunshine provided by the palm trees (*Washingtonia filifera*), and an abundance of flora and fauna, which was expertly used by the Cahuilla peoples in the form of herbal remedies and foods. What more could anyone wish for? The canyon certainly provided me with enchanting painting material; the contrast between the lush green colours and the more dry and brown-ochre shades is fascinating. It provides extremely interesting picture content, as do the finger-like palm shapes. I particularly like the large central boulder which resembles a crusty oven loaf. Because there is a considerable amount of light against dark in this painting, it seemed logical to use gouache throughout.

Stage 1

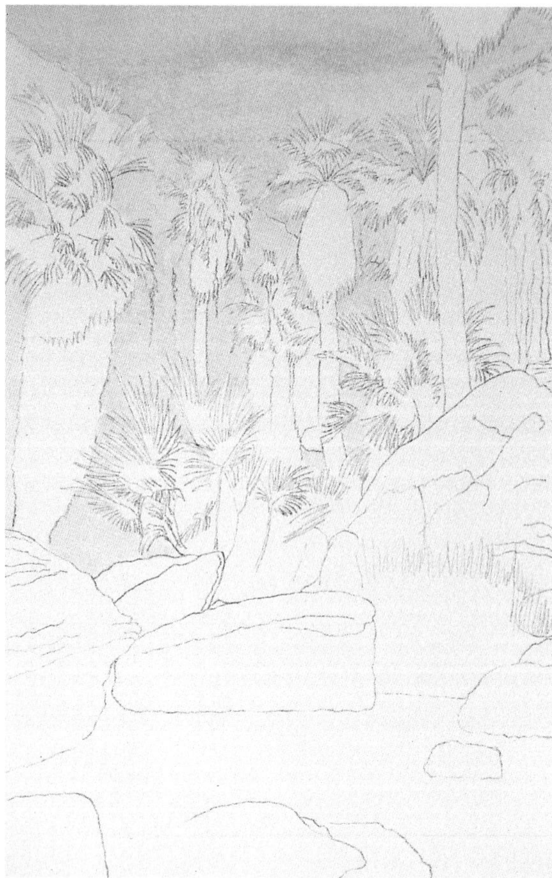

Stage 1 A wash of ultramarine mixed with cobalt is applied to the sky; lifting off with a tissue creates the clouds. When the wash is dry, white is dry-brushed on to the cloud tops in order to produce highlights. Dilute ochre is washed behind the palm trees; detail will be added at a later stage

Stage 2

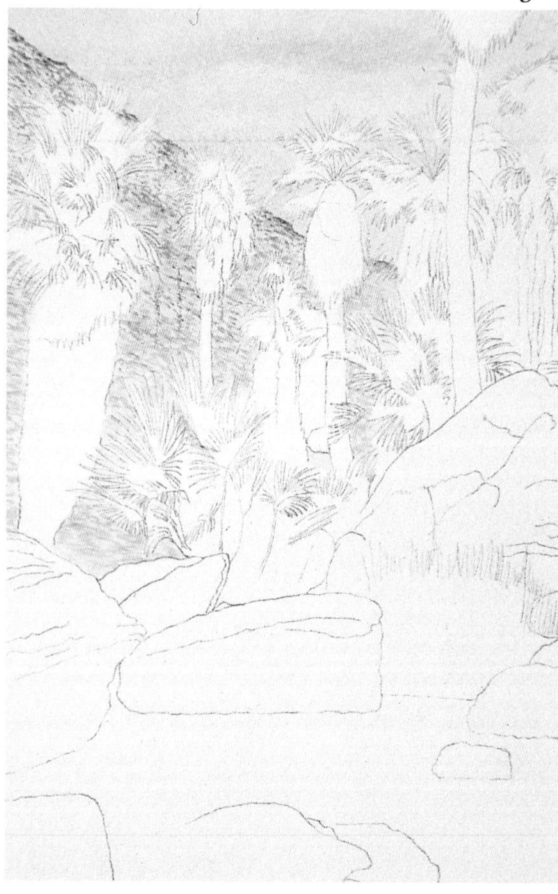

Stage 2 Detailing in the form of dry-brushing continues on the arid hillside which, in essence, is the background. Scree and light scrub are the ingredients of this area; the object here is not to over-detail, but just to create a texture suggesting the subject matter. Mixtures of ochre and burnt sienna are applied with a no 1 round pointed sable

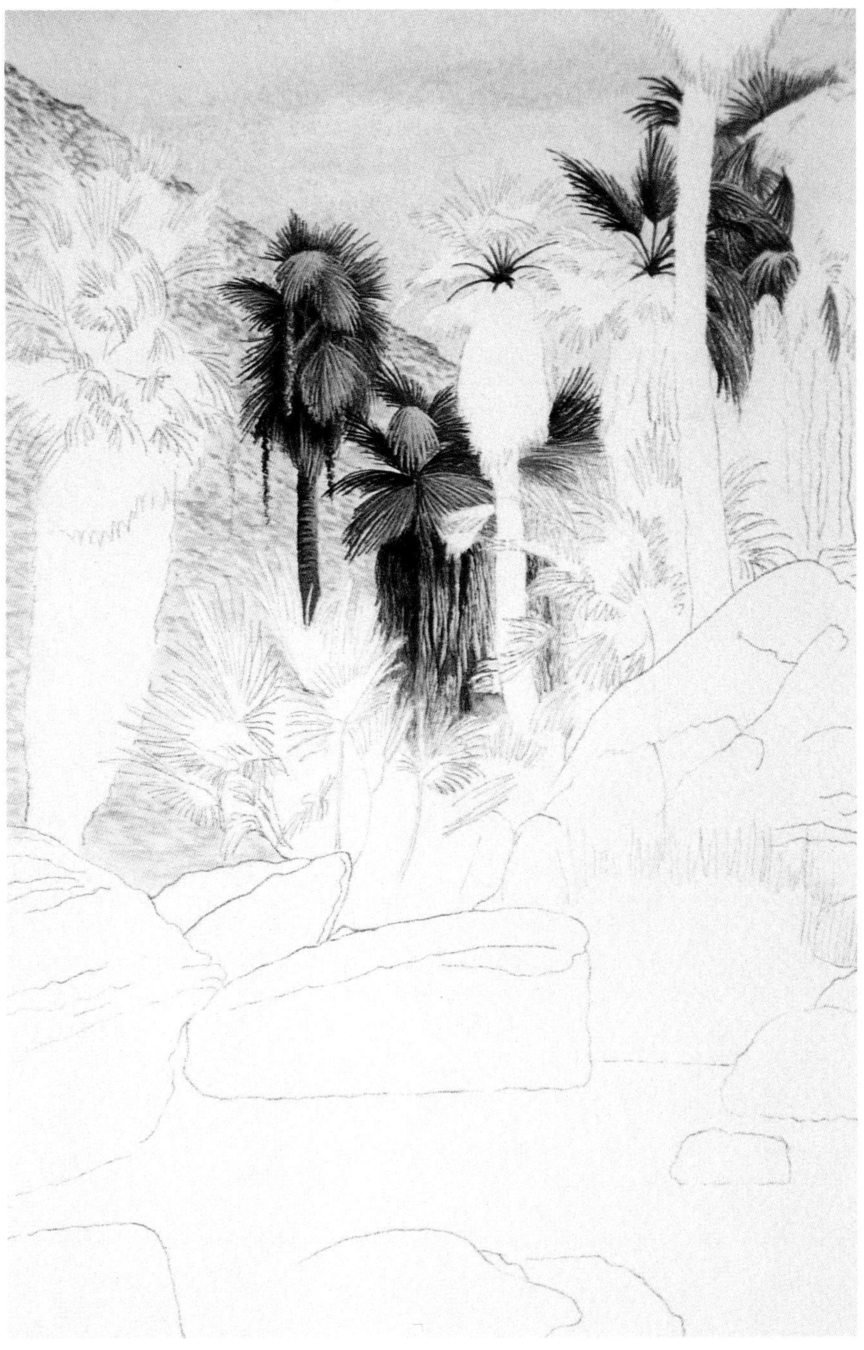

Stage 3

Stage 3 There are a number of palm trees to be painted; being all of one species (*Washingtonia filifera*), naturally the same colours are used. Golden yellow is mixed with ultramarine for the medium tones. Black is added to these colours to make darker tones. Bright highlights are made by adding white to a mixture of golden yellow and ultramarine. Dry, brittle parts of the leaves are created with the use of ochre mixed with burnt sienna. A no 0 round pointed sable creates the spiky shapes. Dead and dying leaves tend to cascade down the trunk of the tree producing a somewhat shaggy appearance. These areas are painted with ochre, burnt sienna and white, with a no 0 round pointed sable

Colours Used
ultramarine cobalt ochre burnt sienna golden yellow black carmine white

Stage 4

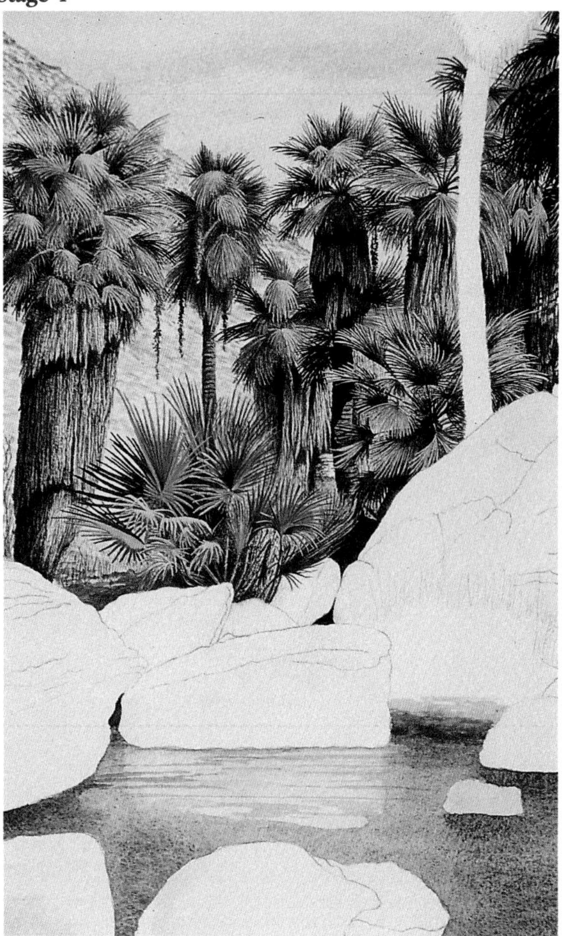

Stage 5

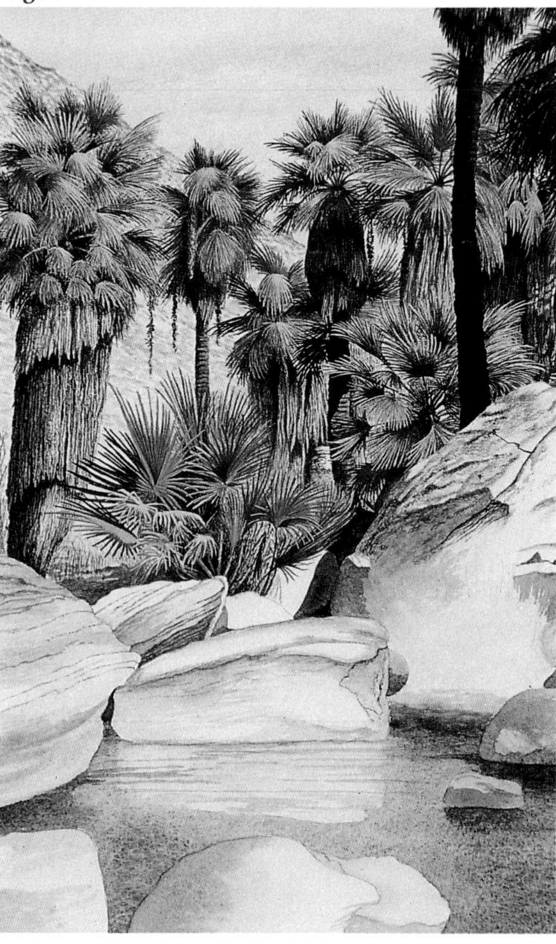

Stage 4 Work continues on the trees; the very dark, shaded leaves at the top right are painted with a strong mixture of ultramarine, golden yellow and black, while below these, ochre, burnt sienna and black depict more dead leaves around the trunks of trees. Note that a little sunlight filters through. When the dark leaves at the top are dry, colour is lifted out with a thirsty brush, creating texture. The central low-growing tree is more yellow in appearance and therefore more golden yellow is added to ultramarine to produce a yellow-green. There is only a tall dark trunk to be tackled now, which will probably be the next stage. A basic wash of black, ultramarine and carmine is applied to the rocks and boulders with a no 6 round pointed sable. When these washes are dry, the cool shaded water is painted with a strong mixture of ultramarine and black; a few reflected shapes are also indicated

Stage 5 Detail is added to the rocks and boulders: shadows in the first instance, then characteristic textures. The shadows comprise a mixture of ultramarine and carmine, applied with a no 3 round pointed sable. Areas of the rocks and boulders will be obscured by vegetation in the final stage, so detailing is only included where it will be visible. Some dry-brushing helps to build detail on the larger boulders. The tall palm trunk which is mainly in shadow is painted with a no 3 round pointed sable and mixtures of burnt sienna, ochre and black

---

Stage 6 The rocks and boulders are completed by adding final details, and it is time to think about the immediate foreground, which consists of grasses and reeds, some of which are green. Mixtures of ultramarine and golden yellow applied with a no 00 round pointed sable create the greens, while mixtures of burnt sienna, ochre, black and white are used for the dry ones. This mass of shapes is produced by working from the bottom, applying the no 00 brush heavily and then lifting off to create the tapered effect. The technique is repeated many times until a density of vegetation is achieved

Stage 6

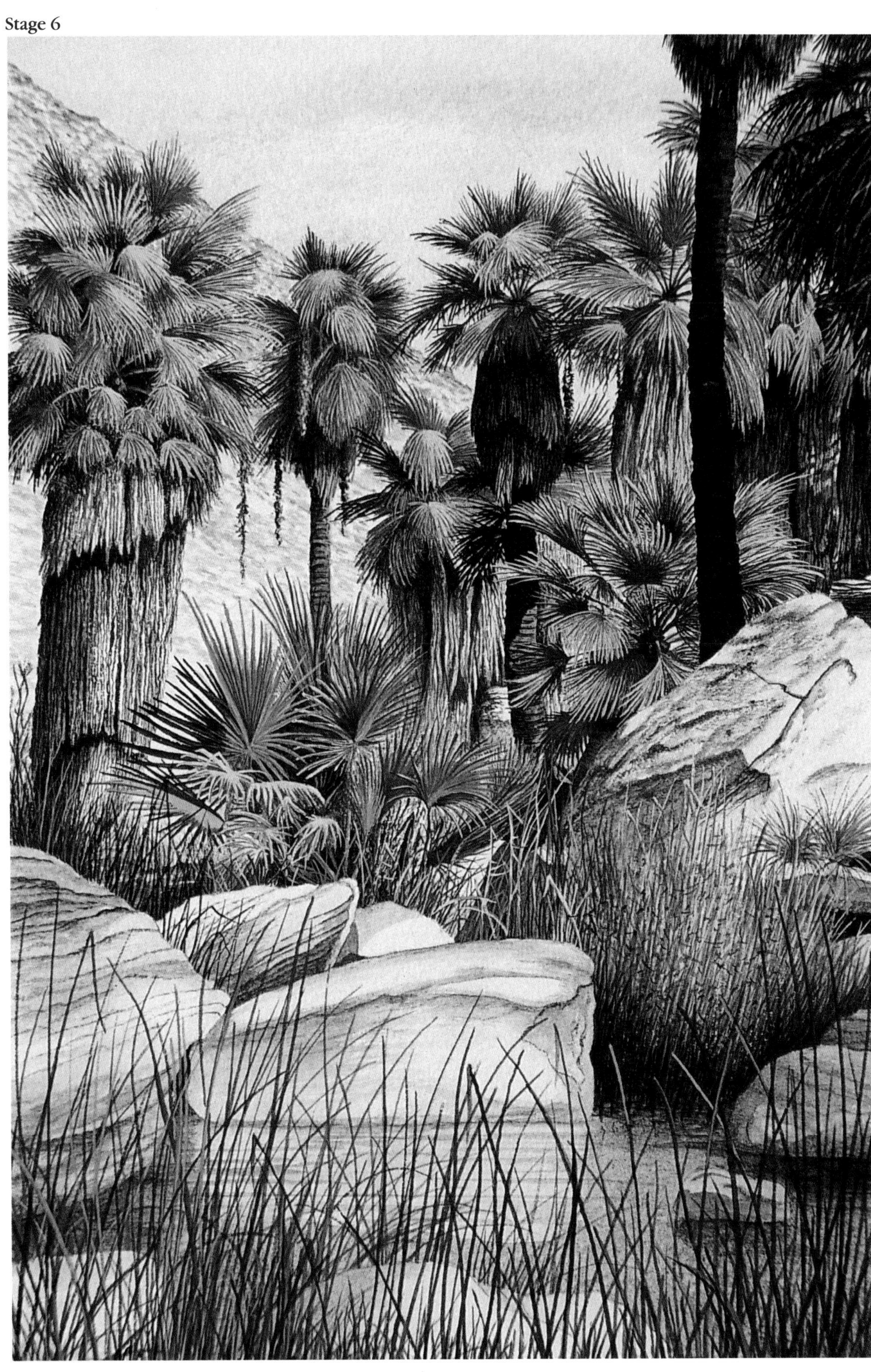

Marina del Rey

This scene attracted me immediately: the combination of distant mountains, the water and the interesting architecture seemed to gel together in a very pleasing way. Marina del Rey is situated in Santa Monica Bay, close to Santa Monica, in the county of Los Angeles. A paramedic, to whom I chatted while I was surveying the scene, informed me that the distant mountains are the San Gabrials, which are about 35 miles (55km) away. A low tide exposes interesting shapes of sand that contrast well with the light, crisp art-deco style houses.

Perspective plays an important role here, leading the eye in from both sides of the picture; the distant mountains prevent us from going too far. The birds in and around the water add life to this painting, and the palm tree is a lovely touch.

Stage 1

Stage 1 The sky area is dampened with clear water ready to take dilute raw sienna and a touch of crimson alizarin directly above the mountains. These colours are fed into the damp wash with a no 6 round pointed sable; moving up into the sky, a mixture of coeruleum and french ultramarine is added with the same size brush. The colour is applied carefully, allowing exposed areas of paper to form cloud shapes. A wash of french ultramarine and crimson alizarin depicts the mountains; the mist above the distant buildings is produced by lifting off damp colour with an absorbent tissue. This light area will provide an excellent background for the buildings at a later stage

Stage 2

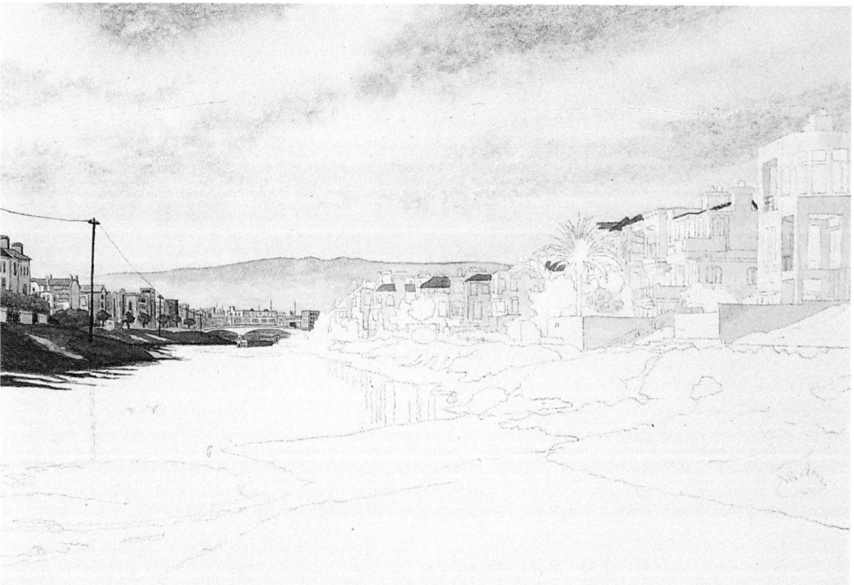

Stage 2 The distant buildings, the bridge and area beyond are painted with french ultramarine, crimson alizarin, Payne's grey and raw sienna, using a no 1 round pointed sable. Payne's grey is a useful colour for depicting detail and outlines in this instance. Darker versions of the same colours are used for the buildings on the left which are in shadow. Mixtures of Payne's grey, french ultramarine and cadmium yellow pale with a no 2 round pointed sable create the dark river-bank. These colours are also used for the row of street-side trees and shrubs. To the right, the buildings are seen in full sunlight, so the colours are much lighter. Many of the buildings are white; their shaded sides are tinted with a mixture of crimson alizarin and french ultramarine. The pink and peach buildings are tinted with dilute crimson alizarin and dilute raw sienna, respectively. The pantile roof-tops are painted with crimson alizarin mixed with warm sepia. A no 1 round pointed sable is used for this work

Stage 3

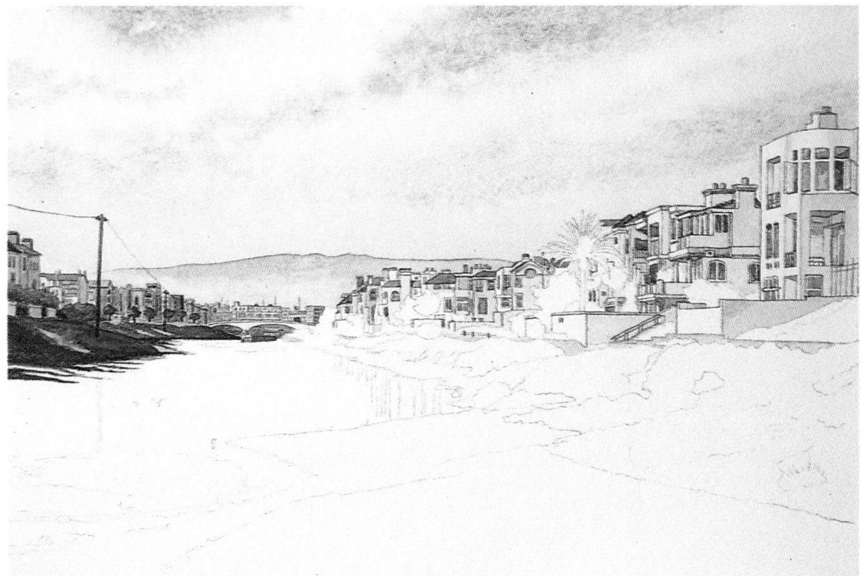

Colours Used

raw sienna
crimson alizarin
coeruleum
french ultramarine
Payne's grey
cadmium yellow pale
warm sepia
burnt sienna

Stage 3 In the main, the windows are depicted with a mixture of Payne's grey and french ultramarine, using a no 00 round pointed sable. Other small details and features are produced with the same colour. Adding architectural detail becomes a fascinating process; you feel that it is possible to walk up to a front door and say 'Hi'! Incidentally, is that an American flag we can see? Detailing continues until the houses and garden walls are complete; a pathway also appears at this stage

Stage 4 It is time to look at trees and shrubs in the gardens and also at the right river-bank. Mixtures of cadmium yellow pale, french ultramarine and Payne's grey are used for the greens in these areas. Application is with a no 1 round pointed sable. The muddy part of the bank is painted with raw sienna mixed with warm sepia and a touch of Payne's grey. This seems to be a logical point at which to conclude this stage

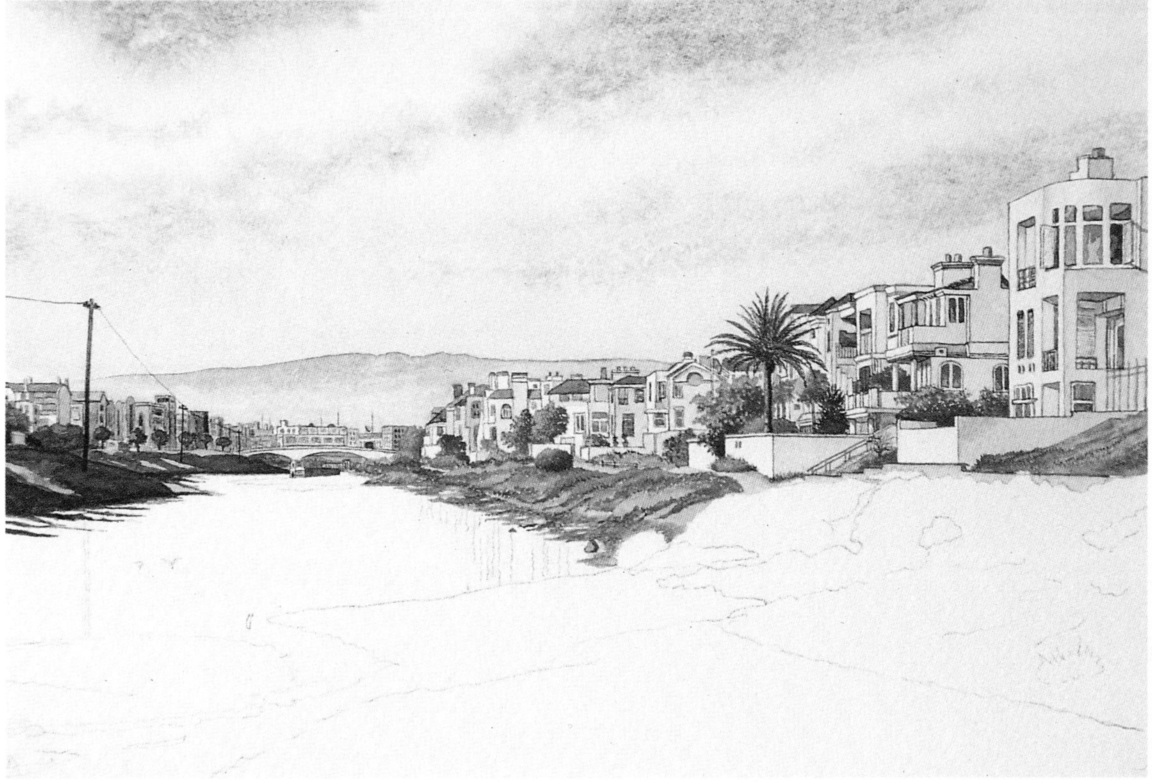

Stage 4

Stage 5

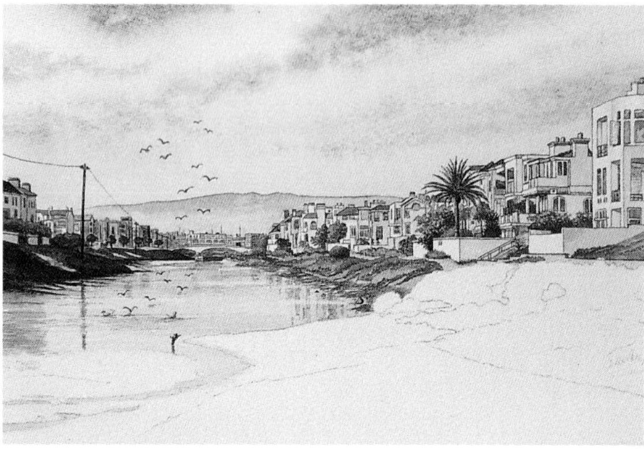

Stage 6

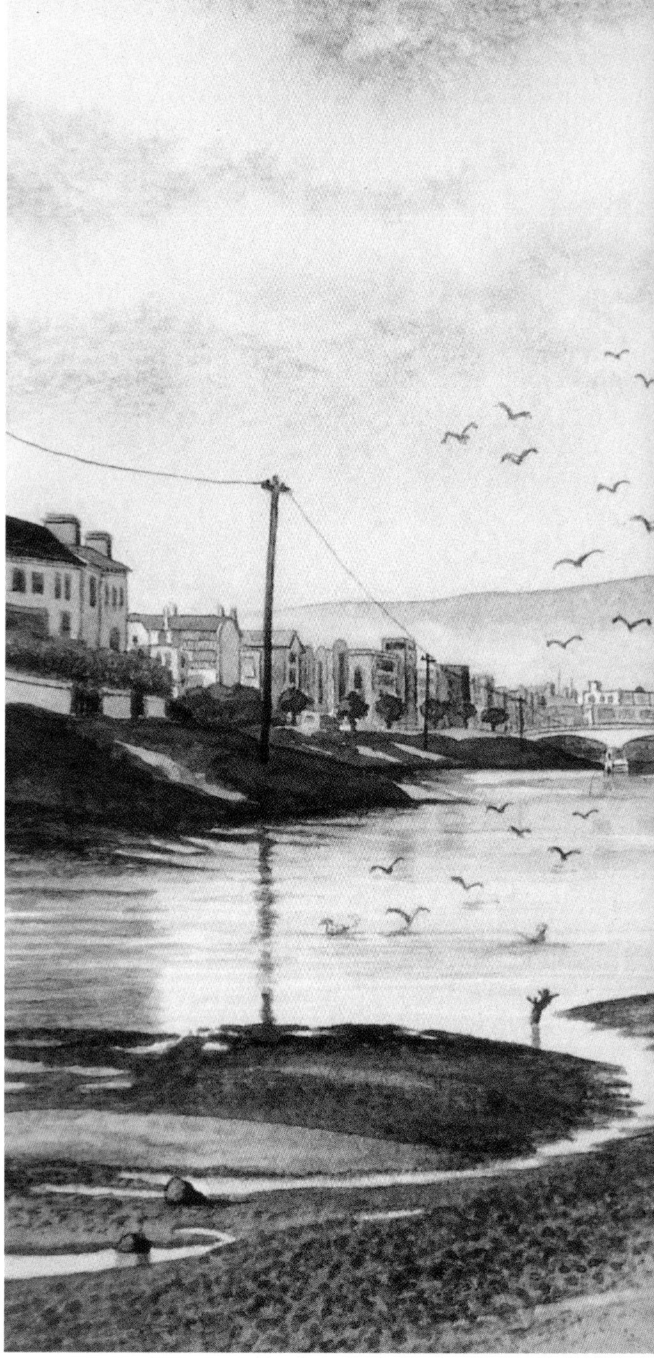

Stage 5 Dilute coeruleum is washed over the entire river area with a no 6 round pointed sable. While this is damp, reflections are painted with Payne's grey and mixtures of crimson alizarin and french ultramarine. There is little movement on the surface of the water and therefore some of the reflected buildings on the right are well defined, as are the two first houses on the left. When these colours are dry, the circling gulls are included with a no 00 round pointed sable and mixtures of Payne's grey

---

Stage 6 A wash of raw sienna is applied to the foreground area with a no 6 round pointed sable. Vegetation on the right, which is growing out of dry sand, is painted with mixtures of cadmium yellow pale, french ultramarine and a no 00 round pointed sable. Payne's grey is added where dark tone is required. Washes of warm sepia, Payne's grey, raw sienna and burnt sienna are used to depict the muddy wet sand. When these washes are completely dry, colour is dry-brushed on in order to suggest pebble textures, holes in the mud, etc. Finally, a wet no 6 round pointed sable is used to remove some colour, which is then blotted away. This technique produces highlights on the wet muddy sand

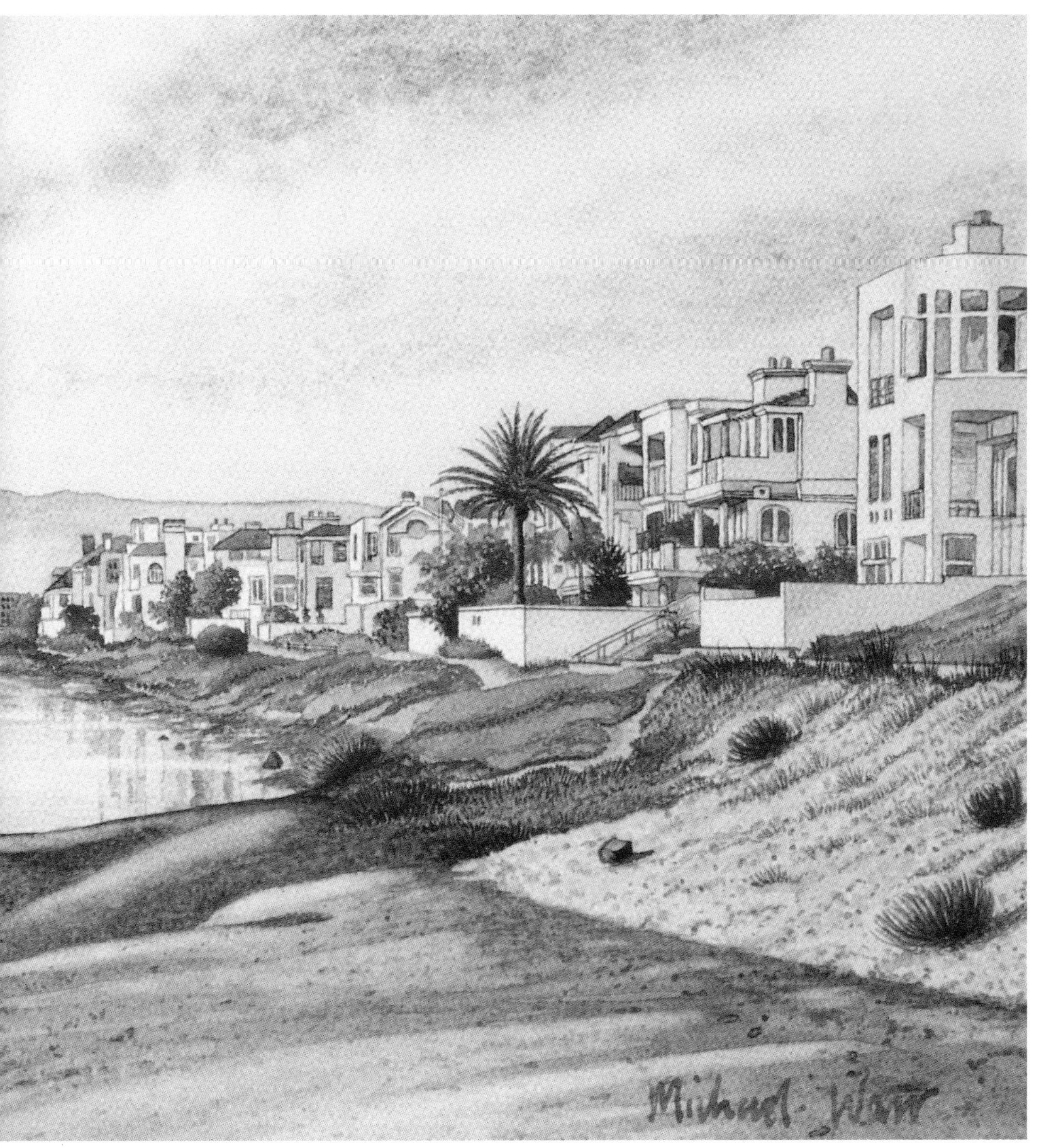

Stracey Arms Wind-Pump

I have travelled past this wind-pump in Norfolk every year since 1948. It may appear very strange that I have not painted it before; maybe it was the complexity of the sails which was off-putting. However, recently it became a worthy painting subject for this book – there is always detail to be found in this type of building. It is important to state at this point that windmills and wind-pumps carried out two entirely different functions: the former ground wheat and grain for flour, while the latter were used to drain the marshes, of which there were many in an area reclaimed from the sea. This wind-pump takes its name from that of a pub standing nearby. Because the surrounding country is very flat, the sails and brick-built tower are seen clearly against the sky, producing an image with impact.

Stage 1

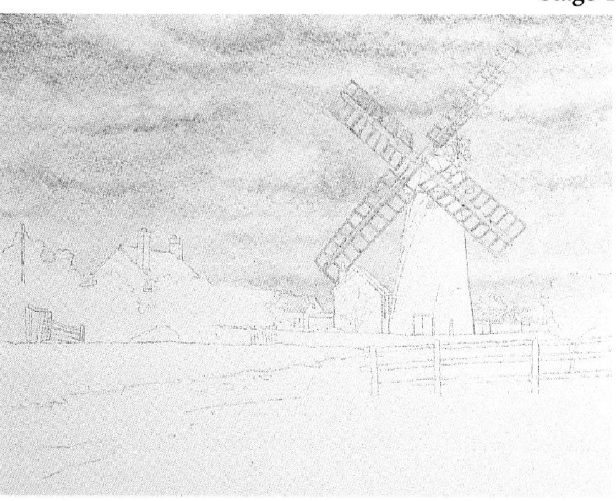

Stage 1 Masking fluid is carefully applied to the accurately drawn sails. They are painted white and therefore it is ideal to retain the white of the paper. White gouache is extremely useful, but there is nothing to beat paper white if it is possible to retain this. A wash of very dilute raw sienna is painted over the sky with a no 20 round pointed Dalon, when the masking fluid is dry. This is left overnight to ensure that the wash is bone-dry before a wash of coeruleum is applied. Above the horizon, an area of raw sienna is left exposed, but other clouds are formed by lifting with tissue, exposing warm raw sienna. When the wash is dry, mixtures of Payne's grey and crimson alizarin are dry-brushed on to the underside of the clouds, giving them weight

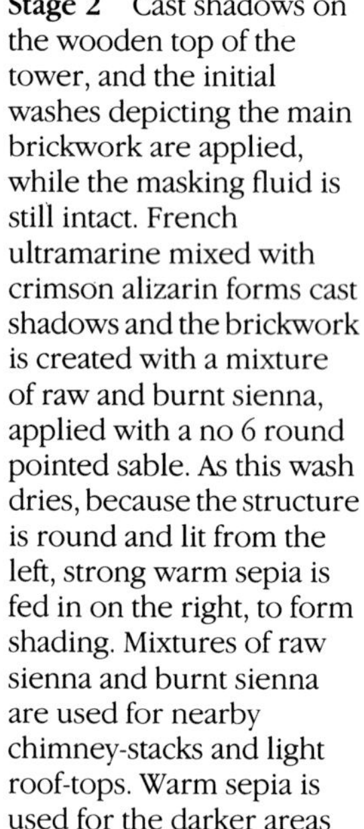

Stage 2 Cast shadows on the wooden top of the tower, and the initial washes depicting the main brickwork are applied, while the masking fluid is still intact. French ultramarine mixed with crimson alizarin forms cast shadows and the brickwork is created with a mixture of raw and burnt sienna, applied with a no 6 round pointed sable. As this wash dries, because the structure is round and lit from the left, strong warm sepia is fed in on the right, to form shading. Mixtures of raw sienna and burnt sienna are used for nearby chimney-stacks and light roof-tops. Warm sepia is used for the darker areas

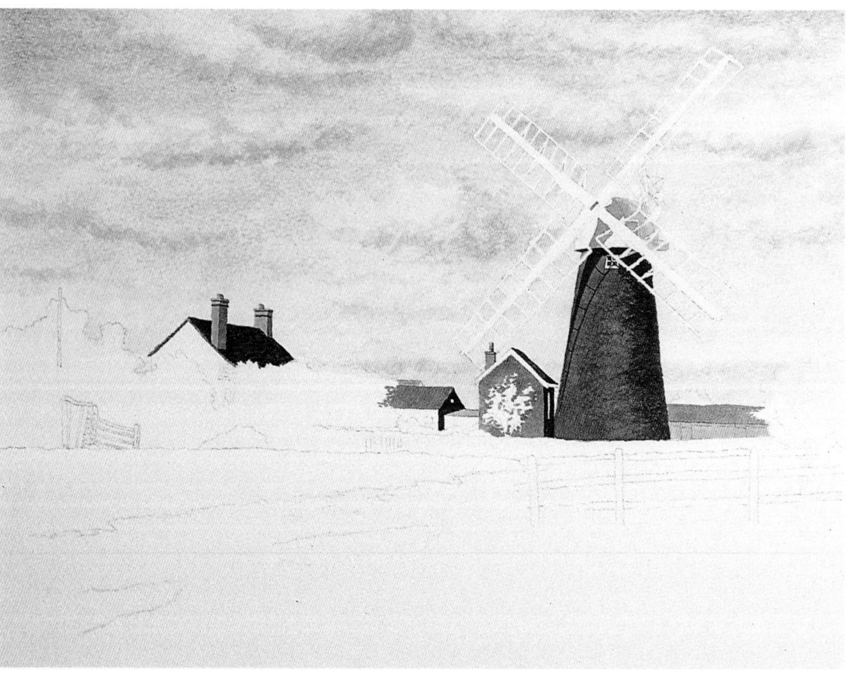

Stage 2

Stage 3

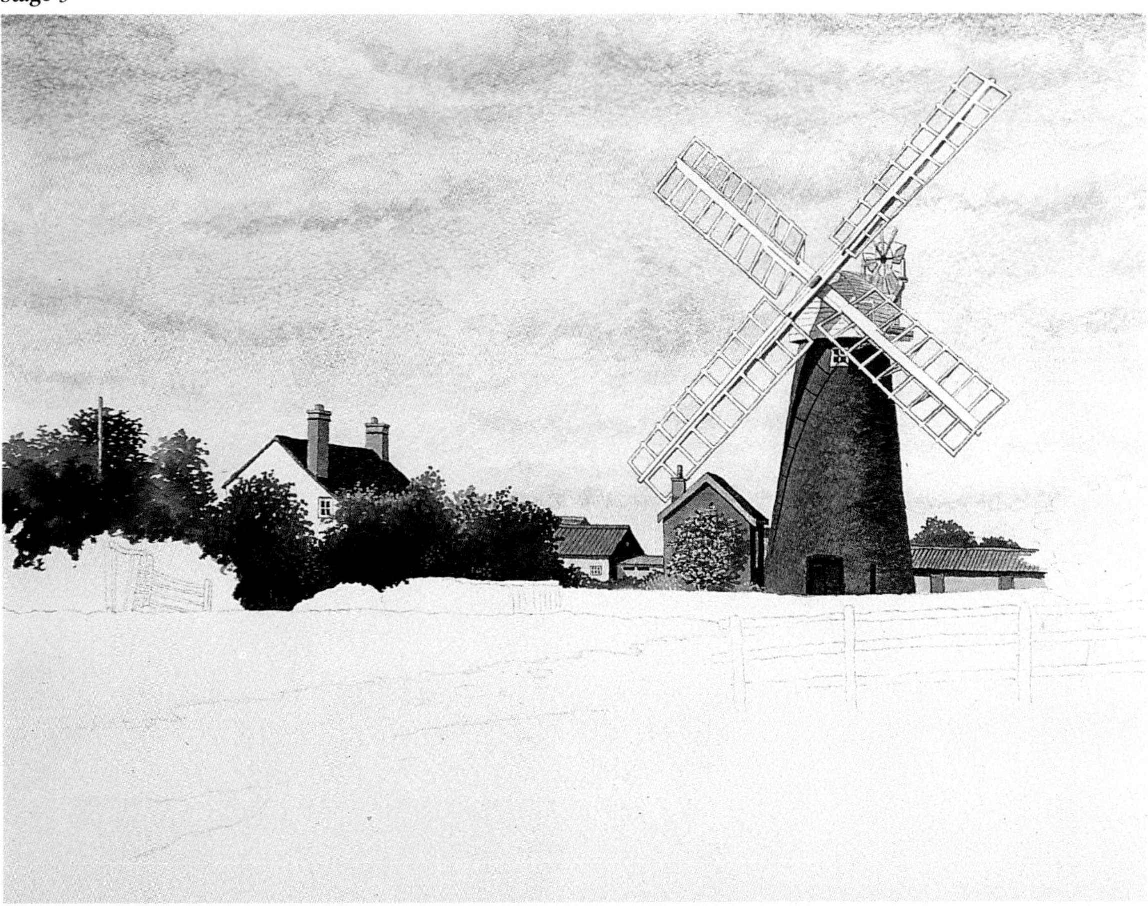

Stage 3 After removing the masking fluid, detail and more shadows are added to the wooden top. Shadows and detail are also introduced into the sails, with mixtures of crimson alizarin, french ultramarine and a no 00 round pointed sable. Small details are added to buildings, doors, windows, etc, and the sails are completed with a no 00 round pointed sable. Shrubs and trees in front of the buildings on the left are painted with mixtures of french ultramarine, cadmium yellow pale and Payne's grey using a no 3 round pointed sable. A rambling rose on the modern pump-house adds a splash of colour to an otherwise bland wall

---

Stage 4 Sluice gates on the left are painted with a no 2 round pointed sable and light colour, which is a mixture of warm sepia and Payne's grey. These are painted first because the tones are much lighter than those of the bushes and shrubs behind. Further along to the right, more foliage and a dike bank are depicted with mixtures of french ultramarine, cadmium yellow pale and Payne's grey. A bridge is also painted at this stage with similar colours to those of the sluice-gate posts. On the right of the bridge, a wash of cadmium yellow pale and french ultramarine is applied; while this is still damp, a little warm sepia mixed with Payne's grey is fed in. Details are added to the wooden bridge and sluice-gate posts and the sunlit meadow on the left is painted with a mixture of cadmium yellow pale and french ultramarine using a no 6 round pointed sable

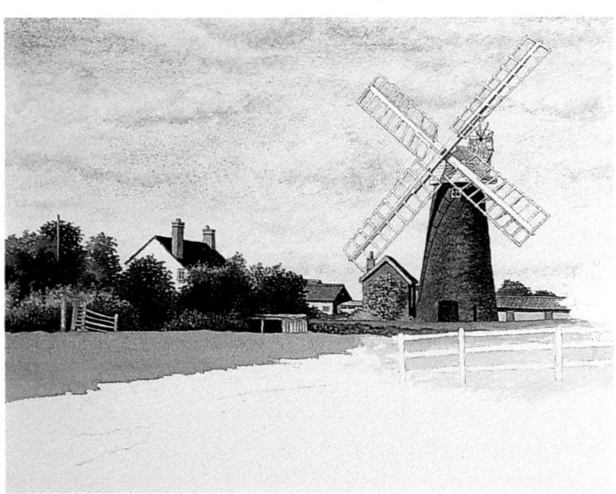

Stage 4

Stage 5

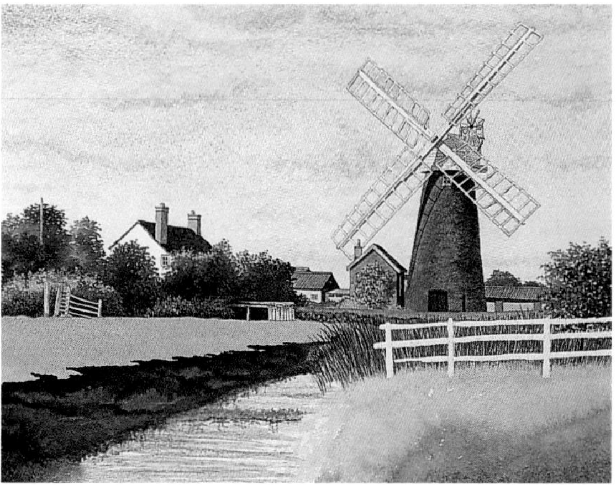

Stage 6

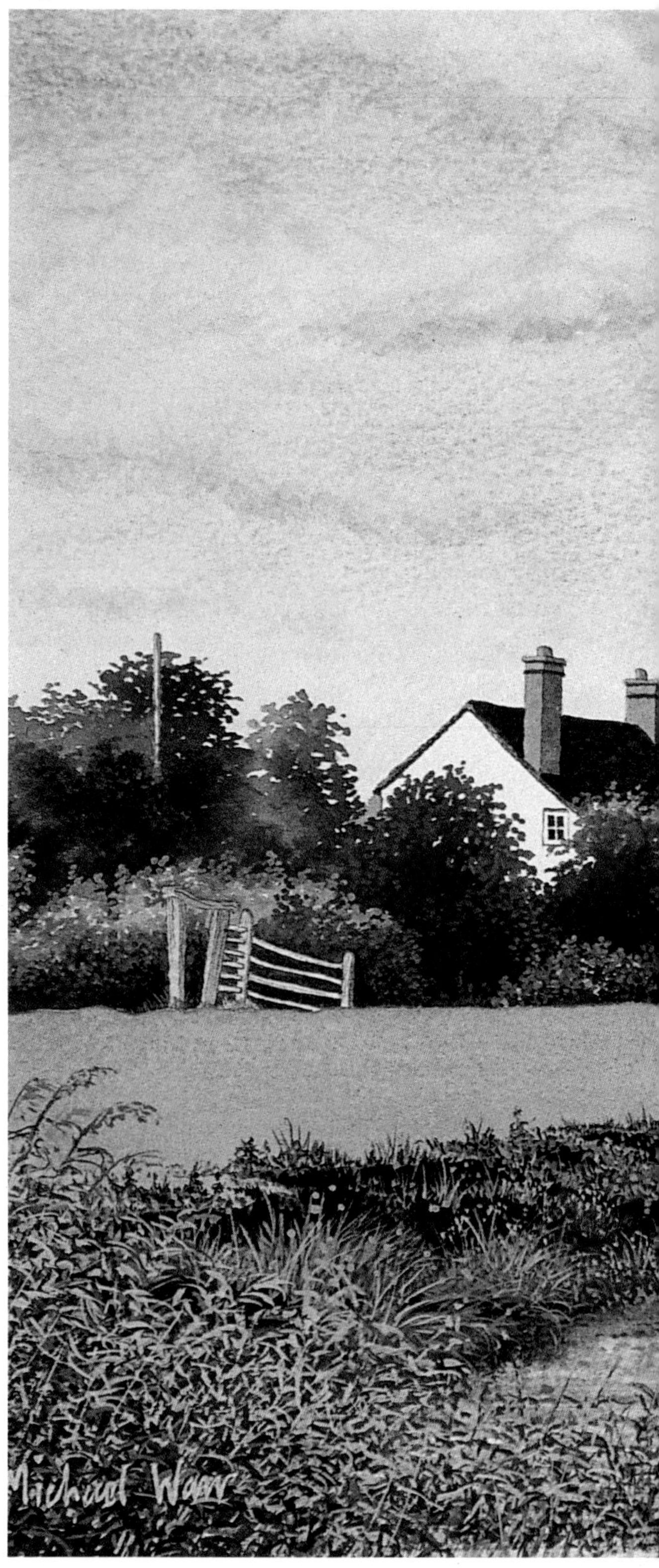

Stage 5 The bank of the foreground dyke is painted with a no 3 round pointed sable and mixtures of warm sepia and Payne's grey. Where sunlight is catching the tufts of grass, mixtures of cadmium yellow pale and french ultramarine are used. A small tree on the extreme right is introduced by using mixtures of french ultramarine, cadmium yellow pale and Payne's grey for the foliage, while the trunk and branches are depicted with mixtures of french ultramarine and warm sepia. Masking fluid is applied to a fence in front of the tree and the tall grasses behind are painted with a no 00 round pointed sable, burnt sienna, french ultramarine and cadmium yellow pale. Water in the dyke is painted with coeruleum and touches of crimson alizarin. A wash of dilute colour is applied to the immediate foreground and when all of the paint is dry, masking fluid is removed from the fence ready for stage six

---

Stage 6 Details are added to the fence-posts with Payne's grey and a no 00 round pointed sable, depicting wood-grain and splits. Grasses and reeds on the dyke bank are painted with mixtures of cadmium yellow pale, french ultramarine and white gouache. A few colours are dotted in to suggest marsh-growing flowers. The silver-green reeds in the immediate foreground are introduced by using mixtures of cadmium yellow pale, french ultramarine, Payne's grey and white gouache with a no 1 round pointed sable. The density of the leaves is built up until the foreground is completed. The silver-green contrasts with the yellow-green meadow behind, which in turn contrasts with the dark green trees

Colours Used

raw sienna
coeruleum
Payne's grey
crimson alizarin
french ultramarine
burnt sienna
warm sepia
cadmium yellow pale
white gouache

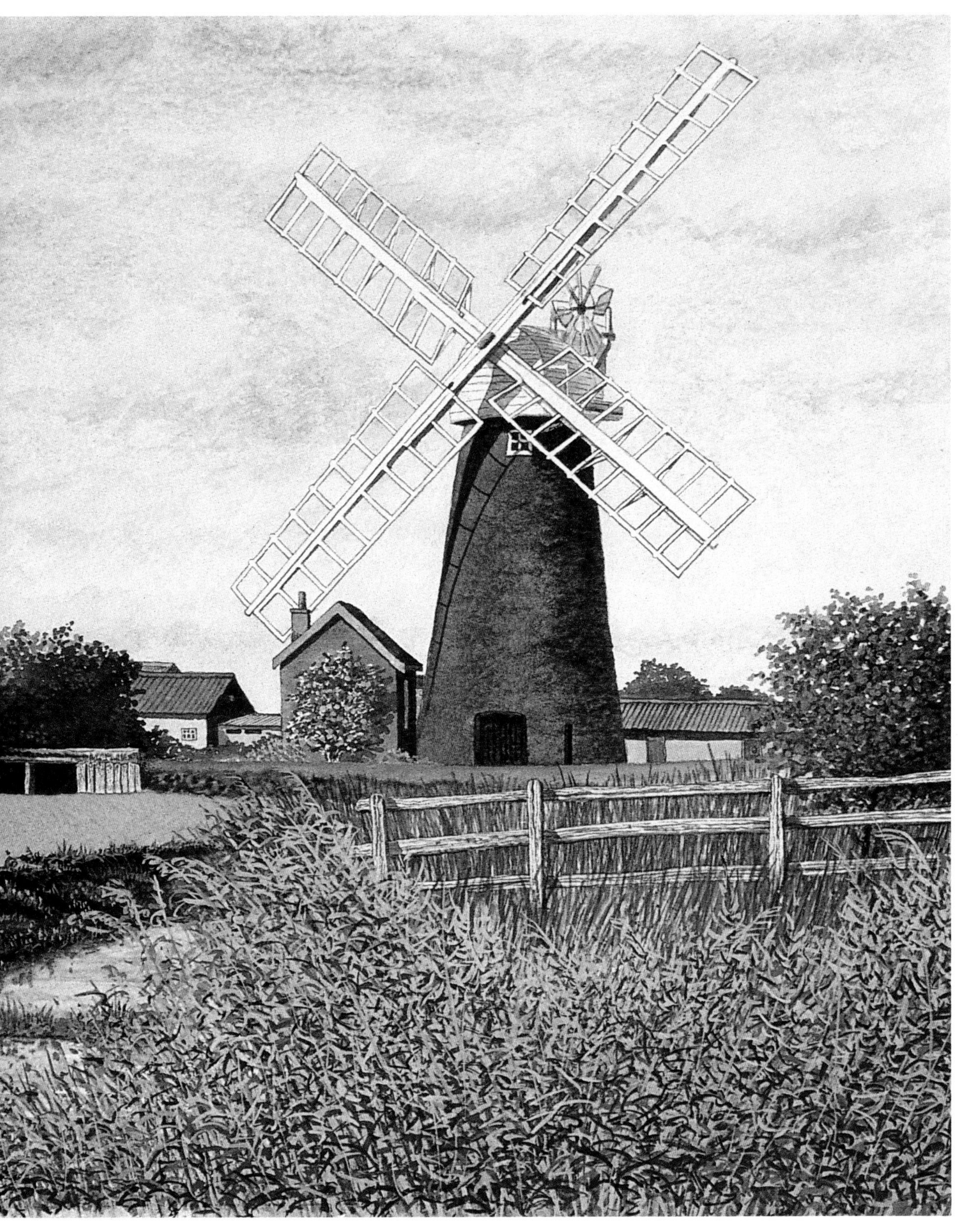

Tijuana Taxi

Crossing the border from the USA into Mexico is a fascinating experience. The town of Tijuana is situated just south of the California state line. Apparently, it is the busiest border-crossing in the world, linking the north continent of America with the south. The change in atmosphere is very marked; the feeling is suddenly Latin and colourful. Advertising signs bombard the eye, competing for attention, while traffic seems to speed along with gay abandon. Drivers shout and sound their horns for little or no reason, but there is a happy, relaxed feel to the place. How to record this atmosphere in visual terms was a challenge. Line and wash seemed to be the answer, allowing me a sense of freedom but at the same time enabling detail to be included. Because there is strength in the subject matter, I opted for ink lines and strong watercolour washes, both of which are strong media. The resulting picture is produced on illustration board, an ideal surface for the chosen technique.

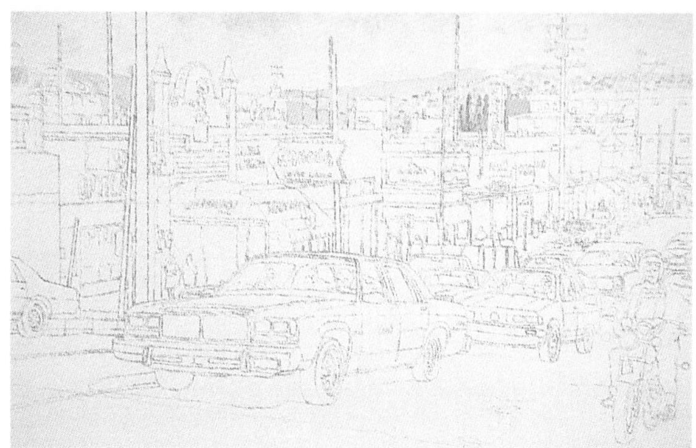

Stage 1

Stage 1 A drawing is produced with an HB pencil. When this is complete, a wash of coeruleum mixed with french ultramarine is applied to the sky. The distant hills are painted by adding Payne's grey to colours used for the sky. Adobe buildings on the right are also included at this stage

Colours Used

french ultramarine
coeruleum
Payne's grey
burnt sienna
crimson alizarin
cadmium yellow pale
monestial (phthalocyanine)
raw sienna
warm sepia
black ink

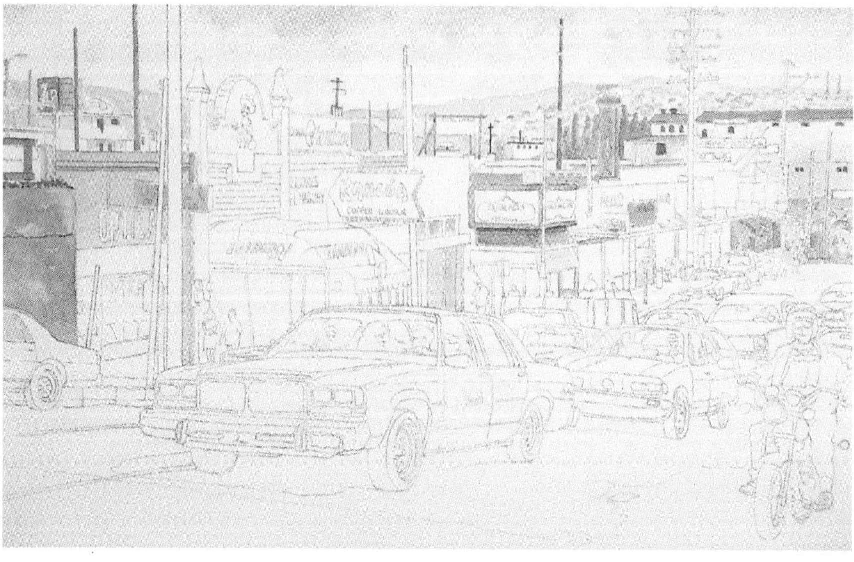

Stage 2

Stage 2 Colours are applied to the distant buildings and to some of the shop-fronts. The wall on the extreme left is a typical Mexican colour and comprises a mixture of burnt sienna and crimson alizarin. Notice that the colours included at this stage are blues, yellows and brown-pinks

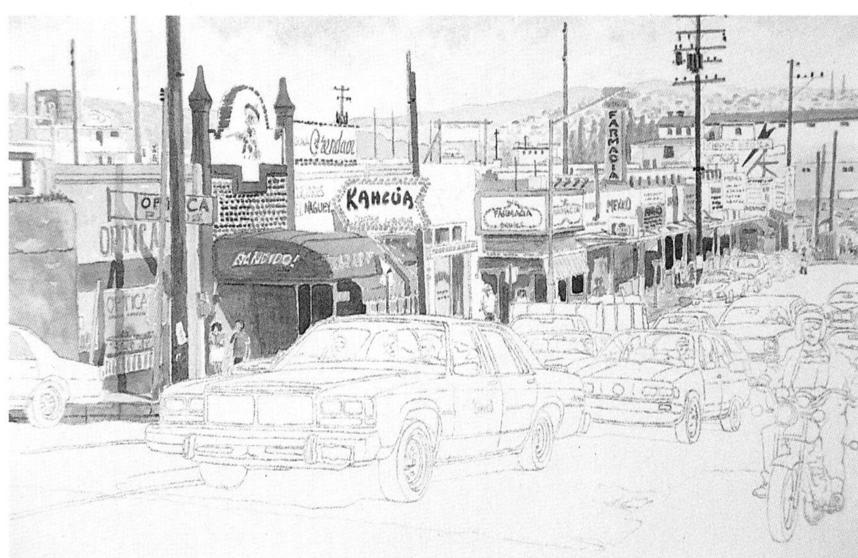

Stage 3

Stage 3 Reds are introduced, being mixtures of alizarin crimson and cadmium yellow pale; there are also greens, mixed by using cadmium yellow pale and monestial (phthalocyanine). Splashes of bright colour are beginning to appear on the shop facades and lettering of the advertising signs. The telegraph poles are completed with mixtures of raw sienna and warm sepia. People on the pavement, or sidewalk, are introduced; these are depicted with little detail, just dots of colour. Cast shadows on the shop-fronts are also included at this stage

Stage 4 It is now time to move on to the vehicles. An assortment of colours is used, including cadmium yellow pale, french ultramarine and red, which is a mixture of cadmium yellow pale and crimson alizarin. The latter depicts the Tijuana taxis, of which there are actually four in this painting! Most of the occupants of the vehicles are in shadow and are painted with mixtures of Payne's grey and warm sepia. The motorcyclist on the extreme right is mainly in dark shadow; the colours used are Payne's grey mixed with various shades of blue. Touches of raw and burnt sienna suggest his face

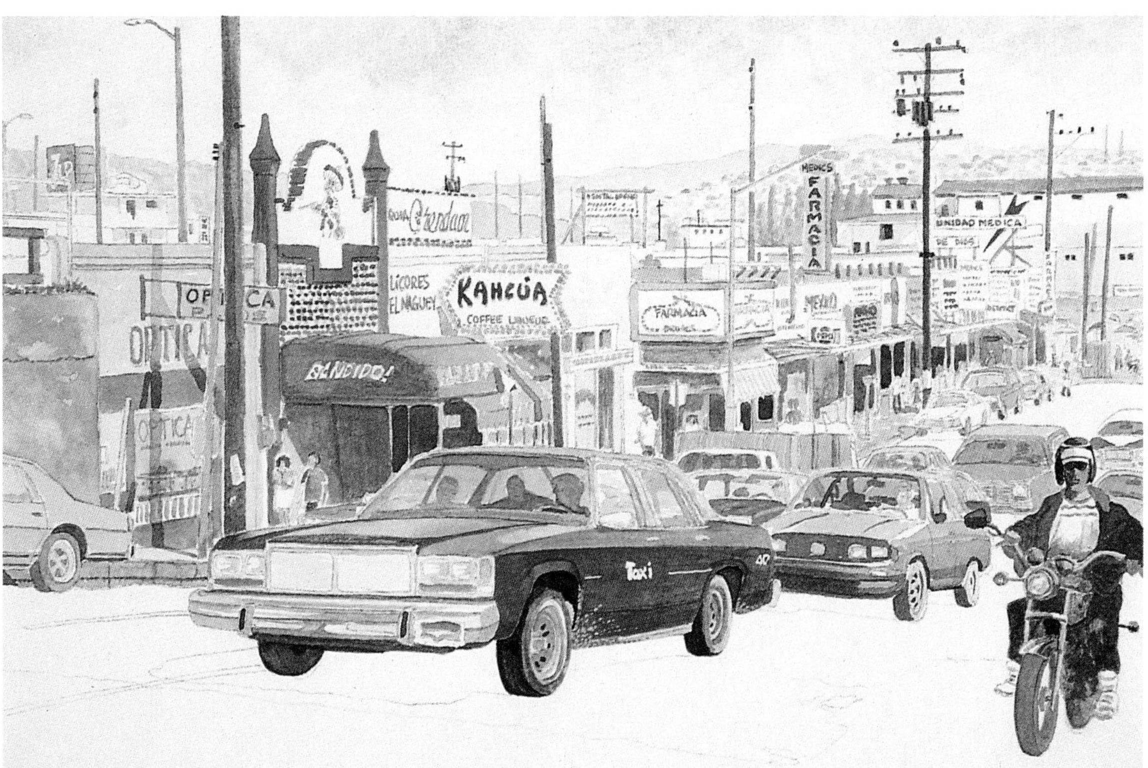

Stage 4

Stage 6

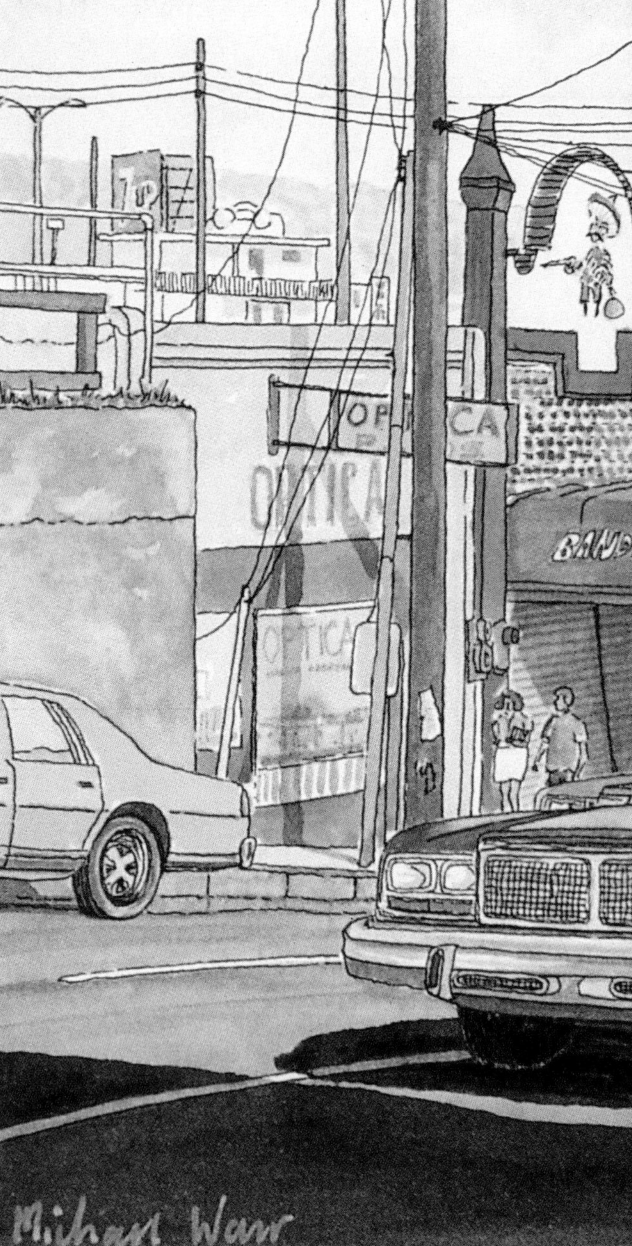

Stage 5

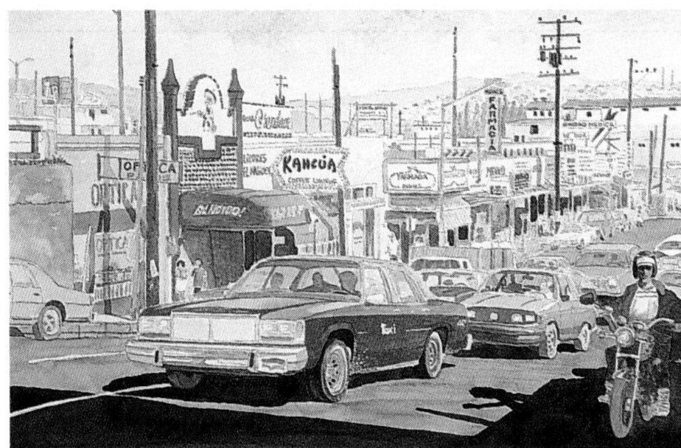

Stage 5 The road surface is painted with a mixture of raw sienna and Payne's grey. When this wash is completely dry, the strong cast shadows of the vehicles and unseen buildings are depicted with a wash of french ultramarine mixed with crimson alizarin. The actual painting work is now complete, and all that remains is the pen and ink work

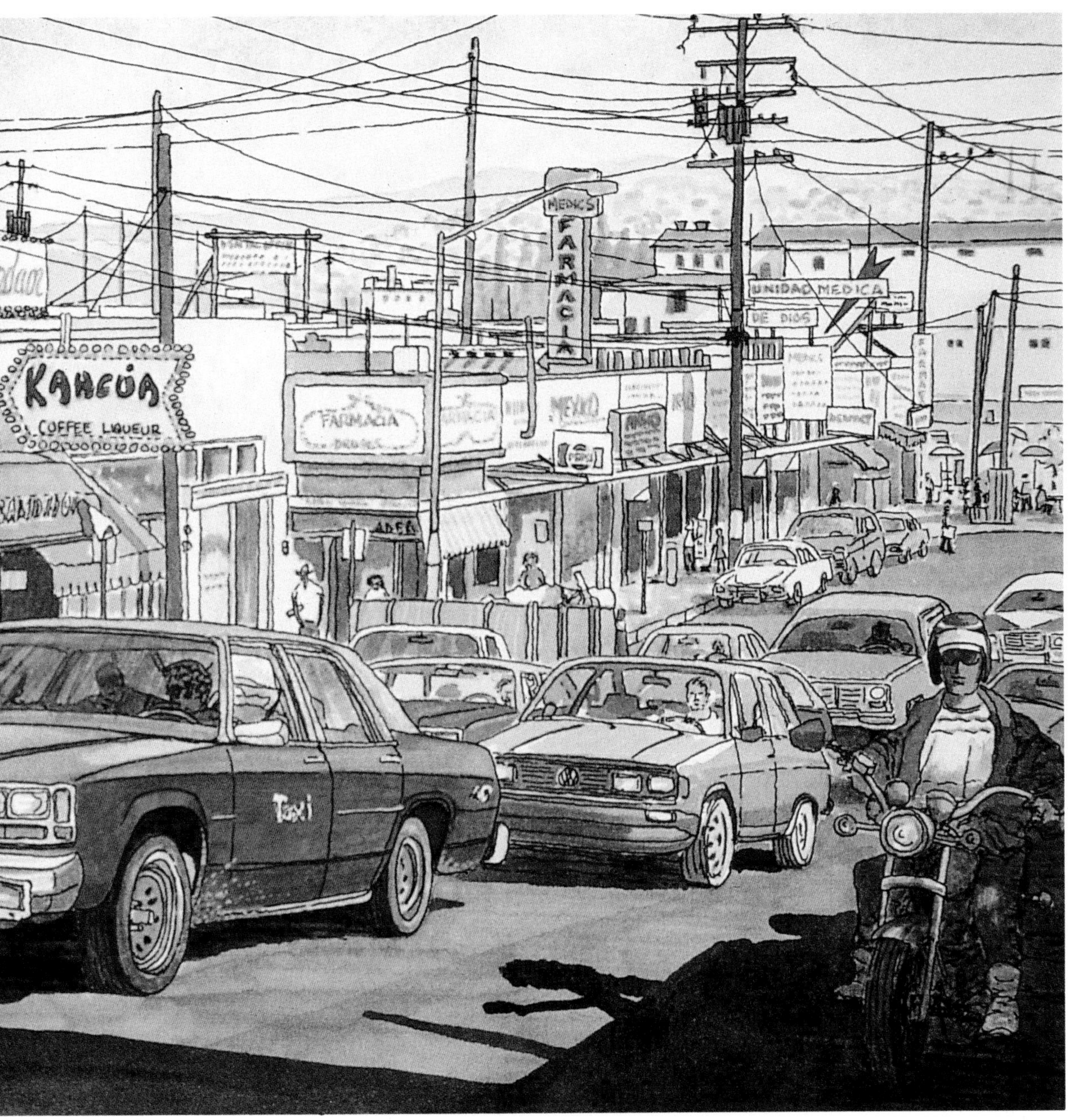

Stage 6 Subjects in the background are treated with a light line – that is, using light pressure on the pen – because of their distance. The shops, people and vehicles are then lined in. There is no need to line every single shape. Be selective and decide what the picture needs. Finally, the fantastic array of overhead electrical wires is included. How they ever disentangle themselves and reach their rightful owners is beyond me

Painting the Seasons

Painting the seasons provides a wonderful opportunity to explore watercolour painting to the full. The four seasons offer so many differing colour combinations; the prospect is very exciting. What other theme allows us to go through the palette so extensively? Reds, oranges, browns, ochres, blues, purples, fresh greens and yellows – the colours are there for the choosing.

The changing seasons provide landscape

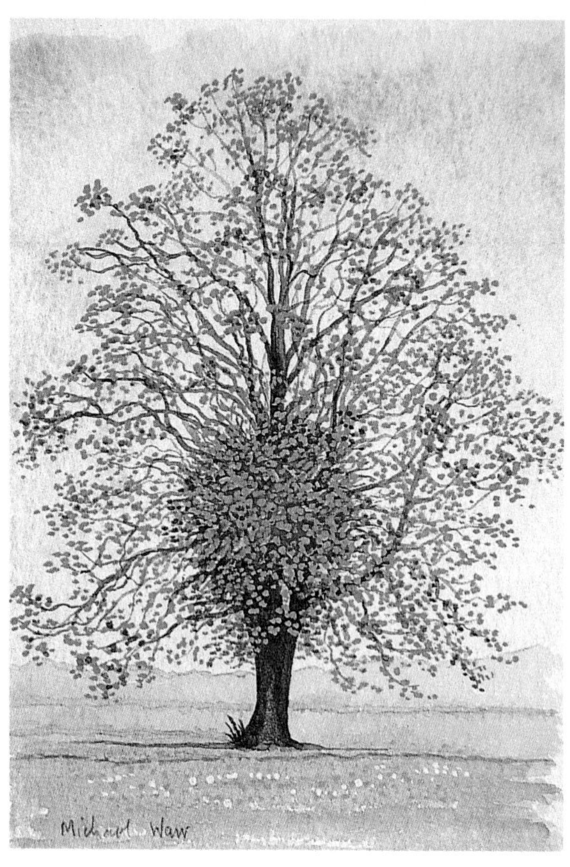

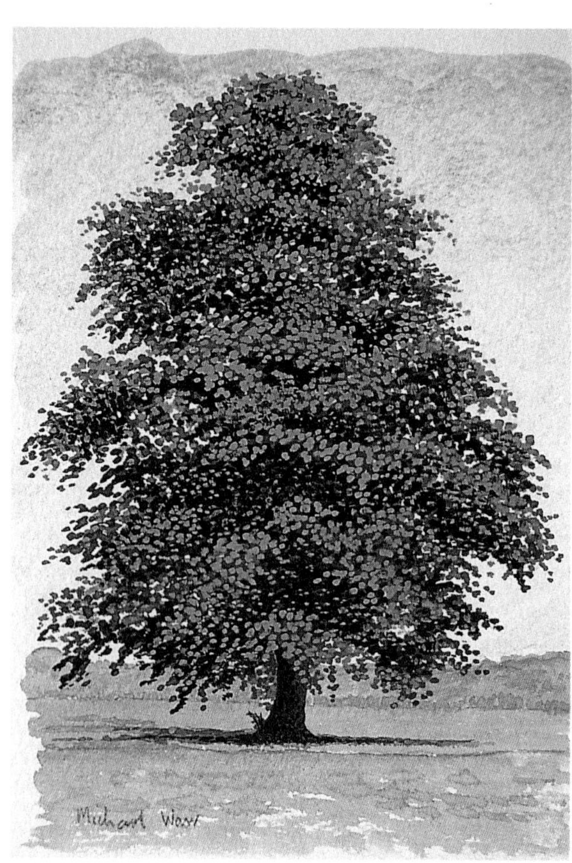

A lime tree studied during the four northern hemisphere seasons makes an interesting subject. This type of exercise is very good for observation; the differences are quite marked.

Spring brings young light green leaves, painted here with mixtures of cadmium yellow pale and french ultramarine. In all four illustrations I used a mixture of light red and french ultramarine for the trunk and branches

By midsummer the tree is heavily laden with leaves and none of the branches is visible. I used the 'three tone system' to paint the foliage: light green (cadmium yellow pale with a touch of french ultramarine and a little Payne's grey), mid-green (less cadmium yellow pale), and dark green (strong Payne's grey with a little cadmium yellow pale and a touch of french ultramarine)

painters with new thoughts and ideas; there is not time to become bored. In fact, very often in the past I have missed a complete season because of being committed to some other project. If you can take advantage of these seasonal changes, do so; they provide such interesting subjects that offer constant inspiration and diversity.

From the practical point of view, painting the seasons helps us to discover new colour mixes as we are forced to deal with the extremes of weather and temperature that require colours which range from very warm to very cool. This is very good experience that enables us to find colours which we didn't know existed.

Shapes as well as colours change with the dawning of a new season. How different the landscape looks under a blanket of snow, or how different a tree appears without its leaves; the structure is there and it is possible to see what holds the leaves in place during the summer. These changes help to sharpen the perception of landscape; anything which aids careful observation has to be good.

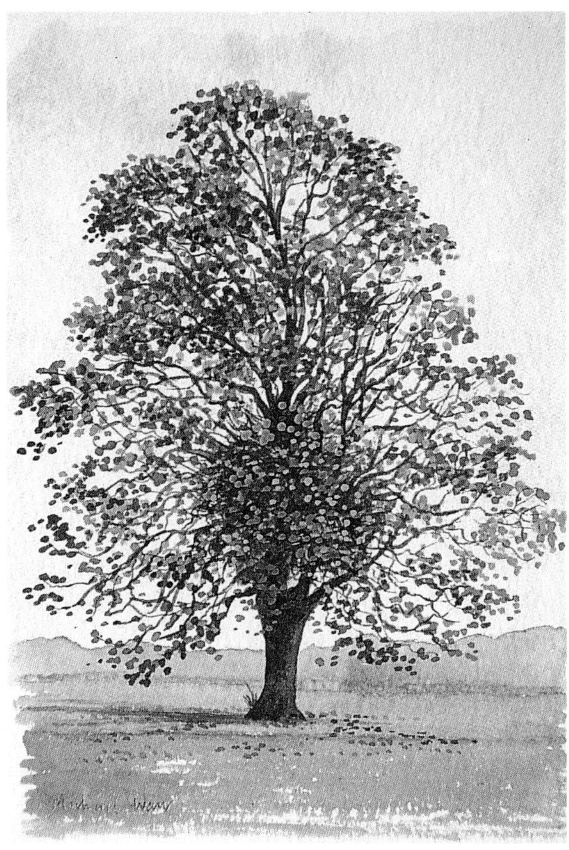

Cool autumn days and nights make the leaves change colour and fall. As a result, the structure can be seen again. The leaves here are painted with mixtures of burnt sienna, cadmium yellow pale and warm sepia.

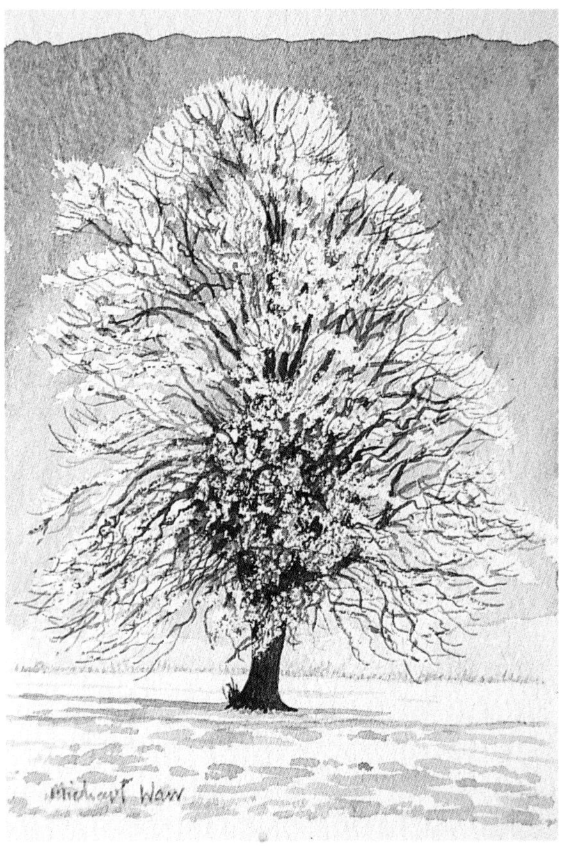

Hard frosts during the winter ensure that all of the leaves disappear. Normally, most of the structure is visible, but in this situation snow and ice cling to the branches almost like white leaves. Masking fluid dry-brushed with a small hog-hair brush over light drawing acts as an effective resist. The sky is painted first and, when it is dry, the tree-trunk and branches follow. When the colour is completely dry, the masking fluid is removed. The result is too much white, so more fine branches and twigs are painted with a no 00 round pointed sable to complete the study

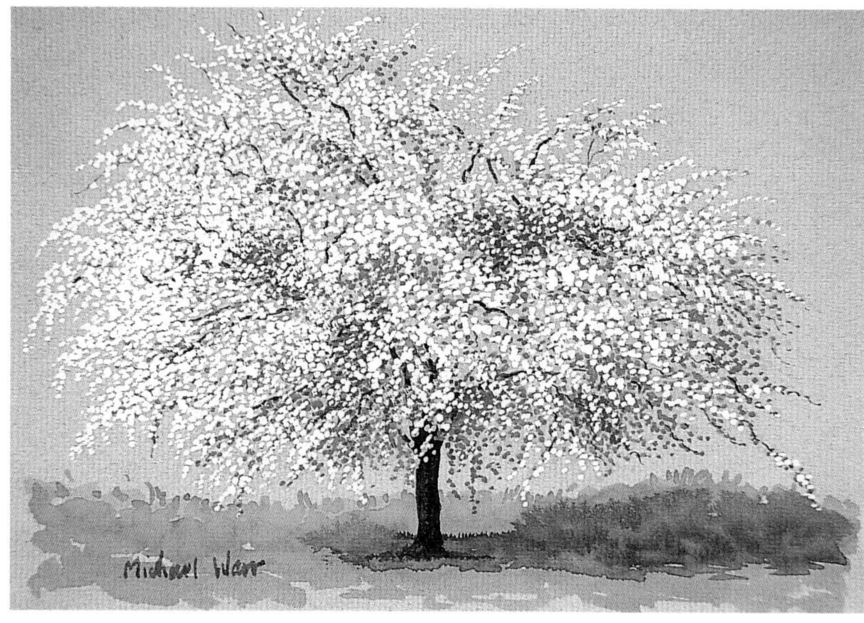

Blossom
Spring is a delightful season. It is full of promise and, to an optimist such as myself, very welcome. A burst of colour is thrust upon us after winter's long haul – something to cheer and gladden the eye. This flowering cherry tree appealed to me: a large splash of brilliant colour just waiting to be captured with paint. Gouache on tinted paper is the chosen media; it has the strength to convey this fresh, eye-catching subject in a powerful manner

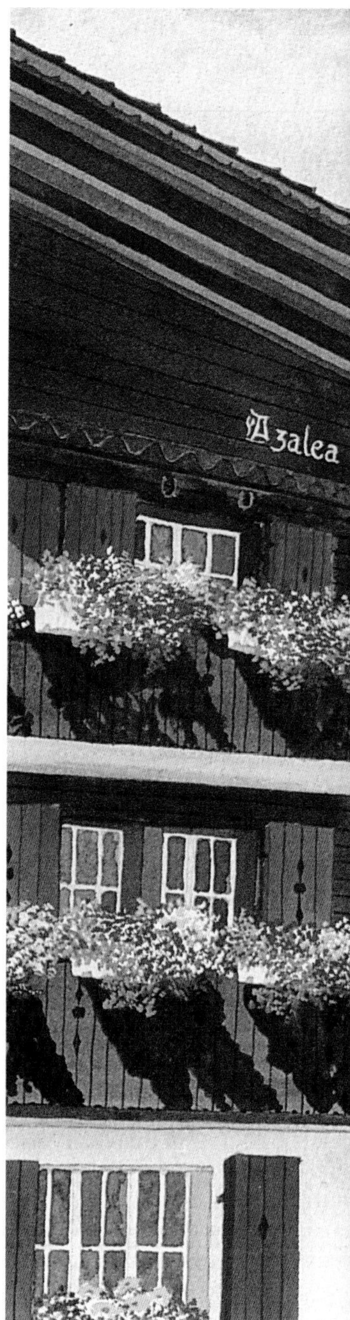

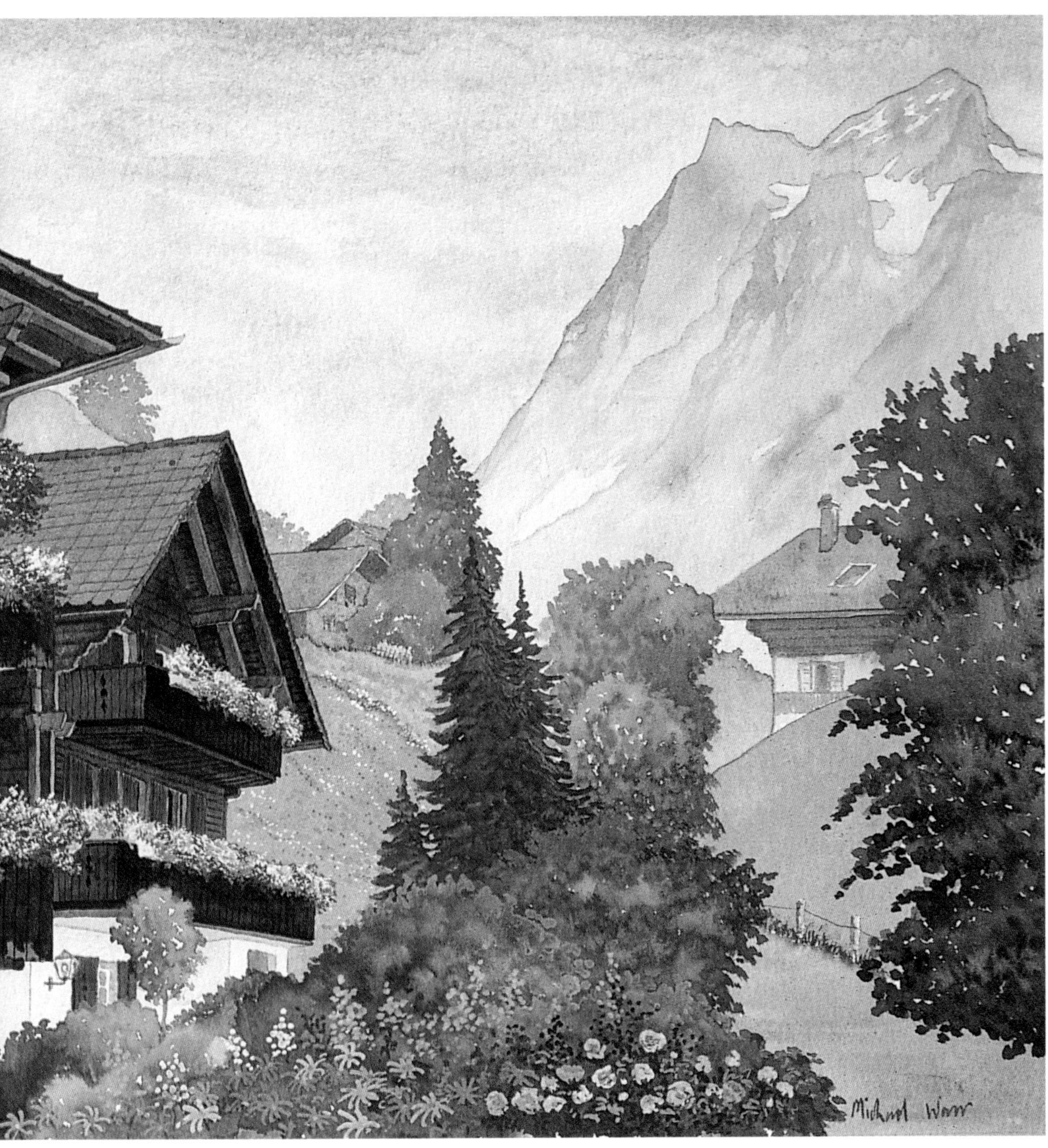

Gaby's Chalet
Frau Schenks' colourful chalet, set in the heart of the Berner Oberland, Switzerland, provides an excellent summer subject. Although this house has appeared on calendars and chocolate-boxes throughout the world, I was commissioned to paint it by the owner. Apart from the colourful summer content provided by the flowers, the balconies are there, presenting a perspective challenge. The background, which includes the mighty Wetterhorn Mountain, remains fairly soft, while the main subject buildings are brought into sharp focus. Approach to the chalet is by means of a narrow road and as the last corner is turned, a stunning array of colour meets the eye. Touches of gouache are used to portray the vivid flowers in an otherwise all-watercolour painting

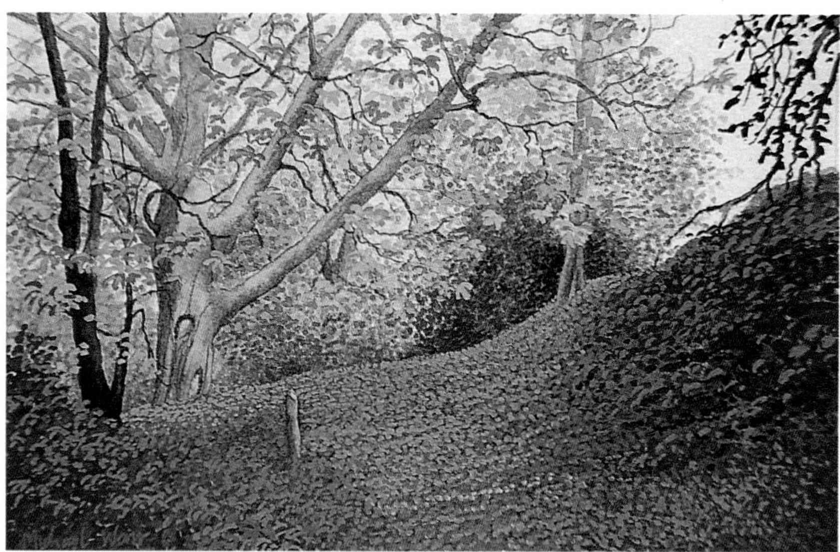

The Rookery
The corner of a childhood haunt named The Rookery is the subject of this autumn painting. It used to give me great pleasure to collect leaves here when I was a member of the Boy Scouts. The ever-present sound of screeching rooks could be heard overhead, as the search was on to find as many different leaves as possible and to be able to name them. It is good to know that the area still survives much the same as it was all those years ago – returning there to paint is a rare privilege indeed.

Silent Night, Kandersteg
This painting was produced out of sheer romanticism, after arriving in the village of Kandersteg, high up in the Swiss Alps. It was Christmas Eve and on the previous day a great deal of snow had fallen, creating a winter wonderland. After settling into a hotel and finishing a satisfying meal, I ventured outside into the crisp night air; the scene was fantastic. Snow-covered mountains were illuminated by a very bright full moon, giving them a yellow-pink glow. Although by this time it was midnight, everything was so breathtaking that it provoked me to return immediately to the hotel and produce a study of the stunning images

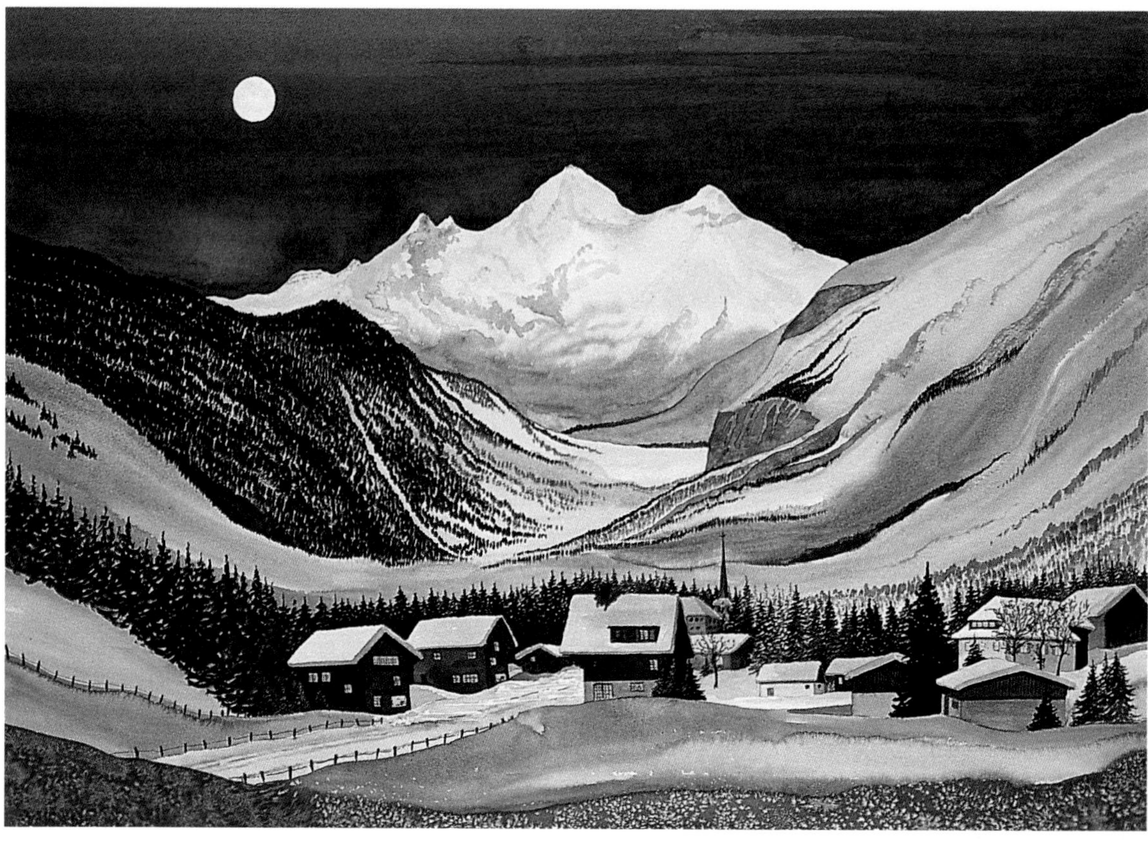

Zooming In

When you survey the landscape, the eye can be used like a zoom lens on a camera or in a similar way to a hawk homing in on its prey, except that the landscape painter will choose one subject within a grand arena. This exercise is fascinating, enabling subjects to be found which otherwise might go unnoticed. The discovery of single elements or small corners in the landscape becomes an exciting quest. It is universal; surprising details are to be found anywhere in the world. Training the eye to spot them is of vital importance – so much is missed without constant observation. I think the word 'observation' is the keynote. Look at the grand vista by all means, but do not ignore the closer, obvious subjects, which is not easy to do when you are in the midst of beautiful scenery.

A few years ago, enormous interest was aroused when I began to allow single landscape elements to become the main subject of a painting. Great pleasure has been derived from hearing people without knowledge of painting exclaim that they did not realise that simple items could be so beautiful. It would appear that focusing on to a certain object changes it from being ordinary into something extraordinary for the viewer of a painting. If this process enriches someone's life, the act of painting has been very worthwhile. The purpose of painting is to share our feelings with the rest of the world.

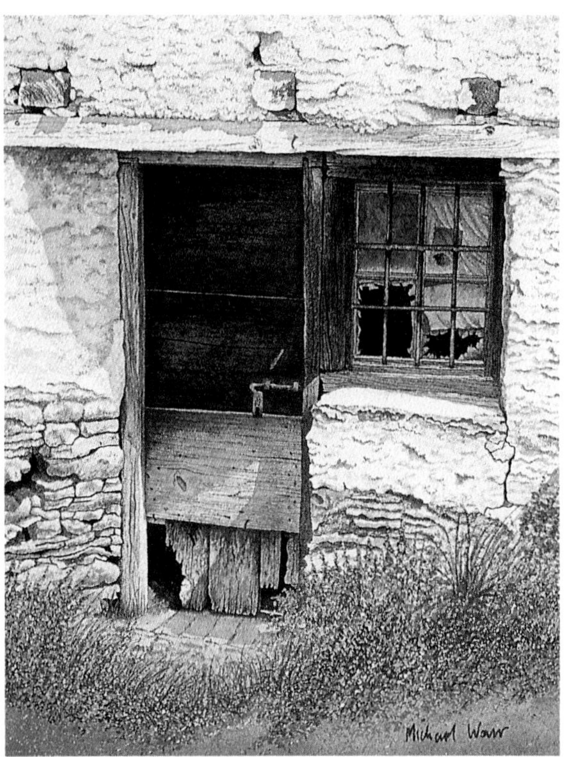

Ticino Rustica
An old doorway in a farm building on the Italian border provides an excellent detailed close-up subject. All the ingredients for a painting are here: texture, colour, shadows and form. The hand of an unskilled decorator has allowed whitewash to flow on to a supporting joist above the doorway, leaving a trace of natural wood showing through. Incidentally, the wooden parts are not treated with preservative, but actually derive their wonderful deep red-brown colour from natural weathering. Remnants of polythene in the window-frame form interesting patterns against the dark tone of the space beyond; the decaying base of the door works in the same way. Dark tones in a painting increase the impact

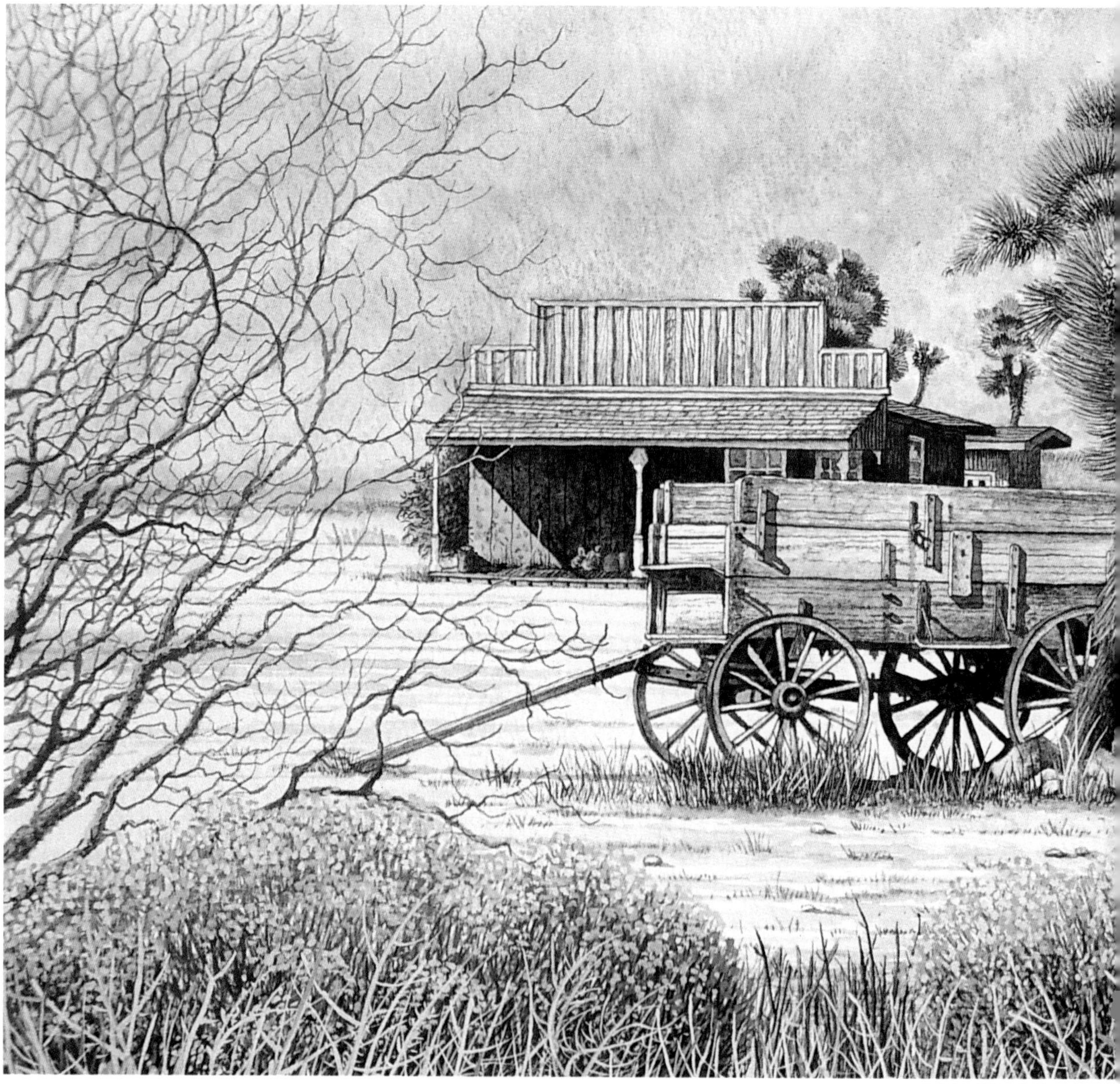

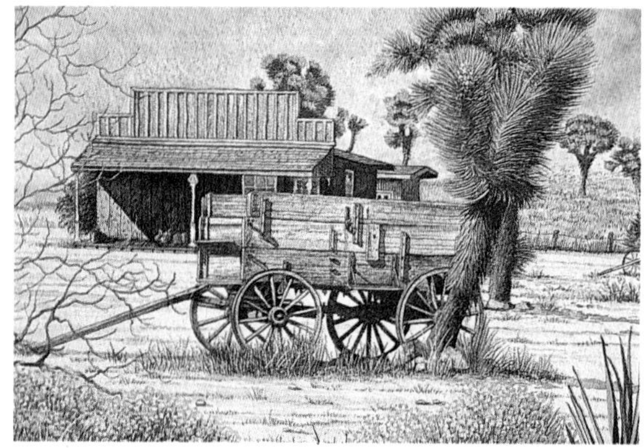

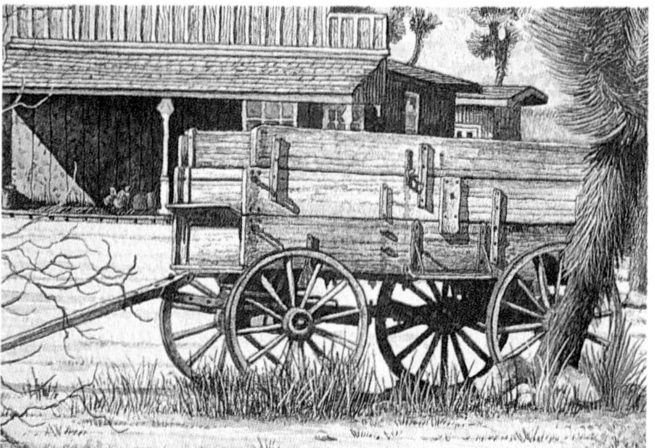

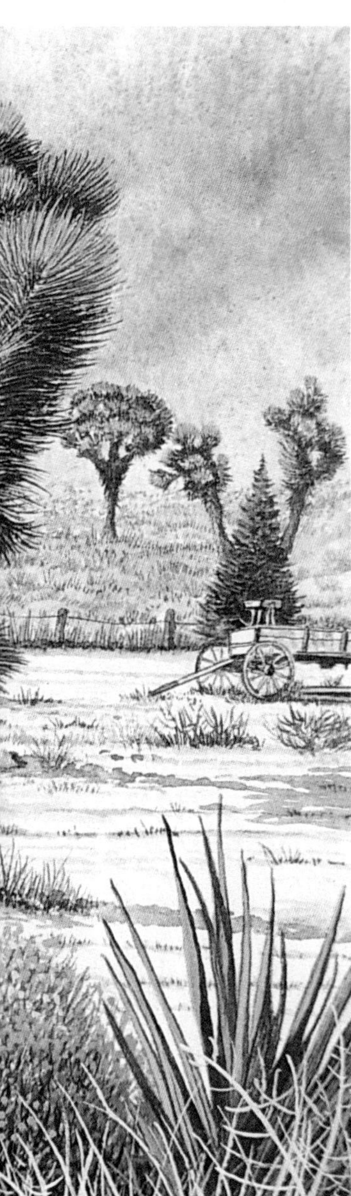

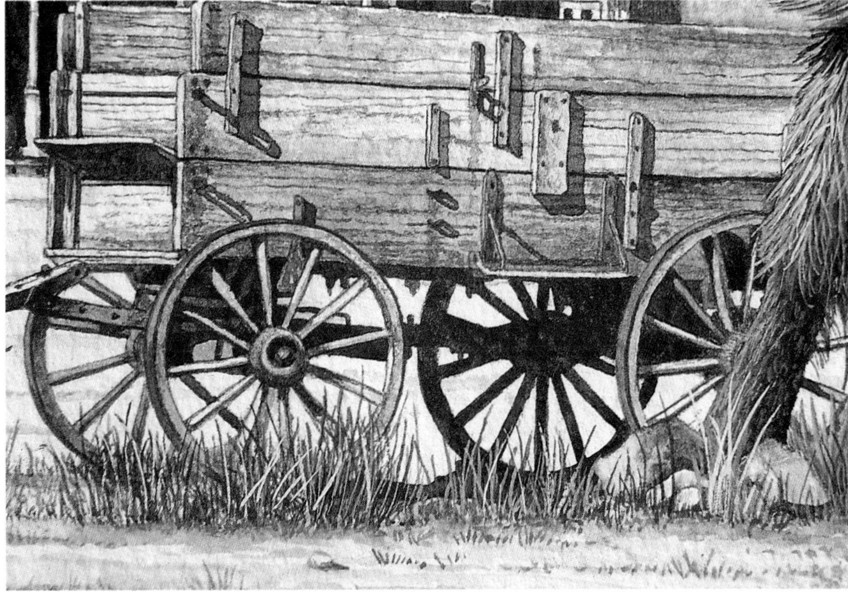

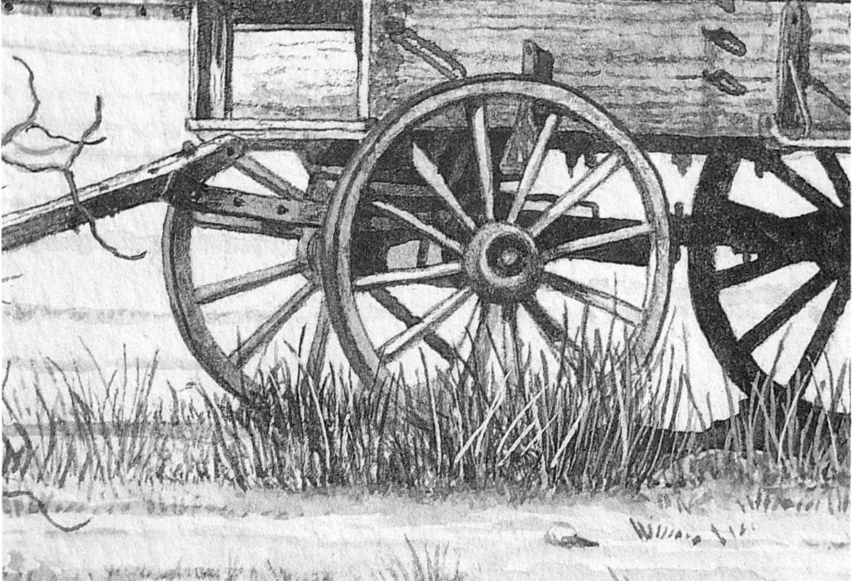

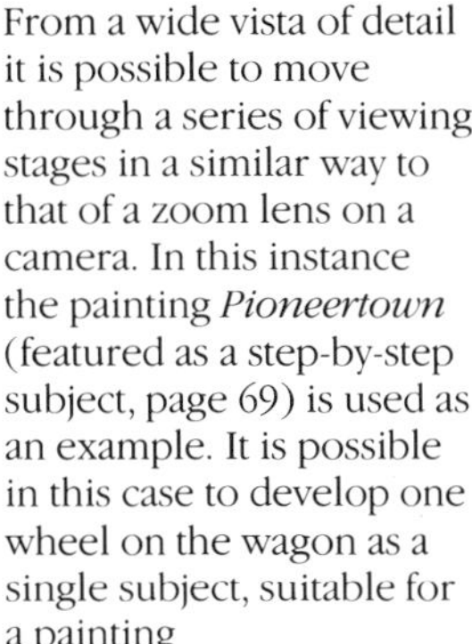

From a wide vista of detail it is possible to move through a series of viewing stages in a similar way to that of a zoom lens on a camera. In this instance the painting *Pioneertown* (featured as a step-by-step subject, page 69) is used as an example. It is possible in this case to develop one wheel on the wagon as a single subject, suitable for a painting

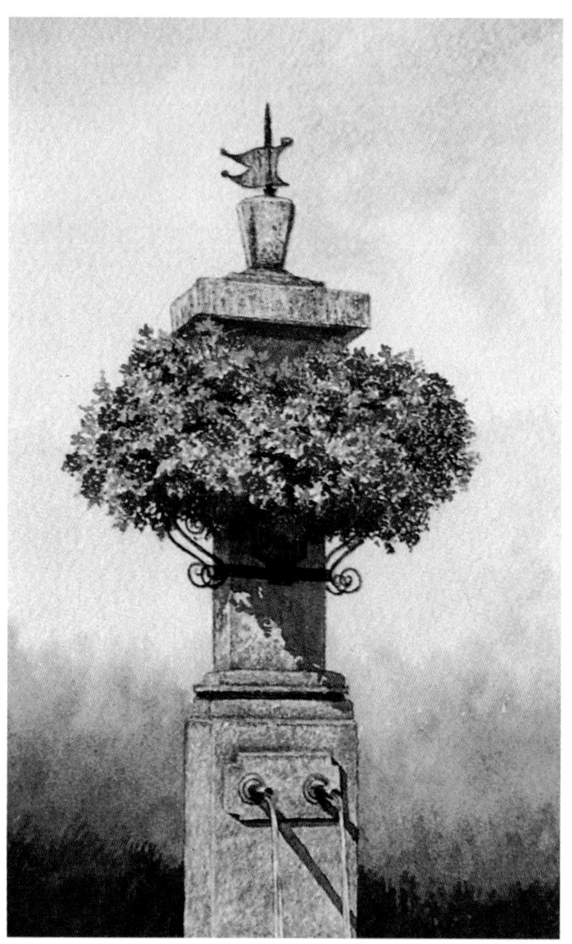

Village Fountain, Wasterkingen
The village of Wasterkingen, near Zurich, is extremely attractive, but I particularly like the village fountain. This is a typical example of narrowing the vision and focusing on a single subject within a vista – in this instance, a picturesque village. The background is fuzzy and out-of-focus, drawing attention to the fountain, complete with its colourful geraniums. Dry brush, a useful technique which works well in a small-scale painting dealing with only one subject, is used to capture the textures of both stonework and flowers

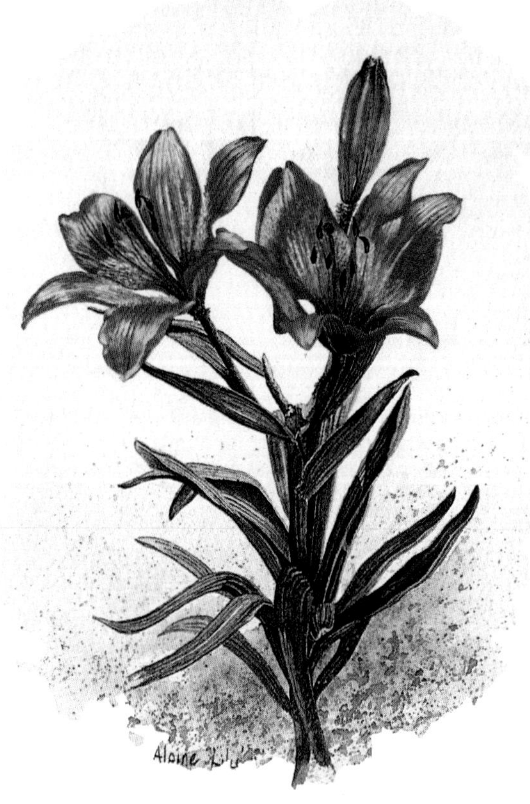

Alpine Lily
This gem of a plant was discovered in the Swiss Alps and makes an ideal subject for close-up work. There is a wealth of detail to be found in the petals and leaves. Note that the background is treated in a simple manner, enabling the main shapes to be seen clearly; all of the detailed work is contained within the main subject. A little texture around the base completes the picture

Presenting Detailed Watercolour Landscapes

After spending many hours working on and completing a painting, many students have no idea how to present their work. For watercolours, the choice of mount (mat) and frame is extremely important, as they have a twofold purpose. First, they have a practical purpose in that they protect the painting against the elements (watercolours are normally glazed) and second, they have an aesthetic purpose in that they create a gradual transition from the picture to its surroundings. Frame and mount (mat) colours need as much consideration as the colour content of the painting itself.

This chapter does not set out to explain methods of making picture frames and mounts (mats), but it aims to assist with the choice of these items. There are many publications on how to make your own picture frames and you can refer to these. I used to frame my own pictures, but lack of time prevents me these days; nevertheless, I still retain an avid interest in framing, and spend many happy hours with a framer making my selections.

Essentially, the frame must be appropriate to the picture; it must not dominate or be too weak. Remember that a good frame will not make a bad painting into a good one, but it can enhance a reasonable picture.

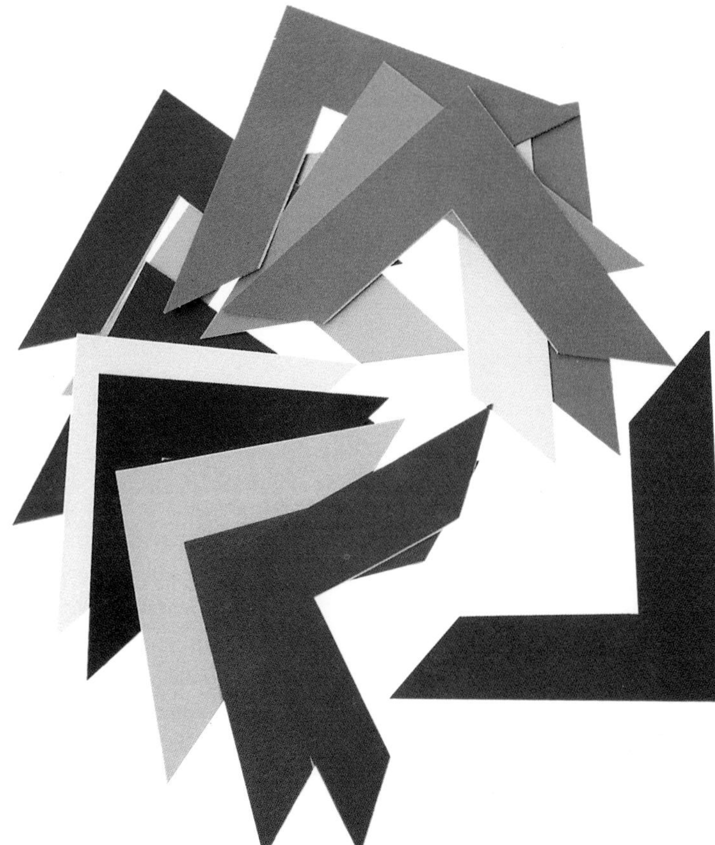

Some of the vast range of mountboard (matboard) colours which are available

Framing Materials

MOUNTS OR MATS

Mounts or mats are normally made from a range of coloured boards especially designed for the job. In the case of watercolours, it is desirable to place them behind a 'window' cut into the board with a blade set at 45°. This creates a bevel or a 'step' next to the painting. The border around the window needs to be of reasonable width, but whatever size you choose, it is a good idea to make the bottom border wider than the rest; if this border remains the same size as the top, an optical illusion will make it appear to be narrower, creating a top-heavy look to the mount or mat. One thickness of board may be used in some instances, but interesting effects can be produced by creating a double mount (mat). This consists of a wide outer and a very narrow inner mount (mat), or slip of a differing colour which may emphasise a colour within the painting. Sometimes this method of presentation can add tremendous vitality to a picture.

There are an infinite number of variations on this theme – for example, treble and quadruple mounts (mats).

MOULDINGS

The choice of mouldings from which picture frames are made can be overwhelming. At the end of the day, it is normally possible to narrow the field down to just a few which are suitable for an individual style of work. However, it is important to select a moulding which is in keeping with the mount (mat) and the painting.

When looking at a range of mouldings, it is not too difficult to sort out the ones which are suitable for watercolours. The wide, very ornate ones are usually better suited to oil paintings, whereas the smaller, unfussy mouldings are better for watercolours. The overall size of a painting and mount (mat) dictates

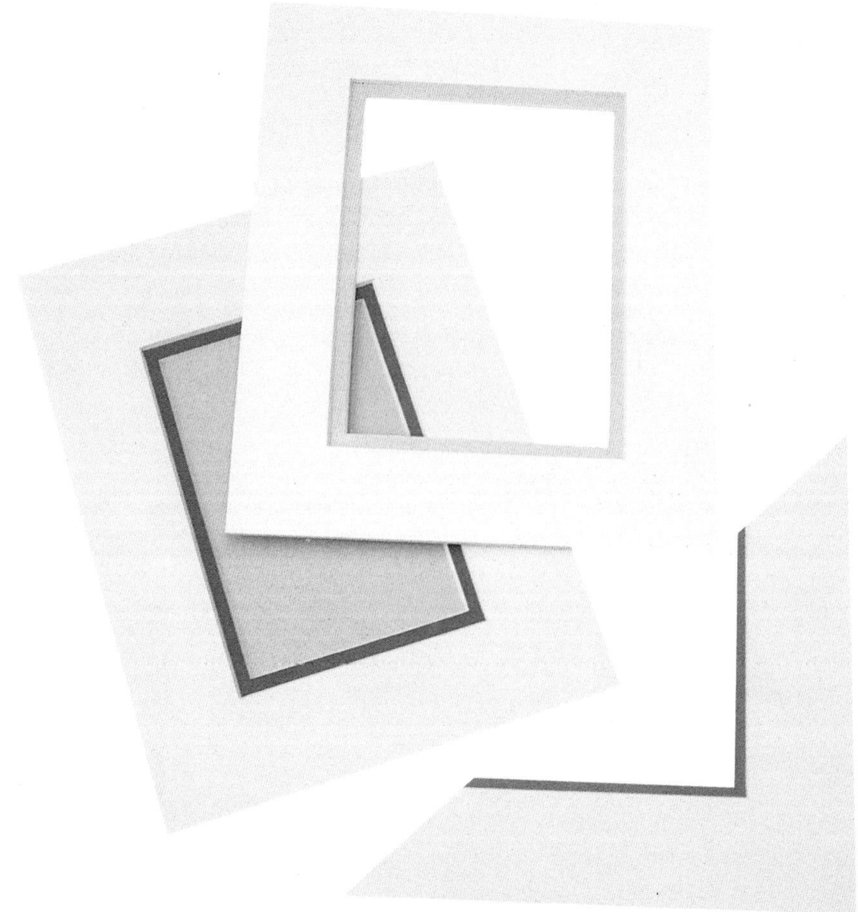

Double window mounts (mats) which can be purchased already cut or made to order from framing suppliers

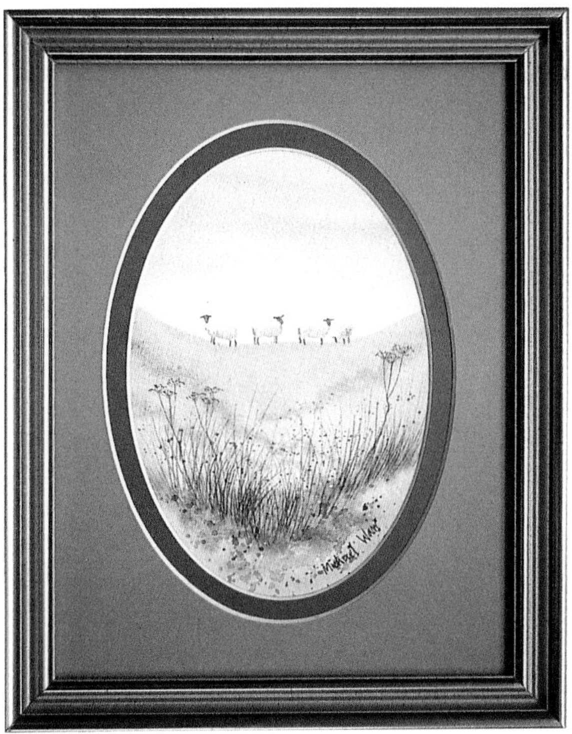

An oval window mount is ideal for this composition. Note how the cow parsley (Queen Anne's lace) on either side helps the balance

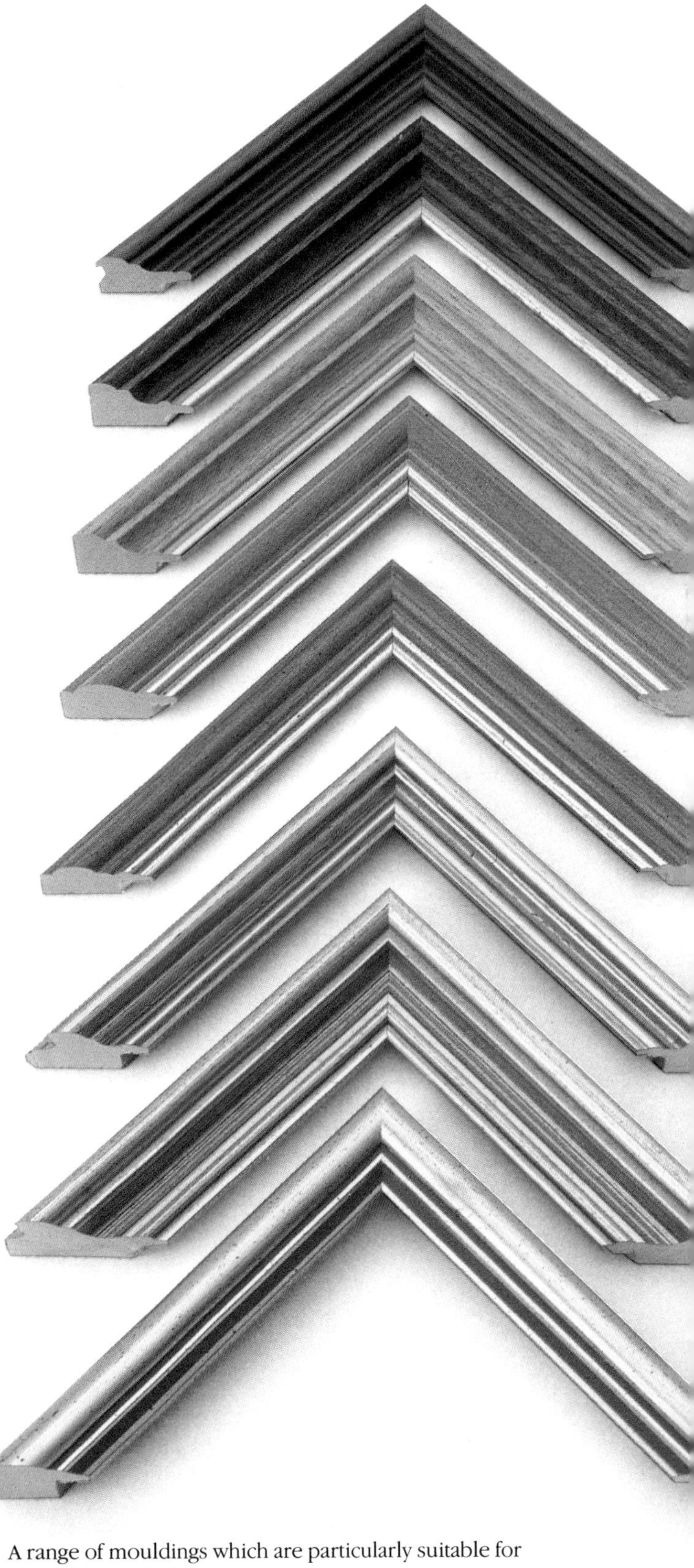

the width of the moulding. A large frame around a small oil painting can work well, but this is not normally the case with watercolours.

Many mouldings which are suitable for watercolours are decorated with a simple line of colour. This is an advantage, enabling a harmony between frame, mount (mat) and painting to be created; it is all part of the finished appearance.

It is possible to purchase ready-made frames in many sizes and styles. They are normally less expensive because they are mass-produced, but the chances of finding one to suit your latest masterpiece are very slim. Painting a picture to suit the frame is a possibility, but under no circumstances should the quality of a piece of work suffer because it is not provided with a suitable mount (mat) and frame.

BACKS

Normally, a framed watercolour needs a back. A suitable material for this is 2mm (1⁄8in) medium density fibreboard (MDF), which has largely replaced hardboard or masonite.

A range of mouldings which are particularly suitable for watercolour paintings

GLASS

Watercolours require glazing in order to protect them. I recommend the use of 2mm (⅛in) clear glass. It is possible to obtain non-reflective glass, but this distorts colour and diffuses detail.

SUNDRIES

I always carry a picture-frame repair kit when hanging an exhibition. This consists of tubes of Rowney 'Goldfinger' metallic finishes (suitable for retouching gold and silver frames) and small tins of coloured filler, usually gold, silver, brown and black (useful for filling larger chips, holes or cracks). A selection of hanging rings, nylon cord, a duster and glass cleaner is always useful.

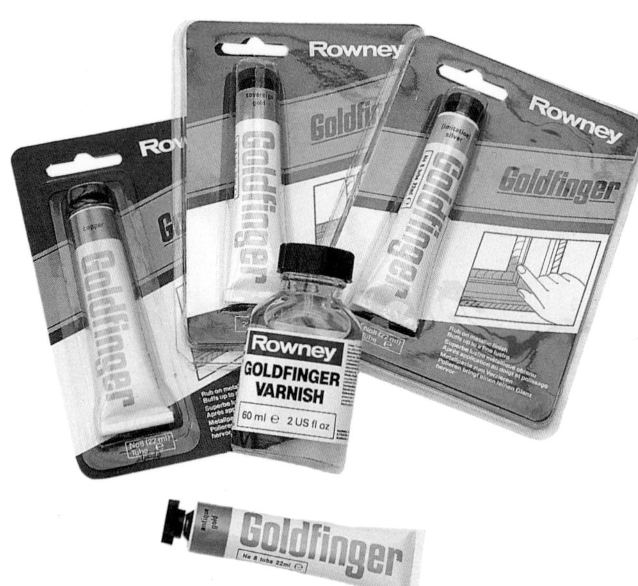

Tubes of Rowney Goldfinger. This range, which includes various shades of gold and silver, is ideal for restoring or repairing the surface of frames. When Goldfinger is dry, the varnish offers extra protection

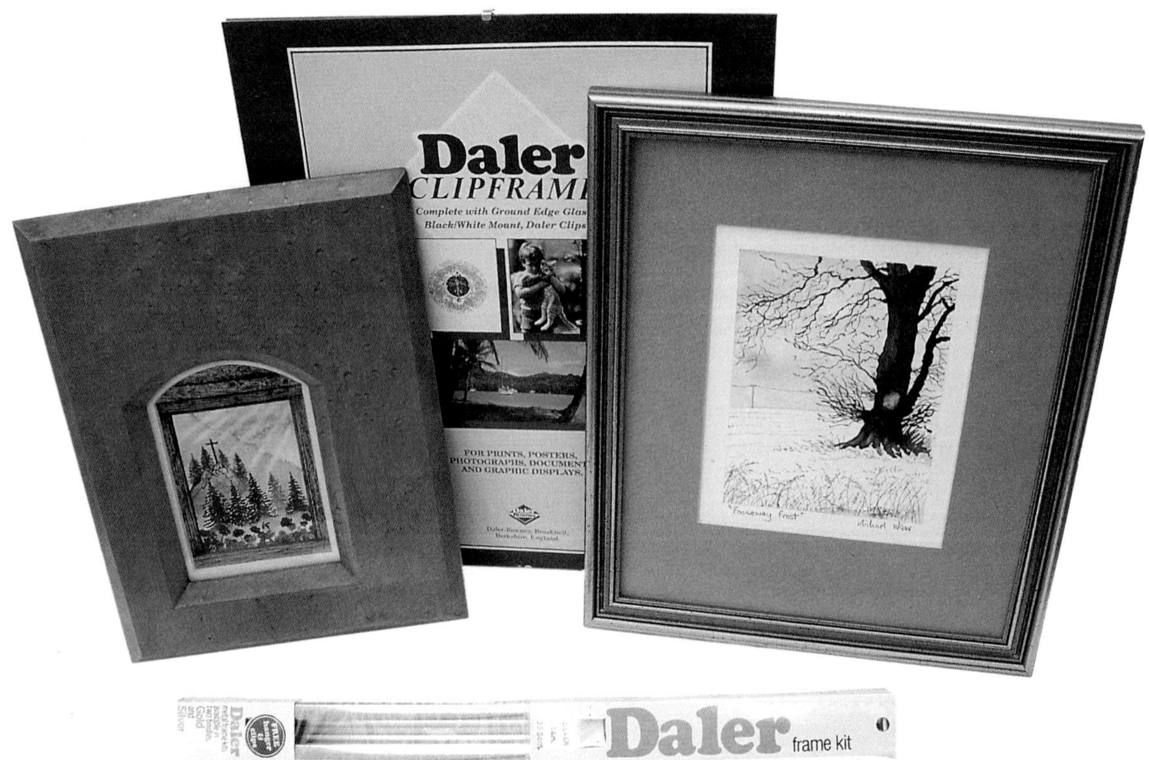

A selection of frames. *Left* An old frame which has been restored. *Centre back* Daler simple ready-made 'clip' frame. After placing the painting in a mount (mat), it is clipped into place behind glass. *Right* Custom-made frame and window mount. *Note* The white border around the painting is retained by keeping masking-tape in place while the painting is in production. When the paint is dry, the masking-tape is carefully peeled off, exposing white paper. This method creates a double mount (mat) effect. *Bottom front* A pack containing a ready-made aluminium frame kit. Easily assembled, it comes complete with instructions

Postscript

Painting is about expressing our feelings through visual imagery, and landscape painting is a wonderful way of discovering nature's plentiful bounty. All the marvellous subjects that are to be found in landscape are there for the asking. Look at the fantastic details in either the man-made objects or in the natural ones which surround us; let these observations become a voyage of discovery, enabling the ordinary, everyday subject to become extraordinary in our paintings. Leaves on a tree, spikes on a cactus, a barbed-wire fence – all have their place in the grand arena of landscape. Let nothing go unnoticed and remember that in looking at the landscape all we take from our natural resources is an idea, and hopefully all we leave behind are a few footprints.

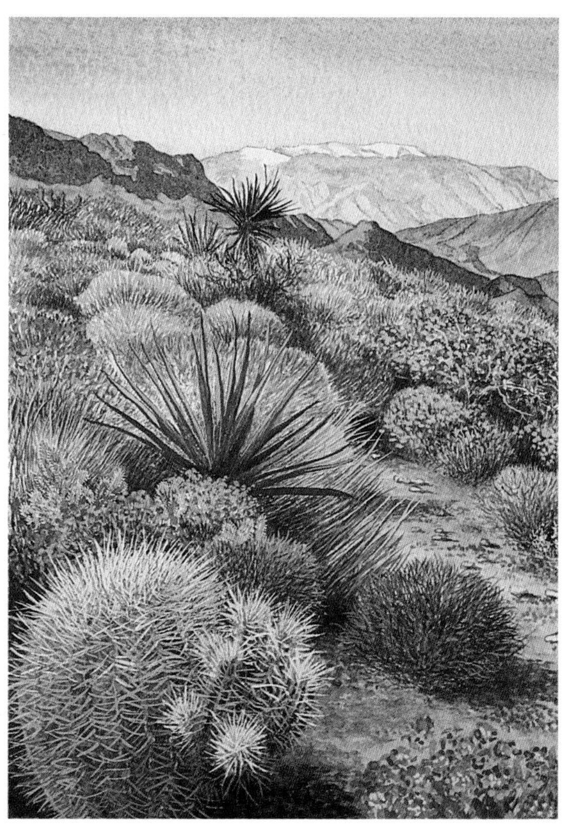

Index